Digital Media Use in Early Childhood

Also available from Bloomsbury

Disabled Children and Digital Technologies, Sue Cranmer
Digital Technologies in Early Childhood Art, Mona Sakr
Digital Personalization in Early Childhood, Natalia Kucirkova
Pedagogical Leadership in Early Childhood Education,
edited by Mona Sakr and June O'Sullivan
Identity, Culture and Belonging, Tony Eaude
More-Than-Human Literacies in Early Childhood, Abigail Hackett
Theorizing Feminist Ethics of Care in Early Childhood Practice,
edited by Rachel Langford
Ethics and Research with Young Children, edited by Christopher M. Schulte
Creativity and Making in Early Childhood, Mona Sakr, Bindu Trivedy, Nichola Hall, Laura O'Brien and Roberto Federici
Using Film to Understand Childhood and Practice, edited by Sue Aitken

Digital Media Use in Early Childhood

Birth to Six

Lelia Green, Leslie Haddon, Sonia Livingstone, Brian O'Neill, Kylie J Stevenson and Donell Holloway

BLOOMSBURY ACADEMIC
LONDON • NEW YORK • OXFORD • NEW DELHI • SYDNEY

BLOOMSBURY ACADEMIC
Bloomsbury Publishing Plc, 50 Bedford Square, London, WC1B 3DP, UK
Bloomsbury Publishing Inc, 1359 Broadway, New York, NY 10018, USA
Bloomsbury Publishing Ireland, 29 Earlsfort Terrace, Dublin 2, D02 AY28, Ireland

BLOOMSBURY, BLOOMSBURY ACADEMIC and the
Diana logo are trademarks of Bloomsbury Publishing Plc

First published in Great Britain 2024
This paperback edition first published in 2026

Copyright © Lelia Green, Leslie Haddon, Sonia Livingstone, Brian O'Neill,
Kylie J Stevenson and Donell Holloway, 2024

Lelia Green, Leslie Haddon, Sonia Livingstone, Brian O'Neill, Kylie J Stevenson and Donell Holloway have
asserted their right under the Copyright, Designs and Patents Act, 1988, to be identified as Authors of this work.

For legal purposes the Acknowledgements on pp. vii–viii constitute
an extension of this copyright page.

Cover image © Pai Shih / Flickr (Licensed under CC BY 2.0)

All rights reserved. No part of this publication may be: i) reproduced or transmitted in
any form, electronic or mechanical, including photocopying, recording or by means of
any information storage or retrieval system without prior permission in writing from the
publishers; or ii) used or reproduced in any way for the training, development or operation
of artificial intelligence (AI) technologies, including generative AI technologies. The rights
holders expressly reserve this publication from the text and data mining exception as per
Article 4(3) of the Digital Single Market Directive (EU) 2019/790.

Bloomsbury Publishing Plc does not have any control over, or responsibility for,
any third-party websites referred to or in this book. All internet addresses
given in this book were correct at the time of going to press. The author and
publisher regret any inconvenience caused if addresses have changed or sites
have ceased to exist, but can accept no responsibility for any such changes.

A catalogue record for this book is available from the British Library.

Library of Congress Cataloging-in-Publication Data
Names: Green, Lelia, author. | Haddon, Leslie, author. | Holloway, Donell, author. |
Livingstone, Sonia M., author. | O'Neil, Brian (Children's media use policy expert), author. |
Stevenson, Kylie, author. Title: Digital media use in early childhood : birth to six / Lelia Green,
Leslie Haddon, Donell Holloway, Sonia Livingstone, Brian O'Neil and Kylie
Stevenson. Description: First edition. | New York : Bloomsbury Academic, 2024. |
Includes bibliographical references and index. | Summary: "Including a glossary of key terms,
this book draws on a three-year research project examining the realities of 0-5 years olds'
experiences of these technologies in the UK and Australia. The authors draw heavily on
Vygotsky and engage with other thinkers including Bronfenbrenner and Bruner. It explores how
parents of young children evaluate these opportunities and concerns, and how they try to
work out ways to parent in relation to technologies they did not experience in their own
childhood. The book examines how digital technologies fit in with other elements of
children's daily lives including their preferences, pleasures and sociability"– Provided by
publisher. Identifiers: LCCN 2023051352 (print) | LCCN 2023051353 (ebook) | ISBN
9781350120273 (hb) | ISBN 9781350226838 (pb) | ISBN 9781350120297 (epub) |
ISBN 9781350120280 (ebook) Subjects: LCSH: Early childhood education–Research. |
Digital media. | Internet and children. | Mass media and children.
Classification: LCC LB1139.225 G74 2024 (print) |
LCC LB1139.225 (ebook) | DDC 372.21072–dc23/eng/20240206
LC record available at https://lccn.loc.gov/2023051352
LC ebook record available at https://lccn.loc.gov/2023051353

ISBN:	HB:	978-1-3501-2027-3
	PB:	978-1-3502-2683-8
	ePDF:	978-1-3501-2028-0
	eBook:	978-1-3501-2029-7

Typeset by Integra Software Services Pvt. Ltd.

For product safety related questions contact productsafety@bloomsbury.com.

To find out more about our authors and books visit www.bloomsbury.com
and sign up for our newsletters.

Contents

List of Tables		vi
Acknowledgements		vii
1	Contextualizing Digital Media Use in Early Childhood	1
2	Conceptual and Other Framings of Children's Media Use	21
3	Screen Time	35
4	Parenting and Digital Media	51
5	Grandparents	69
6	Digital Media in Preschool Settings	83
7	Infants	99
8	Toddlers	119
9	Preschoolers	139
10	The Bases for Diversity in Children's Digital Experiences	163
11	Parents' Evaluation of Children's Learning through Digital Media	173
12	Summarizing Our Research Findings	189
Appendix		208
Glossary		227
Notes		228
References		231
Index		250

Tables

1.1	Participating children in terms of family, country, first name, sibling order, developmental stage, age and birth gender	10
1.2	Assessment of genre of parents' approaches to mediating their child's engagement with digital media, as indicated to researchers	12
7.1	Infant participants	100
8.1	Toddler participants	120
9.1	Preschooler participants	140
A1	Family members participating in digital media use in early childhood – Birth to six	209

Acknowledgements

This book is grounded in work that began in 2013, when Donell Holloway, Lelia Green and Sonia Livingstone wrote *Zero to Eight – Young Children and Their Internet Use* (https://eprints.lse.ac.uk/52630/1/Zero_to_eight.pdf). In that paper, which has since been downloaded almost 50,000 times, we problematized the comparative lack of scholarly attention paid to very young children's digital media use. Thus, one of our first acknowledgements is to the London School of Economics and Political Science and the EU Kids Online project which together offered us the opportunity to establish the need and demand for research in this crucial area.

We also acknowledge a deep debt to the Australian Research Council (ARC) for funding the original research reported in this book via an ARC Discovery Project, DP150104734: *Toddlers and Tablets: Exploring the Risks and Benefits 0–5s Face Online*. That work fed into another grant: DP180103922: *The Internet of Toys: Benefits and Risks of Connected Toys for Children* and into our contribution to an ARC Centre of Excellence that focuses on digital media use by children from birth to eight, CE200100022: *The ARC Centre of Excellence for the Digital Child*. All Australian researchers working on the Discovery Projects were affiliated with, and supported by, Edith Cowan University's School of Arts and Humanities during the data collection. This book is in part an outcome of research time allocated across those periods.

Four of our six co-authors, Lelia Green, Sonia Livingstone, Donell Holloway and Brian O'Neill, a children's media use policy expert, were ARC-accepted Investigators on the *Toddlers and Tablets* project while Kylie J. Stevenson and Leslie Haddon led the fieldwork in, respectively, Australia and the UK. An outline of the different responsibilities taken by the authors is included in Chapter 1. We acknowledge the important contribution made by the three research assistants who supported data collection. Kelly Jaunzems, in Australia, and Svenja Ottovordemgentschenfelde in the UK, helped research the families with very young children. Gianfranco Polizzi helped Leslie Haddon with recruiting parents.

The gratitude all of us feel for the time and trust invested by our participant children and parents, their wider families and the contributing early years' educators, is immeasurable.

Like so many other scholarly endeavours, work on finalizing this book was roadblocked by the Covid-19 pandemic. Indeed, one recent delay reflected our work thinking about how a post-pandemic world might impact our findings. With six authors and a multiplicity of competing priorities, we would never have managed to bring this project to completion without the patience and guidance of Mark Richardson, Publisher (Education), Bloomsbury Academic; and the two Bloomsbury Editorial Assistants involved: Elissa Burns and, before her, Anna Ellis.

The authors gratefully acknowledge the crucial assistance of Linda Jaunzems. Her attention to detail, her deep commitment to getting the manuscript right and her gentle reminders of deadlines looming, and past, were all a vital part of this book's eventual emergence into the world.

Finally, we acknowledge the support of our families and our colleagues and the many discussions we have had about this research with other scholars that helped refine our ideas and understandings. With six authors, it would be unwieldy to name everyone, but if it takes a village to raise a child, it has taken a community to produce this book. Thank you all.

1

Contextualizing Digital Media Use in Early Childhood

The need for this book

This book introduces young children's everyday experiences with digital media. As long-term collaborators, we share a fascination with children's digital activities, especially where the child is self-directed, following their own interests. We're intrigued by what children do with the time and technology they have available to form and express an emerging sense of self. These early experiences, often in domestic settings, resonate through the child's future school and work life, imagining and creating structures for their days, connecting them with others and helping even the very young to formulate, act upon and express personal values and enthusiasms.

Young children's early years provide the foundation for their future lives. Parents and other caregivers often prioritize a young child's digital engagement, hopeful yet also fearful of their digital future (Livingstone & Blum-Ross, 2020). This is the period when young children begin to interact with 'the village' that helps raise them: extended family; neighbours and friends; and key figures in social institutions like parent-and-toddler play groups, libraries and religious organizations. It is an exciting period of diverse and rich influences: a time when children learn to talk about and act in their world, supported by families, friends and educators.

People differ in their views about whether, when, how, and how much; young children should interact with and via digital media. Friends and strangers may hold strong beliefs about what constitutes good digital parenting. Parents tell us that casual contacts in shopping centres, fellow diners eating in restaurants and adults unknown to them sometimes direct stern looks their way if they offer their child a smartphone or a tablet in a public place. As participant Kate Andrews-White (AU) explains: 'When you're just trying to get by sometimes, when you see some of that stuff [other people's disapproval], I would feel very judged.'

Like other ethnographic researchers, we acknowledge the primacy of the family context, whatever the makeup of that family structure may be. The families who contributed to this research came in different shapes, numbers and generations, and the importance of adults' digital practices in families with very young children cannot be over-emphasized. Family composition and dynamics, interacting with the educational, physical and financial resources available to parents and caregivers, create the context in which every child learns about digital media.

Funded by the Australian Research Council grant (DP150104734 *Toddlers and Tablets: Exploring the Risks and Benefits 0–5s Face Online*), we explore the range of ways in which our volunteer parents from Australia (twelve families) and the UK (ten families) harness the digital to help prepare their children for an uncertain future. Recognizing that young children are continuously learning, we discuss our ethnographic data in terms of three indicative developmental categories comprising infants, toddlers and preschoolers.

This book uses the term 'infant' to refer to babies, infants and very young children who are learning to walk, aged roughly from birth to twenty-three months. We acknowledge that older children in this group are often termed toddlers, differentiating them from the non-ambulatory or crawling child on the one hand and the confident walker on the other. Nonetheless, we stretch the term infants to encompass early walkers. Toddlers, aged roughly two and three, are hard to define. We toyed with referring to these children as early language users, since this feature characterizes the age group. In the end we adopted toddler as the more accessible, but arguably less accurate, term. We take heart that the US Centers for Disease Control and Prevention (n.d.) also refer to two- to three-year-olds as toddlers. We embrace the approach advanced by moving image researcher Cary Bazalgette at the beginning of her book *How Toddlers Learn the Secret Language of Movies*:

> We do not want to give the impression that twenty-four to thirty-six months is a precisely defined stage of life. The kinds of behaviour and learning that I describe [...] may develop earlier than twenty-four months and/or carry on after thirty-six months. So although I don't like the term 'toddlers' very much – it seems rather condescending – I do use it sometimes as a reminder that the age-group I am discussing is one that is identified by its capabilities and behaviour rather than by calendars.
>
> (Bazalgette, 2022, p. vii)

A preschooler in Australia, where compulsory schooling starts at six, is generally aged four or five. Formal education in the UK starts a year sooner, with all five-year-olds attending a primary reception class. Our oldest age group is children older than four, but less than six, and we call them preschoolers, whether they are in Australia or the UK. Given these perspectives and the relevance of everyday usage, shorthand terms used for the different cohorts of children in this book are:

- Infants (birth to twenty-three months);
- Toddlers (two and three years old); and
- Preschoolers (four and five years old).

Having addressed the terms we use to refer to child participants, we now explore the relevance of their everyday lives to the research reported here.

The importance of lived experience: What to look for and why we provide detail

The qualitative approach

This book draws principally upon qualitative research methods, ethnographically inspired interviews and close observation to explore digital media use in early childhood. The approaches we use have their foundations in seminal family-based media-use research such as Morley's *Family Television* (1986), Lull's (2000) *Media, Communication, Culture*, Bakardjieva's (2005) *Internet Society* and Clark's (2013) *The Parent App*. Contemporary ethnographies of children's digital media use including Livingstone and Blum-Ross's (2020) *Parenting for a Digital Future* and Bazalgette's (2022) accounts of *How Toddlers Learn the Secret Language of Movies*.

Ethnographic research relies upon small numbers of participants who allow researchers to explore individual and family experiences in significant depth. With a small number of collaborating families (twelve in Australia ten in the UK), this research does not pretend to be 'representative'. What it hopes to achieve, instead, is an appreciation of the meanings our collaborating children and adults assign to digital media use by young children aged up to six. Given that meaning depends upon context, original research in this book is reported in a way that provides in-depth commentary on each child in the context of their family, with an appendix that contains information about the family itself.

The work with individual children and the families that nurture them constitutes the backbone of the research and of the book. At the same time, there is a range of perspectives which can escape the attention of the individual participant family, but which come to the fore when families come together to compare notes or discuss specific issues and aspects of their mediation experiences. For example, individual family experiences, along with commonalities, are often made visible when parents discuss them as part of a group exchange. Accordingly, we complemented individual family-based research investigations with focus group interviews to investigate the role and contribution of common influences across very young children's lives.

Social science research, including the fields of Communications, Media and Cultural Studies, seeks to strike a balance between breadth and depth. Accordingly, we take care as authors to nuance our claims to suit our methods. We focus on the insights we gain via directly citing our interviewees in their own words. We emphasize the importance of direct observations across our different family contributors and use cautious observation in place of offering sweeping generalizations. To complement our qualitative approach, we also consider relevant quantitative findings from Sonia Livingstone and Alicia Blum-Ross's *Parenting for a Digital Future* survey (n.d.) comprising a nationally representative sample of UK parents with children aged birth to seventeen, conducted in late 2017.

A quantitative framework

In the UK *Parenting for a Digital Future* survey (n.d.), the device most available for children's use from infancy through to eight years was the tablet (73 per cent) rather than the smartphone (38 per cent). This pattern reverses by adolescence. Nearly one in ten children (10 per cent) went online via a wearable device, or smart home device, or a smart toy, and just under one-third (32 per cent) used a games console. This suggests dual trends across the birth to eight age range. For very young children, digital engagement involves more shared activities and access to devices within the family; while older children engage in more individualized activities. Qualitative research illuminates nuance around whose devices young children use, in which circumstances, according to whose rules, and how much this changes over time and circumstance.

For children across the *Parenting for a Digital Future* survey age range, digital engagement expands as they get older to feature more digital devices, including some that are not screen-based. Western societies are increasingly constructing a world in which non-screen devices, such as internet- and WiFi-connected toys and smartwatches, are becoming the norm (Kay et al., 2023). This is highlighted in the survey, which also demonstrates that children who access more, and a greater range of, devices (a proxy for better access and connectivity) have parents that are older, more highly educated and/or middle class. Within each socioeconomic segment, children access more devices if the child themself is older and/or has no special educational needs. From this we note that digital access, in practice, means digital inequality (Livingstone & Blum-Ross, 2020). Such inequality builds on established socioeconomic inequalities, which persist unless specific policy interventions counteract the forces of social reproduction (Helsper, 2021).

When we consider device use, we note that even the youngest children may undertake independent digital activities. When the survey asked, 'How often does "your child" use the internet, independently or with help, on any device/in any place?', on a scale from never to almost all the time, parents of a child aged from birth to four chose 'daily' as the most common answer (24 per cent said this). Although on average, parents of older children saw their child as more independent in using the internet, it is worth reflecting that such independence is commonplace for very young children, and this is explored qualitatively in our research with infants. Such independent digital media use was reported more often by older and middle-class parents, with no differences by gender of parent or child, suggesting that more privileged parents see an advantage in independent engagement for their children. Later chapters will illustrate how such independence may be manifest, and in which circumstances it may confer benefits or pose challenges.

Ethical considerations

It is appropriate to note here that our original research took place within a robust ethics framework, overseen by the Human Research Ethics Committees of Edith Cowan University and the London School of Economics and Political Science, respectively. All families are deidentified, while names and some non-material details have been changed to preserve confidentiality. Preschools and other early childhood care and educational establishments have been anonymized, as have complementary services that may have been identifiable, or that might inadvertently have identified participants. Apart from it being a usual requirement of ethics committees, an assurance of confidentiality helps people feel safer when sharing challenging, as well as positive, information. If it were otherwise, participants might be concerned about the possible longer-term ramifications of what they, or their child, might say.

Ethical research is based upon informed consent – parents and children need to understand what the research requires, how it will be conducted and that they have the right to withdraw at any time. While all parents were provided with this information by Ethics Committee-approved Information Letters and gave consent through signing similarly approved individual Consent Forms, we engaged differently with our younger participants and also had some differences in approach between the Australian and UK research teams. For example, although there were some UK interviews where Leslie Haddon worked alone, most interviews with younger children from birth to three used two researchers: one engaged with the parent, while the other focused on the child as the child tired of the adults' conversation and began to act autonomously. This strategy involved prior planning, and Australian researchers would often arrive with play-based items such as hula hoops, flashcards and other tactile resources as described at the start of Chapter 8, Toddlers. Naturally, the parent/s involved first gave their permission, and enabled researchers' interactions with their child.

Children aged three and over would generally express excitement around showing the researcher their favorite digital activities and would sometimes talk about why they enjoyed such play. In Australia, these children actively assented to being part of the research by pointing to a smiley face image, rather than a frowning face, on a purposefully simplified child-friendly consent form. Reassured they could say 'No' if they wished, all child participants' ongoing assent was assessed by their enthusiasm in engaging with us. We regularly offered each child an explicit choice around continuing or not, and we didn't conduct research with children who seemed unwilling or anxious, or with children who were tired of helping. Things didn't always go to plan and the data collection phase involved much discussion within and across the fieldwork sites with active, collaborative engagement between researchers, families and participant children.

Each research interview progressed in a conversational manner, in a venue chosen by the family concerned: often the family's kitchen or lounge room. Once the child began to ignore the adults' conversation and play in a self-directed way, the child-focused researcher would initiate a play-based research activity.

In work with these younger children, parents were enlisted as 'field collaborators' (Holloway & Stevenson, 2017). Older children were invited to take a researcher on a tour of their home, showing them where various digital play activities might take place: family room, kitchen, bedroom, etc. Parents generally stayed in close proximity and researchers were careful to read children's behavioral cues, stopping when the child tired.

Once the interview was over, the team would ask the parent if they could leave a video-capture device for them to record their child's digital engagement. In some cases, especially in the UK when Leslie Haddon was acting as a solo researcher, arrangements were made to return and do some recording. Not every family welcomed the idea of having children's digital media use recorded, and not all families initially open to the loan of a device had time to make a video recording in the weeks before it moved to the next family. This resulted in a dataset of varying depth and breadth that reflected the time that each family could allocate to the research. Those families that took up this additional opportunity to add data constitute a particular subset of informants, providing information relating to children's digital engagement over a period of some weeks and often prioritizing the illustration of activities and perspectives they'd shared in their initial interview. Some families relied on older children to conduct this video-capture, while parents in other families shot the videos themselves. Despite the variation in contribution duration and depth, family-produced videos were included in the research, logged and transcribed, providing additional material regarding very young children's everyday digital interactions.

One research objective was to investigate parents' understandings around mentoring and mediating their child's engagement with digital technology. Parents' ideas about family and family life, their attitudes towards digital technology and expectations around their child's future media use are central to such discussions. For newer parents, learning their role with their first or only child, the interviewers asked about pre-reading and any research done, formally or informally, such as talking with siblings or friends or speaking to early years educators about strategies for children's digital activities. Parents were prompted to recall influences they thought of as important, reflecting upon how these sometimes contrasted with their everyday experiences of digital parenting.

While this book does not include a 'methodology' chapter as such, methodological approaches are outlined throughout this introductory chapter and are also integrated within the chapters themselves. We now turn to the broad-brush aims of this research.

The researchers' brief

The original project motivating this research included the following aims:

1. analyse the ways in which adults are introducing digital technologies to pre-school children (birth to six-year-olds) and the contexts in which these technologies are used;
2. examine the rationales and strategies used by parents in deciding whether and when to allow very young children to play online, as well as what online activities and content they choose as suitable for their very young children;
3. gather video material around children's online play for analysis, involving children in the birth to six age group in research about what they like to do online and why;
4. use an evidence-based media studies perspective to participate in the debate about pre-schoolers' internet use currently emerging in the domains of psychology and paediatrics.

The team had worked together for almost a decade before starting this research, first becoming colleagues on the EU Kids Online project funded by the European Union's Safer Internet Plus Programme, focusing on children aged nine to sixteen (2006–14) (LSE, 2021). It was during the early years of EU Kids Online that touchscreen and smartphone innovations first transformed digital media use, enabling very young children's access. In the consumer societies of the Global North, the very young child is often culturally predisposed to recognize brands, logos, images and sounds as cues for important aspects of everyday life. These readily translate into the language of icon-interfaced digital media.

As touchscreens became prevalent, quickly moving through second and third generations of the technology, adults' upgrades of digital devices enabled a hand-me-down culture that placed digital media (typically WiFi-connected) into the hands of younger children. This phenomenon led members of the EU Kids Online team to explore the evolving digital environment as it impacted the very young. What they found was far more positive and reassuring than the situation implied in the AAP's fear-inducing recommendations of a couple of years earlier (AAP, 2011). In response, EU Kids Online published *Zero to Eight: Young Children and Their Internet Use* (Holloway et al., 2013), a short report with a long-lived impact, with almost 50,000 downloads over its first ten years. The Australian Research Council project which underpins this volume, *Toddlers and Tablets*, was built on these foundations and it benefits from research approaches first forged via EU Kids Online.

Participant children and their families

The original work in this book depends upon the time and commitment of twenty-two families: twelve in Australia, mainly metropolitan Perth and the surrounding suburbs; and ten in the UK, mainly from London. We take this opportunity to express our great gratitude to them for their time and generosity in sharing their experiences. The families were selected via purposeful recruitment with the aim of including a range of childhood development stages and experiences within our categories of infant, toddler and preschooler. Although the balance between age and stage and gender was broadly achieved, few households identified themselves as being blended families, while the homes of parents with higher education qualifications were over-represented. None of the families in the research have non-parents as primary carers, although several have multi-generational care structures that included grandparents. Additionally, a small number of sole-parent households chose to participate. A variety of income ranges and occupations is represented, alongside a range of linguistic and cultural backgrounds.

The twenty-two families contributing to the research include twenty-nine children in the relevant cohorts of interest: nine infants; nine toddlers; and eleven preschoolers. Seven of the families included two children each across the relevant age groups, thus fourteen children have a participant sibling, while fifteen other children made a sole contribution on the part of their family. In terms of binary gender, thirteen of the children are identified as female, sixteen as male.

Table 1.1 (overleaf), ordered according to the child's age, can be used to reference the children and families involved in the project, with outline information about parents' principal approaches to children's technology use supplied in Table 1.2. The Appendix provides a thumbnail sketch of all participant families, by pseudonymous surname. The index includes entries categorized by participant names and family groupings, along with sibling order.

In our research, firstborn and only children have parents who are more focused on their child's digital engagement. That focused attention reflects parents' decision-making around their child's journey towards digital competency. The interview data demonstrates that many parents take tentative steps in enabling their first child's engagement with digital media. As Danny Greenfield (UK) remarked to Leslie, 'it doesn't make any approach more right or more wrong, it's just kind of what works'. Second and subsequent children, however, enter an established digital milieu forged with and for their older sibling. The rules that are applied by parents to second and subsequent children often differ from those first applied to the eldest child's digital media use.

Table 1.1 Participating children in terms of family, country, first name, sibling order, development stage, age and birth gender

Family	AU/UK	Name	Sibling order	Category	Age	M/F
Govender	AU	Eliza	1	Infants	4 mths	F
Campbell	AU	Julia	1	Infants	11 mths	F
Cullen	AU	Finn	4	Infants	14 mths	M
Langridge	AU	Cecilia	2	Infants	19 mths	F
Kramer	UK	Owen	2	Infants	19 mths	M
Cheung-Yeo	AU	Samuel	1	Infants	21 mths	M
Greenfield	UK	Andrew	1	Infants	21 mths	M
Lim-Park	AU	Emily	2	Infants	23 mths	F
Mansi	UK	Sergei	1	Infants	23 mths	M
Tosetti	UK	Leopoldo	1	Toddlers	2 yrs	M
Davis	AU	Emma	3	Toddlers	2 yrs	F
Brown	UK	Simon	1	Toddlers	2 yrs	M
Zhang/Chen	AU	Lavinia	1	Toddlers	2 yrs 4 mths	F
Andrews-White	AU	Scott	3	Toddlers	2 yrs 6 mths	M
Ross	UK	Penny	2	Toddlers	3 yrs 3 mths	F
Langridge	AU	Jasper	1	Toddlers	3 yrs 5 mths	M
Jameson	UK	Evan	2	Toddlers	3 yrs 6 mths	M
Bernard	AU	William	5	Toddlers	3 yrs 6 mths	M
Kramer	UK	Libby	1	Preschool	4 yrs 1 mths	F
Spinner	UK	Imelda	3	Preschool	4 yrs	F
Lim-Park	AU	Michael	1	Preschool	4 yrs	M
Brent	UK	Ellen	3	Preschool	4 yrs 6 mths	F
Palmer	UK	Leela	2	Preschool	4 yrs 6 mths	F
Andrews-White	AU	Liam	2	Preschool	4 yrs 11 mths	M
Lawe-Tammell	AU	Ben	3	Preschool	5 yrs	M
Bernard	AU	Connor	4	Preschool	5 yrs	M

Family	AU/UK	Name	Sibling order	Category	Age	M/F
Davis	AU	Phoebe	2	Preschool	5 yrs	F
Petersen	AU	Freya	2	Preschool	5 yrs	F
Jameson	UK	Floyd	1	Reception*	5 yrs 4 mths	M

*In Australia, children aged five are still preschoolers, whereas in the UK they enter the primary reception class in the year they turn five.

Parents' perceptions of their approach to supporting children's digital engagement

Table 1.2 indicates parents' self-perceived and self-proclaimed overall approach to digital parenting. While every parent we spoke to wanted to provide the best-possible opportunities for their child, some described themselves as more concerned about the downsides of digital engagement, while others focused on supporting their child to embrace a digital future. Not every family had parents who agreed about such matters. Indeed, in our work with older children whose parents may have separated/divorced and gone on to set up separate households, different approaches to digital parenting were often especially evident, a situation also illustrated by other research (Livingstone & Blum-Ross, 2020).

We acknowledge that parents and families might at different times resist, balance and/or embrace their child's technology use. In our experience as researchers, no families invariably represent one or other of these approaches in its purest, unwavering form. The terms 'resist, balance and embrace' are genres of digital parenting styles introduced in the book, *Parenting for a Digital Future* (Livingstone & Blum-Ross, 2020). They are further discussed in Chapter 3.

The parents contributing to our project were keen to talk about issues encountered in mediating children's digital engagement. Acknowledging that digital parenting is an evolving journey that responds to experience and context, some parents describe themselves as being in protracted negotiations with their partner: in terms of their child's digital engagement and also, sometimes, in regard to their own media habits. As parent Francoise Jameson confided in Leslie: 'we've tried … I've … mostly me … to have a sort of detox, digital detox'.

Given that parents' mediation styles shift in response to events and new information, Table 1.2 (on the following two pages) indicates their approaches as shared in the interviews.

Table 1.2 Assessment of genre of parents' approaches to mediating their child's engagement with digital media, as indicated to researchers

Style	Chapter	Family	Name/s	Age/s	Mother	Father
Resisting	Toddler Preschool	Jameson	Evan & Floyd	3 yrs 5 yrs	Resisting*	Resisting
Resisting	Infant Preschool	Lim-Park	Emily & Michael	23 mths 4 yrs	Resisting	Resisting
R/B	Toddler	Ross	Penny	3 yrs 3 mths	Resisting	Balancing
R/B	Infant	Greenfield	Andrew	21 mths	Resisting	Balancing
R/B	Infant	Mansi	Sergei	23 mths	Resisting	Balancing
B/R	Preschool	Spinner	Imelda	4 yrs	Balanced**	Resisting
R/B	Toddler	Zhang/Chen	Lavinia	2 yrs, 4 mths	R/B	Balancing
R/E	Infant	Govender	Eliza	4 mths	Resisting	Embracing
B/B	Infant Preschooler	Kramer	Owen Libby	19 mths 4 yrs 1 mths	Balancing	Balancing
Balancing	Toddler Preschool	Davis	Emma & Phoebe	2 yrs 5 yrs	Balancing	Balancing
Balancing B/E	Preschool	Petersen	Freya	5 yrs	Balancing	B/E
B/E	Toddler	Brown	Simon	2 yrs	B/E	B/E
B/E	Infant	Campbell	Julia	11 mths	Balancing	Embracing
B/E	Toddler Preschool	Bernard	William & Connor	3 yrs 5 yrs	Balancing	Embracing

Style	Chapter	Family	Name/s	Age/s	Mother	Father
B/E	Preschool	Lawe-Tammell	Ben	5 yrs	Balancing	Embracing
E/?	Infant	Langridge	Cecilia & Jasper	19 mths / 3 yrs 5 mths	Embracing***	Not known
E/B	Preschool	Brent	Ellen	4 yrs 6 mths	Embracing	Balancing
Embracing	Infant	Cullen	Finn	14 mths	Embracing	Absent
Embracing	Preschool	Palmer	Leela	4 yrs 6 mths	Embracing	Absent
Embracing	Infant	Cheung-Yeo	Samuel	21 mths	Embracing	Embracing
Embracing	Toddler	Tosetti	Leopoldo	2 yrs	Embracing	Embracing
Embracing	Toddler	Andrews-White	Scott & Liam	2 yrs 6 mths / 4 yrs 11 mths	Embracing	Embracing

*Resisting: these parents tend to focus on the perceived downsides of their child's digital media use.

**Balancing: these parents express a conscious attempt to balance perceived positives and negatives of digital media.

***Embracing: these parents tended to talk about benefits and opportunities arising from their child's media use.

Many parents find themselves negotiating a balance between maximizing the positive benefits of their children's digital activities while trying to minimize possible drawbacks. In effect, these parents are engaging in a local variant of a global discussion that argues for a balance of protecting children from digital risk while encouraging skill development and participation. Regulatory settings in this area encompass complex and overlapping restrictions and guidance regarding all ages of children under eighteen years old, seeking to balance protection for minors with the development of resilience and safe forms of participation (O'Neill et al., 2013). There are many different parameters that impact what children can and cannot do in digital domains including contractual capacity (typically eighteen, though children and parents may agree to informal family-based 'contracts' around digital media use) and providing consent for organizations' collection and processing of personal data (different jurisdictions typically assign children this capacity between the ages of thirteen and sixteen: Pasquale et al., 2020, and also see Livingstone, Stoilova & Nandagiri, 2019). Such discussions also encompass guidance on age appropriateness, which were applied largely voluntarily at the time of this research but are increasingly the focus of regulation via age verification mechanisms (Pasquale et al., 2020). As the next section notes, however, a focus upon prohibition runs counter to a rights-based discourse that is gathering momentum in the context of the United Nations' *General Comment (No 25) on Children's Rights in the Digital Environment* (UNCRC, 2021), which recognizes children's entitlement of access to and engagement in digital domains (see Chapter 2).

The structure of this book

This book has been a joint collaboration among experienced researchers across three countries who have worked together on the *Toddlers and Tablets* project and shared other research endeavours for more than a decade. Leslie, Kylie and Donell were heavily involved in the original data collection for *Toddlers and Tablets*. All authors engaged fully with all chapters and the team generously and collectively gave feedback to one another. There was nevertheless some division of labour in the writing. In particular, Sonia focused on screen time issues; Brian specialized in policy inputs and implications; Leslie took on responsibility for literature reviews; Lelia made sure the voices of individual families were heard and Kylie applied a keen editorial eye to individual chapters and thereafter worked on the entire volume to integrate material across the book.

Setting the scene for what follows in the book's exploration of parents' mediation of young children's digital lives, this introductory Chapter 1, 'Contextualizing digital media use in early childhood', has explained the background of the ARC-funded *Toddlers and Tablets* project. It identifies the aims, research methods and approaches used in the research while providing information about participant families. Positioning parents, grandparents, early years' educators and children as having specific expertise grounded in everyday life, the chapter details the contributing families, the twenty-two households and the twenty-nine children, from birth to almost six, whose digital experiences inform the research findings. The importance of matters, such as family size, educational background, cultural heritage, resource access and sibling order, is introduced. Finally, this chapter provides an outline of the book's structure.

Chapter 2, 'Conceptual and other framings of children's media use', addresses the seminal theorists and foundational concepts that inform our approach and underpin our understandings of the research we discuss. Recommended approaches to adults' management of children's digital media use are also important, prefiguring debates to be addressed in 'Screen time' (Chapter 3). Prescriptive guidelines around children's media use are often at odds with the everyday practices of parents and children detailed in following chapters, while the suitability of such advice and its mutability in practice have been brought into sharp relief by the Covid-19 pandemic, which saw younger children go online for longer, and more often, as parents struggled to respond to challenges posed by lockdowns and home-based isolation. While our ethnographic research concluded prior to the pandemic, Covid-19 informs ongoing interpretation of our work. It also raises issues of geographical and other differences inflected within the context of the Global South and the Global North: consideration of these matters concludes Chapter 2.

'Screen time', Chapter 3, positions research on digital parenting and young families in relation to hotly contested debates over children's media use. It argues that parents are exhorted simultaneously to control their child's screen time and to ensure their child keep up in the race to prepare for a digital future. Since it is easier to monitor and police screen time than to judge and enhance the quality of children's digital engagement, parents are tempted to do the former. Yet this results in a moral burden that parents find difficult to implement in practice and that children seek to evade, leading to domestic conflict. Moreover, researchers and policymakers are no longer convinced that simply controlling screen time is advisable, necessitating a more nuanced approach that recognizes the diverse pressures families face, their choices to embrace, balance or resist technological change and the rights of children to be heard within the debate.

Starting with an overview of research on young children's experiences in engaging with digital media, including parental mediation and parenting styles, Chapter 4 'Parenting and digital media' reviews contemporary sources of parental ethnotheories which guide how parents address their concerns about digital media and their use of technologies to occupy children. The *Toddlers and Tablets* project reveals the sources of ideas used by parents as they learn to parent, including drawing on online advice from experts and bloggers, noting how parents critically construct ideas about parenthood and technologies. A discussion of the complexities of parental concerns around children under six years old and how these overlap with, but differ from, concerns about older children follows, given that parents of younger children focus on the role of digital media in children's development, rather than on online risks. Finally, the chapter considers the use of digital content to keep children occupied and parents' assessments of this practice.

Chapter 5, 'Grandparents', discusses a relatively new area of interest compared with that of digital parenting, yet demonstrates the complexity of and changes in grandparenting experiences, roles and differing approaches: the shifting norms of grandparenting. The *Toddlers and Tablets* research reinforced this picture of diversity while providing examples that challenge a stereotype of grandparents as having low digital skills by virtue of being older. Grandparents reflected critically on changes in parenthood and pressures on parents, and were no more conservative than their children in approaching their (grand)parenting duties. They had an equivalent range of views about the role of digital media, for example, with mixed evaluations of using connected technology to occupy children. The example of a grandparent's discussion of their concern around 'interfering' in their child's parenting decisions illuminates why so many grandparents try to avoid this. Even so, some grandparents try to create a haven from technology when their grandchildren visited them.

The 'Digital media in preschool settings' literature, Chapter 6, illustrates a historic lack of engagement by preschool staff with digital media. Staff taught technology use with scant guided interaction and had limited appreciation of how digital media use might aid cognitive development. Our research illustrates factors that still limit preschoolers' digital engagement, such as financial constraints, lack of training, limited time, the priorities of the individual nursery and the relevant regulatory frameworks. Nurseries use digital media to varying degrees – sometimes including staff members' personal devices – and staff who used technologies least aspired to use them more. While it appeared that children's home use stimulated interest, preschool workers had to manage that interest carefully to ensure it became educationally productive. Confirming previous findings, early years' educators had limited knowledge of children's digital media use at home and parents and staff were sometimes concerned about each other's use of digital media to occupy children.

Chapter 7, 'Infants', explores the factors that parents consider when enabling digital media use by children up to two. It recognizes that early motor skill development can include touching and swiping before a first birthday. Family vignettes show how children's agency manifests early, contextualized within differences in parents' approaches and experiences. The analysis considers how adults say they learn to parent and how their experiences of parenting may differ from expectations. Some parents say mediating children's digital engagement makes them aware of their own habits, including using media as a distraction or 'babysitter'. Media practices that connect young children with absent family are valued, but parents occasionally feel that educators working in childcare and nurseries are wasting educational opportunities if they use digital media with infants. Describing young children's digital media skills as 'natural', parents seem unaware of current policy settings, or that designers and industry could do more to support their digital parenting practices.

Investigating how parents see their toddler's media use as creating or constraining possibilities for the future, the 'Toddlers' cohort comprises nine families (Chapter 8). Vignettes of toddlers engaging with digital media reveal their growing capacity to make deliberate choices and negotiate their wishes with the adults who set rules around media use. Parents worry about toddlers having an optimal balance of activities, while some fear that digital engagement might be 'mesmerizing'. They express a range of attitudes: from suggesting digital media can be deferred until compulsory school begins, to believing a child steeped in technology from their earliest days will have a clear advantage in the future. Many parents embrace videocalls for connecting with distant family and also use digital devices to support toddlers' exposure to non-Anglo language and culture, helping build multi-lingual competencies. Policy relating to toddlers is less contested than for infants, but families feel generally unsupported by the private sector.

Chapter 9, 'Preschoolers', explores how children's use of digital media may help develop social and emotional skills and their ability to relate to others. This is reflected in four- and five-year-olds' greater understanding and awareness, and their capacity to contribute more reflexively and knowingly to the research. As a result, the chapter addresses the expanded research methodology adopted for this age group and some of the issues arising from this, before discussing the family-based vignettes. The ethnographic accounts offer various examples of family practices: social co-play between children and adults; children's projection of sociability onto favoured devices; parental use of digital access as a reward mechanism; digital engagement as shared cultural capital; children's identity exploration and self-care; and the confidence-boosting benefits of digital skill-development. It also details some parents' fears around inappropriate content, digital 'addiction' and the priming of consumerism, all of which have emotional components. The chapter concludes with some policy considerations.

Looking beyond differences in children's experiences of digital media influenced by factors such as gender, socioeconomic status and ethnicity, Chapter 10 considers the less well-covered 'Bases for diversity in children's digital experiences'. Family observations reveal how the technological orientation of parents may impact their personal evaluation of digital media, with implications for parents' mediation and their enabling of children's access and opportunities. Such dispositions interact with parents' more general approach to parenting, and their mediation styles, while cultural and linguistic considerations also influence how parents try to encourage and manage their children's technology use. Siblings have a bearing on young children's digital media experiences since they can be enablers and supporters of each other's use, as well as competitors. Finally, problematic relationships between parents may adversely impact children's access to communication media, for example, in the case of divorced parents, where children spend time in two households.

Chapter 11 reviews the literature on 'Parents' evaluation of children's learning through digital media' and parents' own place in that process, contrasting and critiquing the frameworks of Piaget and Vygotsky. While some parents in the *Toddlers and Tablets* study are sceptical, most are positive about the role of digital media. Parents' hopeful evaluation of the potential of educational apps to support children's learning is implicit in the fact that most parents have bought these, even if they don't use them. Borrowing from the forms of learning identified in the literature, we show how parents construct their children's learning as a matter of learning dispositions, developing operational skills, learning about the world and engaging with cultural values and practices. Lastly, drawing on video evidence, three case studies illustrate ways in which parents scaffold their children's learning with technology, sometimes building on that process by asking additional questions that stimulate children's thinking.

The book's final chapter (Chapter 12) 'Summarizing our research findings', brings together our findings on the development of the young digital child. Acknowledging the growing importance of siblings and friends as children get older, we argue that young children progress in digital skill development and diversify their digital engagement in parallel with developments in walking and motor skills (roughly, Infants); talking and an increasing awareness of self (roughly, Toddlers); and negotiation and identity differentiation (roughly, Preschoolers). We highlight that most parents of young children focus on how they can support their child's development, but have concerns about whether technology use might undermine that process. Parents, grandparents and early childhood educators apply rules around preschoolers' digital media use that arise from their often-unstated techno-imaginaries for their child's future. While parents sometimes view young children's digital media use with trepidation, sometimes with enthusiasm, there are many reasons to be optimistic about parents' support of young children's digital media use.

2

Conceptual and Other Framings of Children's Media Use

Having introduced our book in Chapter 1, noting why we focus on infants', toddlers' and preschoolers' digital media use, Chapter 2 offers a range of theoretical and other frameworks that guide the empirical research that follows in later chapters. These framings are informed by our shared disciplinary backgrounds as media, communication and cultural studies scholars, although each of us also acknowledges other influences, such as psychology, social anthropology and education. For readers without expertise in digital matters, we can recommend a comprehensive disciplinary glossary such as that produced by the Digital Futures Commission (Atabay et al., 2023).

Social constructionism

This book is grounded in social constructionism – the view that humans construct and refine their ideas of what is real through social interactions with others. Berger and Luckmann (1966), who are widely accepted as foundational influences upon social constructionism, argue that we are actors within our social contexts, co-constructing shared understandings that underpin what we know, our views of the world, and our place and agency within it. Since the world is complex, changing and diverse, we also agree with Burr (2015, p. 4) that 'the ways in which we commonly understand the world, the categories and concepts we use, are historically and culturally specific'. This includes concepts such as child, parent, family, technology and digital media. Take a simple example – a 'mobile', half a century ago, might reference a toy hung over a baby's pram. Nowadays it references a portable connected multimedia device (except in American English, where the more common term is cell phone, with less emphasis on mobility).

Berger and Luckmann wrote as sociologists with an interest in ontology, the philosophy of 'being'; of understanding what is. Epistemology complements ontology by considering how we know what we know, the philosophy of 'knowledge'. The epistemological implication of social constructionism is that we may understand more about what we know, and the ways in which we know it, by examining people's accounts of how they come to the knowledge they have about specific matters of interest (Crotty, 2020). In social constructionism we might aim to 'undo the social' (Game, 1991) as a means of understanding our participants' perspectives. In this book, we particularly attend to the meanings that parents, caregivers, educators and children themselves assign to young children's digital media use.

The social construction of reality does not assume that all views are equal, however. Some perspectives are pervasive, playing a dominant role in meaning construction within particular social settings, while others are heavily contested. Scholars might offer different 'ways of seeing' (Berger, 1972) or suggest a range of metaphors for a particular social institution, as with organizations (Morgan, 1986). In the same way that Berger and Luckmann's views have influenced us, we acknowledge a particular contribution to meaning making in this area by key scholars in the socio-cultural tradition, including Vygotsky, Bruner, Bronfenbrenner and Flewitt. These thinkers have contributed much of the conceptual framework that underpins this book. Accordingly, it is to these thinkers and key theories that we next turn.

Lev Vygotsky

Vygotsky wrote in Russian and while his ideas were formed mainly in the 1920s–30s, they only began to impact Western understandings around child development in the 1960s when his work was translated and made widely available. His theories have some resonances with those proposed by Berger and Luckmann (1966) in that he argues that language and culture shape children's cognitive abilities (1962), suggesting these develop through children's engagement in social and cultural practices. Building upon his notion of 'the social origin of all human mental processes' (Eun, 2019, p. 18), Vygotsky developed the idea of 'the zone of proximal development'. This captures the idea that children are always ready to stretch themselves to learn the next thing, without trying to learn too much at once; hence, there is value in their interacting with a more experienced guide, such as a parent, teacher or mentor.

In the context of this book, we hold that the child works with their guide at the boundaries of their knowledge and competence, to the point where the child internalizes a new understanding which offers opportunities for further development. This has some similarities with the idea of the 'scaffolding of knowledge', which was subsequently put forward by Bruner (see Wood et al., 1976; also Margolis, 2020), and which raises clear questions about uses of digital technology to scaffold learning. Vygotsky's work (1978) is also discussed in Chapter 11, contrasting his approach with that of Jean Piaget (1952, 1954), whose work was known to him.

Jerome Bruner

Jerome Bruner's work (2006) in developmental psychology focuses upon the active processes through which a child perceive their world, and the impact of the child's sensory and tactile engagement in everyday life. Beginning around the mid-1960s, and referencing Vygotsky's work, Bruner started investigating what he called the 'scaffolding' of children's learning. Scaffolding describes the process through which an educator, a parent, teacher and/or another child might carefully guide a learner to start with the skills and competencies they already possess, while supporting the gradual and structured development of new or augmented knowledge.

Bruner's conceptualization of how this knowledge is experienced or 'represented' in the child's learning process encompasses action-based, image-based and symbolic (language-based) representation. Bruner's suggested spiral curriculum delineates how a particular skill may be developed through successive periods of practice that cement established knowledge while adding new elements that become increasingly sophisticated over time. Bruner also argues that humans learn more quickly and easily when they are interested in the subject matter. This perspective energized his late-career pioneering work in the 1980s exploring the minutiae of children's learning through their everyday interactions in home settings – then assumed to occur face to face – using (the then innovative method of) videotape recording.

Urie Bronfenbrenner

Independently of Bruner's work, developmental psychologist Urie Bronfenbrenner dedicated his career to developing what is now known as the ecological systems theory, built around his emphasis on the wider, societal ecology which contextualizes human development (Bronfenbrenner, 1979, p. 21). This theory positions the child at the centre of concentric circles of influence, to delineate and explore different layers of environmental impacts across four concentric dimensions. These move outward, from the child at the heart of the model to the microsystem, the mesosystem, the exosystem and the macrosystem. While subsequent researchers have interrogated a range of social and contextual factors that potentially impact that child's development and maturation, Bronfenbrenner's theoretical concepts are broadly applicable to every aspect of children's lives, including digital media.

The child themself is individuated in having been born in a particular time and place with specific sexual, emotional, cognitive, and socio-cultural characteristics. While some of these are determined by history, geography and genetics, the individuals and institutions within the microsystem (Bronfenbrenner, 1979, p. 22) temper and emphasize certain aspects of that individuality. Chief among the microsystem influences is the family, and this informs the focus that this book places on each child's individual family context. As he developed his theory, Bronfenbrenner became so persuaded of the importance of the child's biological heritage that he went on to refer to his model as the bioecological theory of human development (Bronfenbrenner, 2005, pp. 3–15).

As children get older, their lives are increasingly influenced by other social institutions. These include the educational context: their childcare centre, their pre-primary or school, the peers they interact with, the opportunities they have for physical and exploratory outdoor play, and the religious and political frameworks that both enrich and circumscribe their lives. Effectively, the mesosystem (Bronfenbrenner, 1979, p. 25) describes the interactions between these different frameworks that constitute a neighbourhood and the social and other resources that the family draws upon for its parenting, and for important aspects of their child's daily life.

But mesosystems themselves operate within exosystems (Bronfenbrenner, 1979, p. 25). These are not influenced by individual child participants but nonetheless they impact upon children. Exosystems include the political organization of the community and of the cultural setting; such elements as the mass media, the economic context for the family, and the resources made available to the child and their parents, including matters like childcare, libraries and a public education system. Encircling and supporting the exosystem, Bronfenbrenner conceptualized the macrosystem (Bronfenbrenner, 1979, p. 26) as the physical manifestation of the attitudes and ideologies of the dominant culture in which the child and their family live: systems such as capitalism and a free market economy. Clearly, as well as influencing the child, their family and children's development opportunities and trajectories, the different elements within these expanding contextual circles also influence the child's interactions with digital media.

Rosie Flewitt

Rosie Flewitt has a specific influence on the research reported in this book through her work on 'the respectful and inclusive involvement of children in the research process' (Flewitt, 2005, p. 553). Flewitt describes in detail the approach she takes to working with four three-year-old children on naturalistic, ethnographic, video-based case studies exploring the children's lives and experience as they began their preschool education. Noting that children of this age may be perceived as too young to 'consent' to such research, Flewitt counsels against this, arguing that such child participants' 'responses indicated strongly that although only three years old, they were "competent" and confident enough to grant or withdraw consent – with some more outspoken and enquiring than their parents' (p. 555). While our research was mainly conducted via audio-recording supplemented by (mainly) family-initiated video-recordings, we followed Flewitt's approach to adopting ethics-based practices that helped build trust between participants and researchers, noting that 'those relationships in turn shaped the nature and quality of data collected' (p. 564).

More recently, Flewitt and her colleagues have explored children's engagement with digital media. In Kucirkova and Flewitt (2022), the authors make recommendations for adopting a posthumanist perspective on socio-materiality in which the social (and psychological) practices that contribute to a child's digital interaction are contrasted with the 'physical, technological and design-related properties of resources used in the interaction', arguing that an assemblage constructed via the interaction produces 'truths, realities, knowledges and relationships' (Kucirkova & Flewitt, 2022, p. 164, citing Kuby & Rowsell, 2017, p. 285). They suggest that 'nuanced understanding' of children's digital media should be based on an appreciation of 'socio-material entanglement' and 'time-space dynamics' (2022, p. 175) and it is these details that we seek to capture in the book via the deep attention paid to the individual child case studies (although we do this via the theoretical framework of social constructionism rather than posthumanism).

Having explored some of the key influences and approaches that inform our research (and others will be introduced in later chapters), we next consider the importance of developmentally appropriate practice, within educational policy, before addressing other dominant policy settings that frame young children's digital engagement. These include the global influence of the American Academy of Pediatrics' statements around these issues, taking a public health approach, and the UN Committee on the Rights of the Child's General Comment (no. 25) on Children's Rights in Relation to the Digital Environment (UNCRC, 2021), which implements the UN Convention on the Rights of the Child in digital contexts.

Educators, developmentally appropriate practice and early years' education frameworks

The United States' National Association for the Education of Young Children (NAEYC) offers a range of guidelines and resources for the care and education of children from birth to eight. Its book *Developmentally Appropriate Practice in Early Childhood Programs*, now in its fourth edition (NAEYC, 2022), sets the US benchmark for meeting the needs of individual children in the early childhood sector. The NAEYC framework supports teachers' strategies and competencies across a range of practices to aid them in 'creating a caring community of learners, engaging in reciprocal partnerships with families and fostering community connections, and enhancing each child's development and learning' (Jeon et al., 2022, p. 1367).

The NAEYC position statement (NAEYC, 2020) identifies six key focus areas for enacting developmentally appropriate practice, requiring educators to apply knowledge of child development and learning across a range of contexts:

1. creating a caring, equitable community of learners;
2. engaging in reciprocal partnerships with families and fostering community connections;
3. observing, documenting and assessing children's development and learning;
4. teaching to enhance each child's development and learning;
5. planning and implementing an engaging curriculum to achieve meaningful goals; and
6. Demonstrating professionalism as an early childhood educator.

The position statement also provides a useful glossary of terms relevant to the area.

In sum, developmentally appropriate practice is achieved by the holistic goal of meeting the needs of the individual child across all 'domains and content areas' (Jeon et al., 2022, p. 1367) including social emotional learning and early childhood special education settings. Developmentally appropriate practice mirrors the emphasis on the child's 'evolving capacity', rather than their chronological age, as is appropriate in a child-rights approach. Jeon et al. (2022, p. 1375) argue that the practice is most effective when adopted by organizations as a framework that is applied across shared contexts. A belief in the efficacy of developmentally appropriate practice has been associated with lower rates of job burnout and psychological stress in American early childhood special needs educators, possibly because of more effective teaching, classroom and behaviour management strategies, alongside better communication with parents, families and communities (p. 1367).

While the formal statement about 'developmentally appropriate practice' is a dominant influence in North America, other frameworks are found in equivalent early years' contexts in alternative national settings. In Australia, for example, the early childhood education and care framework aims to instil 'social, physical, emotional, personal, creative, and cognitive learning in children' (Education, 2023) and operates from birth to the commencement of compulsory schooling, usually the school term in which the child turns six. In England, the Department for Education (education.gov.uk, 2023) publishes a *Statutory Framework for the Early Years' Foundation Stage: Setting the Standards for Learning, Development and Care for Children from Birth to Five*.

Having considered some of the professional frameworks supporting young children's educational experiences, we move on to address the part played by expert medical advice in children's experiences of digital media.

Medical statements around young children and digital media use

Whereas most educational curricula see some merit in the teaching and integrating of digital media in relation to children in early years' settings, medical perspectives have generally been more conservative. One set of recommendations in particular – from the American Academy of Pediatrics (AAP) – has had a disproportionate influence on public and policy perceptions both within the United States and across the globe. The research in this book overwhelmingly addresses the global North, as do the AAP guidelines. In these richer countries, parents and families typically live in communities where, although characterized by significant inequality, digital technologies are relatively plentiful and comparatively affordable. In other countries, and in earlier times, the policy focus was and still is more on bridging the digital divide and enabling access for children in a range of settings and age groups.

While the AAP guidelines have changed over the years, perceptions of these recommendations have not kept up with those changes. One impact is that it has made 'screen time' a hot button topic for parents, for the public and for policymakers. Our research is motivated by a desire to understand parents' approaches to introducing and supporting very young children's use of digital media, and the aspects of digital media use valued by young children themselves. Yet it's the 'don't do it' statements, such as those in the AAP guidelines, that still capture the public imagination and this prohibition may lie behind judgemental responses from others that unsettle parents when they support their young child's use of digital media outside the home. Such negative perspectives have led to an emphasis on restricting 'how long' a child might interact with a screen rather than focusing upon the quality of the content with which they interact, and the various benefits, including fun and skill development, that a child may derive as a result.

Chapter 1 addressed Bazalgette's (2022) work in detailing the skills developed by infants and toddlers in understanding 'the secret language of movies', calling into question the notion of 'passive' media use. Analogously, parents from language groups and minority cultural contexts contributing to this research deliberately use media from their countries and cultures of origin to support their child's understanding and appreciation of cultural and linguistic diversity. This deliberate harnessing of content to teach culture is an active use of digital media to support children's learning. The current AAP guidelines on 'Media and young minds' (AAP, 2016) are more nuanced than the original AAP guidelines 'Media use for children younger than 2 years' (AAP, 2011). But it is still the dictum of the earlier guidelines – summarized as 'no media use under two' (AAP, 2011, p. 1040) – that retains a hold on the global public consciousness. That approach has also been formally and informally adopted into many government policy frameworks. The distorting impacts of blanket screen time rules are addressed more centrally in the next chapter, Chapter 3, but this section has highlighted the potential of medical models to influence public debate more strongly than is the case with educational or culture-based perspectives.

Children's rights in the digital environment

While the AAP guidelines continue to counsel caution in relation to younger children's engagement with screens and digital media, scholars around the world have been asking what a rights-based approach to these issues would look like, thus building on the authority of international soft law addressed to states worldwide. Indeed, completion of this book closely follows an auspicious date in the journey towards a rights-based framework for children growing up in a digital world.

In 2021, the United Nations Committee on the Rights of the Child, a sub-sectorial responsibility of the United Nations Office of the High Commissioner on Human Rights, concluded many years of discussion and consultation with its publication of a 'General Comment'. That General Comment (No. 25) on Children's Rights in the Digital Environment (UNCRC, 2021) moves the discourse forward from a dominant focus upon the protection of children from harm in digital contexts to primarily requiring jurisdictions to promote children's full range of rights including those of participation and engagement in digital contexts. This rights-based approach includes but is not limited to an affirmation of children's rights to protection and privacy (Livingstone & Third, 2017). Such rights are conceived as intersecting with a child's age and evolving capacity, as well as requiring the provision of opportunities (fairly, for all children) related to infrastructure, education and technological access. By incorporating the UN's child rights framework into national law and policy, governments and other national and supra-national organizations can chart their progress in delivering better paths for children's digital engagement, protection and citizenship.

The research reported here can be construed as supporting that aim. Our original intention was to augment existing research around very young children's digital participation with an evidence base derived from and representing the everyday knowledge of contemporary parents and children. While a range of health, education and policy-promoting authorities offer parents and caregivers guidelines and cautionary advice, there is comparatively little evidence that draws upon the intrinsic knowledge held by those who live with the impacts of their everyday decisions in relation to children's everyday digital media use. This dearth of the lived experience of children's mediatization (Livingstone, 2014) is especially evident in the case of children below the age of six. This book addresses that gap in the evidence base.

Raising young children in a (post-)pandemic digital world

The foundational family-based face-to-face research in this volume was conducted before the seismic shift in digital device use fostered by community-wide Covid-19 lockdowns. This section sketches some of the early research emerging from those events in relation to very young children. It seeks to explore the implications of Covid-19 for the fieldwork reported in subsequent chapters. As we contextualize our data for the post-pandemic era, we also use the paragraphs that follow to reflect upon the possibility (or not) of extrapolating our findings from Australia and the UK to other nations. Ultimately, we argue that rich, deep research findings require original data from many more settings than those represented by the twenty-two families reported on in this book. At the same time, there is a dearth of ethnographic studies investigating the digital lives of children under six years, and it is better to have made this start than to bewail the impossibility of achieving comprehensive coverage.

Although there may be a general lack of ethnographic studies, the lives of very young children are deservedly attracting increasing research attention not least because, as Wade et al. (2023, p. 115126) recognize (citing Nelson & Gabard-Durnam, 2020), 'the first three years of life are a period of heightened neuroplasticity and vulnerability to stress'. Su et al. (2022) conducted a bibliometric analysis of global trends in early childhood education research during Covid-19. They identified 242 relevant English-language early childhood education articles on the World of Science database and 265 on Scopus (with many overlaps). Three of the four most-cited publications were articulated around gendered divisions of labour related to parents' early years' nurturing and education practices during the pandemic. The overall second most-cited publication, Dong et al. (2020), focused on 'Chinese parents' beliefs and attitudes relating to young children's online learning during the pandemic'.

Noting a disproportionate quantum of publications from six countries – the United States, Canada, Germany, China, Australia and the UK (in descending order) – Su et al. comment that this indicates a 'publication bias towards authors from less developed countries' (2022, p. 5). Even so, the insights from the papers that follow indicate many shared features characterizing young children's lives online, even as we recognize that millions of children around the world remain unable to access digital media. Using Bronfenbrenner's schema, however, we now consider a range of studies that address digital media use by young children whose families can provide those opportunities.

Bergmann et al. (2022, p. 1) researched 2,209 infants and toddlers aged between eight and thirty-six months, recruited by fifteen labs across twelve countries, and concluded that toddlers 'were exposed to more screen time during lockdown than before lockdown'. In the United States, during the 2020-1 lockdowns, Findley et al. (2022, p. 1095) argue that parents, and especially mothers, lessened restrictions around screen time for children under six. Facing the 'extraordinary task of managing competing demands such as illness, economic hardship, fatigue, working remotely and supporting their children's learning' (Minson & McLean, 2023, p. 118, discussing Australia), parents allowed their children to go online younger, for longer. While this made some parents feel guilty, Findley et al. (2022) found that many parents justified screen time as a strategy for prioritizing their own mental health while allowing children to socialize with peers, engage in educational activities and connect with extended family members.

In Japan, Shinomiya et al. (2021) surveyed over 5,000 parents and caregivers of children aged between eighteen and thirty months, seeking information about any changes in sleep quality and activities relating to an eight-day period before (2019) and during (2020) the pandemic. They concluded that, in the early stages of the pandemic in Japan, 'outdoor play decreased significantly while media use time significantly increased among infants staying at home during the daytime. In addition, the caregivers of these infants showed more stress' (Shinomiya et al., 2021). Children also slept less well.

Working with older children (ten- to eleven-year-olds) during the pandemic, Indonesian researchers (Temban et al., 2021) argue that YouTube Kids allowed 'young children to be curious and make sense of their new-found information within a controlled environment'. Adopting a child-rights lens they suggest YouTube Kids is an 'ideal' learning environment given that children have 'autonomy to direct their learning' (2021, p. 284). Temban et al.'s (2021) arguments could also apply to children under six viewing YouTube Kids and would support Bazalgette's (2022) observations that even 'passive' viewing involves active learning. We suggest in the chapters following that this learning includes self-discovery: children's agentic exploration of their personal interests and enthusiasms.

The studies mentioned above indicate that within the microcosm of the family, digital media was often used to compensate children for Covid-19 impacted activities that could no longer be enjoyed, such as outdoor playtime and catching up with friends and family. Older preschoolers would have been able to harness these opportunities to explore and build social and cultural capital, engaging with content they could talk about with others (Stevenson et al., 2021), online and off. For parents, children's digital media use could offer some respite and an opportunity to focus on other responsibilities.

Moving to a consideration of the mesosystem impacts upon children's media engagement, Ford et al. (2021) surveyed over 500 educators who had taken part in the virtual teaching of children under six. These early years' specialists identified a range of challenges, including factors that confounded their ability to use developmentally appropriate practice. Amongst other issues, teachers noted: 'Low levels of participation [by children ...] limited social interaction and developmentally appropriate ways of engaging children [...] lack of knowledge and skills for virtual teaching [...] limited technological support and unstable internet access' (Ford et al., 2021, p. 7). Educators regretted that many parents used the remote teaching periods to attend to other priorities, with the implication that children would have benefitted from parents scaffolding children's digital media use, helping their children understand the digital learning environment, and assisting with education around some of the content.

An analogous study of Australians whose children engaged with early years' education online noted parents' concerns that children wanted '*to run around, not participate in the conversation*' (Parent 18, Levickis et al., 2022, p. 5). Parent 5 from this same study thought their child was put off by the teacher's digital presence because '*you can't see into the room, you can't see anything so just have no sense of, it's like a black hole that you're sending [your]child in*' (P5) (2022, p. 5). These challenges may have been less of an issue in families where parents weren't trying to work remotely, and who weren't anxious about the necessities of life in a pandemic. But many parents were concerned about both these things and more, and Ford et al. (2021) note that lockdown learning risked exacerbating educational inequality. That argument links the mesosystem issues of children's educational interactions with the exosystem parameters of economic, digital and infrastructure resources, and the macrosystem influences of dominant ideologies, such as a free-market economy and the availability (or otherwise) of accessible healthcare and social security.

Minson and McLean's (2023) Australian work contrasts and complements Ford et al.'s (2021) US-based research. Referencing neighbourhood resources and interactions, the mesosystem, Minson and McLean discuss the digital delivery of virtual 'caregiver-led community-based playgroups' during a series of strictly enforced lockdowns in the Australian state of Victoria. They note that many families successfully used digital media 'to support play-based learning opportunities for their preschool children' (2023, p. 118). The community playgroup model assumes a parent, usually the mother, facilitates their child's engagement and it's reasonable to suggest that the community playgroup's capacity to reposition itself online reflects that parent-per-child support, with each child helped by their parent working with them in their zone of proximal development. Families who had played and learned together within physical playgroup spaces were able to harness (variously) Zoom, Facebook and Messenger to maintain 'trusted networks' and 'familiar traditions' while enabling 'meaningful play-based opportunities' (Minson & McLean, 2023, p. 128) online.

Considering these playgroup and childcare papers together, it's possible that home-based young children engage more freely via digital media when their co-communicators are other parents and children who fit into their understanding of a domestic context. Young children may feel less at ease communicating with formally trained educators from early care and education settings when these are repositioned in quasi-domestic, or a 'neutral'-seeming visual space, and where the microsystem of the child's home is infiltrated by the mesosystem of the structured childcare education setting. It is also likely that exosystem-level 'state and local policies issued in response to the Covid-19 pandemic altered ECE [early childhood education] environments, teacher-child interactions, and activities' (Pic et al., 2023, p. 194, referencing the United States).

The body of work investigated in Su et al.'s (2022) bibliographic analysis, referenced at the start of this section, indicates that existing inequalities of access to early years' care and education were exacerbated during the pandemic by 'factors such as race, culture, language, technical literacy, family background, and economic status [widening] gaps in learning outcomes between privileged and underprivileged children' (Su et al., 2022, p. 15). Ethnographic family-based research takes some time to reach publication and while there are a few examples of this work in Covid settings (e.g. Levickis et al., 2022; and for some older children, as in Pearce et al., 2022), these are comparatively sparse. What evidence there is, however, including the material cited above, indicates that once the pandemic lockdowns began, children would likely have had:

- differing experiences as a result of geography, wealth and educational advantage;
- parents who were preoccupied and tired, juggling a range of stressors such as finances, work, health, social isolation and lack of childcare;
- reduced outdoor playtime and poorer quality sleep;
- less formal educational instruction; and
- more screen time, at a younger age.

These factors indicate that the pandemic has increased the relevance and importance of a detailed understanding of very young children's lives online. The rest of this volume responds to that challenge, and that opportunity. Chapter 3 starts our journey by considering one of the dominant discursive tropes relating to children's digital media use: screen time. It seeks nuance within the 'one size fits all' injunctions and argues for a discussion around quality, rather than quantity.

3

Screen Time

There are many reasons to be optimistic about children growing up in a digital world and many reasons to be concerned. Both the opportunities and the risks of technology deserve society's attention, for significant and wide-ranging changes are needed if children's opportunities to benefit are to be maximized and the risks of harm are to be minimized. Problematically, potent myths in circulation confuse public debate and divert policymakers from the tasks ahead. One is that children are 'digital natives' supposedly better able to manage the digital world than the adults around them (Bennett et al., 2008). For sure, some adults may lack the confidence or proficiency to engage with the latest apps, though many – including parents – do not. Yet the digital native myth can be used to justify the lack of intervention on the part of those with the power to improve children's digital lives: surely, it is blithely held, children can be left to get on with it themselves, society need not devote attention or resources to their needs. Another myth is that the internet is just for adults – children have no business being online anyway and, if they go online, their parents are responsible for keeping them safe (Livingstone & Third, 2017). While parents are indeed responsible for their children, educators are also key actors in this space. Governments have responsibilities to support parents and children, as do the commercial providers of digital products and services. Moreover, to leave matters solely to parents exacerbates the inequalities that already shape children's lives, since parents are not equally resourced to manage complex technological change. Also important, children have the same rights as the rest of us to participate fully in today's digital world, so leaving them out is not an option.

Drawing on Isaiah Berlin's (1969) analysis of liberty, we could say that the digital native myth undermines actions designed to optimize children's positive freedoms – for digital learning, creative expression, sociability and participation. Meanwhile, the internet-is-not-for-kids myth undermines efforts to improve children's negative freedoms – to engage safely and without undue barriers or discrimination. These myths, along with others, have become wrapped up in two overarching and contradictory injunctions to parents. First: control screen time! This breaks down as: allow them up to two hours a day but no more; police what they do; if anything goes wrong, it's your fault. Second: keep up! Since children will grow up to do jobs that haven't been invented yet, parents must invest to ensure their children don't fall behind, so they are prepared for the digital future. As research shows, in their efforts to keep up, parents buy the latest devices, upgrade their connectivity, search for educational apps and enrol their children in coding clubs. But all the while, they worry about screen time and about not reproducing the idyllic childhood of yesteryear, itself another myth used to criticize parents. Thus, they keep a daily tally of screen time hours in their head, unsure whether homework or zooming grandparents 'counts', offering and withholding device use as behavioural rewards and punishments. Screen time calculations wear parents out, blinding them to the specificities of how and why children engage with what's actually on the screen, leading to conflict within the family. Parents feel anxious and guilty about screen time and this is not helped by the critical judgements of others, whether friends or strangers, who may call them out for failing to control their children.

Not only does screen time become a catch-all concept for highly diverse technologically mediated activities but, as Livingstone and Blum-Ross (2020) argued in *Parenting for a Digital Future*, it can become a focal point, a catalyst even, for families' negotiation of the many and often non-technological challenges they face – whether due to poverty or family breakdown or ethnic discrimination or special educational needs and disabilities, or any of a host of further causes. Whatever the problem, technology gets the blame – teenage mental health problems are caused by their smartphones, toddlers' bad behaviour is due to playing computer games, families don't talk to each other because everyone's on their own device. And whatever the problem, a technological solution offers itself – invest in a computer to overcome the risk of exclusion, sign up to digital media classes to get ahead when formal education is failing your child, play the latest computer games to become a professional games designer in future. No wonder digital technology has become the terrain on which parents centre their hopes and fears for their child's development and negotiate their values, expectations and practices of everyday life.

Many aspects of society shape families' practices and prospects, along with children's well-being. In crucial respects, families are complex and diverse, impeding simplistic generalizations about 'children these days' or 'what's wrong with parenting'. Moreover, both techno-utopian and techno-dystopian ideas are impossible to live with. Under the radar of panicky public discourses, families must get on with raising their children in ways that accommodate life's complexities, uncertainties and necessary compromises. This means recognizing that today's world is increasingly reliant on digital technologies, that there is no going back to pre-digital days, but that there is some latitude for choice and that it's worth thinking about this carefully. This is not to say that all's well: the commercial pressures on families to accede to the digital marketer's dream are considerable; the narrow focus of governments on e-safety and basic skills instead of, also, creative and participatory digital literacies, lets families down; the long-standing sources of inequality and exclusion in society are perpetuated and even exacerbated in the digital realm.

This chapter will first look back to see how the focus on screen time came about before considering its role in family life. Then we will widen the frame, draw on available survey findings to complement the ethnographic approach of this book and identify more constructive ways of conceptualizing today's digital parenting dilemmas. This allows us to consider the normative question – what does 'good' look like for young children's digital lives – and point to themes that the rest of the book will address.

The rise and fall of screen time

> Deep anxieties about technological and social change go back to Plato's worry that writing would erase memory, to the Catholic church's fear that the printing press would undermine its authority by democratising access to knowledge and to public anxieties over the circus, comic books, the cinema, radio – each in turn feared for unleashing the unruly or immoral impulses of the weak-willed.
> (Livingstone, 2021, p. 89)

The prominence and persistence of the concept of screen time in parents' talk about childhood socialization – often expressed as some unattributed version of the American Academy of Pediatrics' famous 2×2 rule (no screen time for under twos, no more than two hours per day for older children: Council on Communications and Media, 2016) – was examined by Livingstone (2021) to excavate its origins. It emerged that, while 'moral panics' about technological innovation are nothing new, a means by which the privileged express their concerns about and exert control over those who are less powerful (women, children, the working class), screen time is, paradoxically, not only an old concept but also a new one (Butsch, 2000). For it is also a modern product of the postwar rise of psychology and its statistical techniques to measure the everyday behaviours of the population (including exposure to the then-new medium of television) and correlate these with the societal problem of the day (whether body weight, fitness, reading skills, educational attainment or crime rates). In practice, the effort to correlate television viewing with a host of social ills proved fraught, with the results being both inconsistent and heavily contested. But as techniques to measure viewing time developed, providing the currency for the marketing spend of mass media advertising, they also added the gloss of scientific precision to the popular appeal of that simple measure – time. Whether exposure to particular contents (such as violent cartoons) could be incontrovertibly linked to problematic behaviour (such as aggression) received less attention than the reliable division of people into 'light' or 'heavy' viewers and the public and expert castigation of the latter. Influenced by the public health model of diagnosis and treatment, the idea took hold of a 'dose-response relationship – so that for every hour (or quarter-hour, even) that the limit was exceeded, the outcomes for the child would be worse; even though the research does not support such precision and even though the adverse outcome itself was generally unspecified' (Livingstone, 2021, p. 98).

The World Health Organization's (2019) *Guidelines on Physical Activity, Sedentary Behaviour and Sleep for Children under 5 Years of Age* found little convincing evidence that screen time *per se* was the problem. This is not least because screen time is not inevitably sedentary: young children may play, dance or run around in front of a screen; moreover, some sedentary activities can have value (think of reading a book). However, referring specifically to 'sedentary screen time', WHO advises no screen time for infants less than one year old and no more than one hour for one- to four-year-olds, preferably accompanied by reading or storytelling with a caregiver. They also emphasize the importance of moderate to intense physical activity and good quality sleep. In other words, while sitting still for extended periods is not advised, it is more critical that positive activities known to contribute to well-being are not displaced.

Running through the debates about screen time is the difficulty of controlling for many possible confounding factors that may explain the observed association between screen time and health, notably socioeconomic status or underlying health or family problems. For example, the UK's Royal College of Paediatrics and Child Health concluded from its systematic review of evidence reviews that 'the contribution of screen time to wellbeing is small when considered together with the contribution of sleep, physical activity, eating and bullying as well as poverty' (Stiglic & Viner, 2019, p. 3). In other words, screen time may play a role for both good and ill but other factors make a greater difference to well-being and so should take precedence when it comes to policy interventions to improve children's lives. Similar results have been found in the United States.

> The most recent and rigorous large-scale preregistered studies report small associations between the amount of daily digital technology usage and adolescents' wellbeing that do not offer a way of distinguishing cause from effect and, as estimated, are unlikely to be of clinical or practical significance.
> (Odgers & Jensen, 2020, p. 336)

The emphasis on methodological rigour here is significant: the news is full of shocking headlines about screen time and children's well-being; however, it does a poor job of examining the evidence claimed to link the two in a cause-effect relationship. Corkin (2021) compared two large-scale studies, both based on the Growing Up in New Zealand longitudinal cohort study, to illustrate the problem. One study found no relationship between 'excessive' screen time and poor well-being when it correlated 'excessive' screen time (more than two hours per day) among children aged two to nearly four with measures of poor well-being (inattention and hyperactivity) when the same children were four and a half. A second study used the same measures at four and a half, finding a significant association. Since the first study showed that excessive screen time did not precede poor well-being, one must conclude from the second study that poor well-being leads to excessive screen time (rather than the other way around). As Corkin comments, 'it may be that children struggling with inattention and hyperactivity find screen time calming or satisfying, or that parents find it offers opportunities to occupy their children, whether as a sole or joint activity'.

What does this mean for the concept of screen time? We are left with a paradox:

> The idea of screen time worked because it is simple, measurable, memorable, needed by parents facing new technological uncertainties and has science behind it. But it didn't work for similar reasons: its simplicity overrides the specifics of screen content and context; the focus on time measurement precludes attention to the quality of a child's engagement with the screen; it does not, in fact, help parents either in skilling their child for a digital future or building their resilience to technologically-mediated harms.
> (Livingstone, 2021, pp. 98–9)

No wonder parents think parenting is harder today than twenty years ago, precisely because of the advent of social media and smartphones (Pew Research Center, 2020).

Parenting for a digital future

The concept of screen time can be seen as one instance of technological determinism – attributing significant causal power to technology while neglecting the role of humans as agents in appropriating technology in diverse ways and the importance of the social context in shaping and constraining the possibilities for those human agents. Like all determinisms, it doesn't fit the complexities of real lives. We need to reorient our analysis and our advice to parents in ways that recognize people's meaningful actions and the contexts that constrain them, contexts often not of their own making. Seeking an alternative, media ethnography builds on calls for non-technologically centric approaches that, quite literally, seek to put technologies in their rightful place in our lives. It aims neither to overemphasize technologies nor to overlook them; instead, the ethnographic approach explores how they 'are situated as part of the routine, habitual, tacit, normally unspoken sensitivities of everyday life' (Pink & Leder Mackley, 2013, p. 678), critically examining why this matters and what difference the digital makes. This approach has particular value for the research participants of this book, for whether a child, parent, grandparent, early years' educator or other caregivers, none of their voices are prominent in public debates about 'the proper way' to bring up children in a digital age. Yet, all can offer the voice of experience and the distinct insights of those involved.

In their *Parenting for a Digital Future* research, Livingstone and Blum-Ross (2020) invited parents to look back to the remembered past of their childhood and then forward to an imagined future of their children's adulthood. This revealed how parents themselves highlight particular hopes or fears, articulate the values that matter to them and account for their everyday practices in general and around digital technology on a broader canvas than just screen time. This broader canvas itself is shaped by the historical process of individualization in the late modern risk society. Beck and Beck-Gernsheim explain:

> On the one hand, individualisation means the disintegration of previously existing social forms – for example, the increasing fragility of such categories as class and social status, gender roles, family, neighbourhood etc. [… on the other hand] new demands, controls and constraints are being imposed on individuals.
>
> (2002, p. 2)

In other words, families can no longer count on established traditions and norms to guide their parenting and socialization, for they are freer than ever before to express their individual preferences and lifestyles. On the other hand, they lack the support of established communities and institutions and must face alone the new challenges of globalization, innovation and precarity, including carrying the risk personally if things go wrong. Of the many consequences for family life, one is that 'parenting' has become a crucial means by which society explores pressing dilemmas over how to live, what constitutes well-being and what 'good life' to hope for. Another is that parents attempt to optimize their imagined future by establishing family values and practices designed to improve their child's life chances, drawing on diverse and highly unequal resources to do so. Notably, investing in digital technologies emerges as a distinct pathway for many parents, albeit one that also compounds adult anxieties about innovation, authority and control.

Livingstone and Blum-Ross identified three genres of 'digital parenting' as follows:

- embrace, in which parents seek out digital technologies for themselves or their children to ease family life or to gain valued professional skills or, for some, 'future-ready' identities and lifestyles;
- balance, in which parents try to hedge their bets by encouraging some digital practices and not others, often ad hoc, weighing opportunities and risks salient in the present or future;
- resist, in which parents articulate their efforts as attempting, at least some of the time, to stem the seemingly unstoppable incursion of digital technology into family life. (2020, p. 11)

Note that this is not a categorization of parents, for one family might exhibit all three genres, while another might oscillate between two. Instead, these digital parenting genres captured the culturally shared ways in which particular values, imaginaries and practices tended to cluster together in the everyday lives of their research participants. Moreover,

> each genre brings its own anxiety, as parents ask themselves: Did I get it right? Will it pay off? *Embracing* means positioning oneself ahead of the curve and so one may feel exposed, acting before the social norms and resources are in place to offer support. *Balancing* is an active and effortful process, like standing on a rolling log. Not simply a compromise, it invites constant self-questioning and adjustment: Is this right? How can I tell? *Resisting* may mean worrying about missing out professionally or personally, or that one is going out on a limb, taking a risk by *not* doing what everyone else seems to be doing.
>
> (Livingstone & Blum-Ross, 2020, p. 13)

In such ways, the digital preoccupies parents' attention and emotions, leading them to seek advice from others, debate and sometimes conflict with others within the family and invest yet further in whatever technology that promises to serve their needs better. In turn, this necessitates that parents wrestle with the particular affordances of the digital itself: the complexity and opacity of the interface, its widely networked connections, its constant innovation and change, its heavily commercial motivations, its creative forms of expression and its radical challenge to our privacy.

In no small measure, parental views of technology influence their actions. The *Parenting for a Digital Future* survey (n.d.) asked for their views in recognition of how digital parenting in the here-and-now is motivated by parents' deeper understanding of the changing digital world. Parents were broadly but not hugely positive about technology, judging that the benefits to their child are likely to outweigh the harms. This was particularly the case for the benefits of learning about technology, supporting school learning, pursuing hobbies and interests, being creative and expressive and preparing for future work. Parents were a bit more doubtful, but still not negative overall, about possible benefits to their child in developing relationships with family or friends, or learning social and emotional skills. More about why this is and how parents manage to balance the pros and cons of technology as they see them unfolds in the chapters that follow.

Survey findings support qualitative insights

Several of the themes developed in this chapter are supported by the findings of the *Parenting for a Digital Future* survey already referenced above and in the previous chapter. This includes the finding that screen time rules can result in family conflicts. Top sources of difficulty or conflict between parents and children were bedtime/sleep, 'their behaviour' and screen time, closely followed by eating, homework (especially with sons) and chores (especially mothers). Less problematic were money, friends, clothing (more for daughters) and how they use technologies. The child's age made the greatest difference to screen time conflicts – infants and toddlers occasioned the least conflict (15 per cent of parents of birth to four-year-olds said that the amount of screen time leads to conflict) and this is fewer than parents who find bedtime (26 per cent), behaviour (24 per cent) or what they eat (23 per cent) difficult. Among parents of five- to eight-year-olds, however, screen time was in joint third place for what results in family conflict, with what they eat (27 per cent) behind bedtime (35 per cent) and behaviour (30 per cent), but ahead of homework (25 per cent) or chores (17 per cent). Screen time was perceived to be more problematic among older parents and those from higher socioeconomic status households. Interestingly, the amount of screen time was reported as much more problematic by parents than what children actually do with digital media, which was seen as leading to difficulties or conflict by just 3 per cent of parents of birth to four-year-olds and an average of 9 per cent across the entire age range birth to seventeen.

Digital parenting strategies focused on the content and context of children's digital engagement thus appear promising. For this, parent-child shared activities are particularly important. Gee, Takeuchi and Wartella (2017) show that 'joint media engagement' has a range of benefits for children's digital engagement and well-being (including for improving digital safety) and for family life more generally. It likely also benefits the parents and grandparents who get involved (Nimrod et al., 2019), as explored in this book. The *Parenting for a Digital Future* survey found that shared child-parent play with video games was more common in middle childhood than for older or younger children. Still, one in five parents of a child aged birth to four reported playing computer or video games together. Watching TV or films together was a much more common form of joint media engagement – more than three-quarters of parents said they did this, whether their child was a toddler or a teenager. Learning about something on the internet together was least common among parents of birth to four-year-olds (one in three) and most common in middle childhood (one in two parents of five- to twelve-year-olds say this). We can compare these figures with nondigital activities, where the most commonly shared activities include eating meals together (four in five parents, irrespective of the child's age) and playing with toys or games; the latter also reported by four in five parents of birth to four-year-olds, though this tails off as children get older, as do reading together and creative activities (practised by seven and six in ten parents of birth to four-year-olds respectively).

These and other forms of parental mediation or joint media engagement are significantly facilitated by the fact that parents themselves live digital lives. This point is too often neglected as if parents were all unskilled 'digital immigrants' rather than, in truth, the first generation 'born digital' (Palfrey & Gasser, 2008). But of course, parents today have multiple digital skills. They may gain these at work or through their own activities, but they are keen to use them to benefit their children. The *Parenting for a Digital Future* survey found that, of seven activities that might enable children's learning at home, parents reported undertaking an average of two, but more for younger children and with no gender differences. For instance, nearly half of the parents of children aged birth to six watch a video to help them or their child learn something new. Three in ten parents of birth to four-year-olds and four in ten of five- to eight-year-olds downloaded an educational app or game to support their child's internet use. Parents of children in the middle years (five to twelve) report doing most activities, as do middle-class parents, while a third of parents from the lowest socioeconomic group said they did none of them.

Such enabling activities also include accessing parenting support. Asked, 'When you have a question or concern about your child or family, where do you go for advice?', the most popular answer was to search online or just figure it out for themselves. Strikingly, while 28 per cent of parents of birth to seventeen-year-olds said they could turn to their own parent(s) for general advice, only 9 per cent could do this for digital problems, suggesting a generation gap in support. Wealthier parents were more likely to turn to online sources, while the poorest parents are most likely to have 'nowhere' to turn, as were parents of birth to four-year-olds. In consequence, more parents of very young (birth to four) than older children (five to seventeen) go online to search for information or advice about their child's health (41 per cent vs 23 per cent), to connect with other parents for advice or support (23 per cent vs 14 per cent) and to find local activities and events (51 per cent vs 40 per cent).

Having recognized parents' increasingly rich digital lives, it becomes more obvious that parents are positioned to mediate their children's digital activities by doing more than just imposing rules. The survey found that parents, on average, reported 'sometimes' doing a wide range of enabling and restrictive forms of parental mediation (Livingstone et al., 2017). Their activities varied little for sons and daughters, but a lot by the child's age. For infants and toddlers, preferred parental mediation involved rules about screen time, using parental controls or apps to manage their use and also sharing activities online together. For five- to twelve-year-olds, parents did more overall compared with parents of younger and older children, often using restrictive strategies such as screen time rules, parental controls and apps. However, they were also more likely to enable their child's digital media use by encouraging their child to explore online, suggesting how to use the internet safely, talking to them about what they do online, sharing online activities with them, pointing them to good resources and last, resorting to treating device access as a reward or punishment depending on their child's behaviour. As younger children use devices more and more, it will be necessary for policymakers and professionals to encourage parents to undertake enabling forms of parental mediation – for example, advising, guiding, sharing, monitoring and using parental controls – rather than restrictive ones based on content-blind and outdated screen time rules.

What does 'good' look like for young children's digital lives?

This chapter has examined the popular and scientific concept of screen time and found it wanting as a way of characterizing young children's digital engagement and as a guide for digital parenting. Not only does it fail families and policymakers in achieving their purposes, but its technologically determinist mindset promotes what Third et al. (2019, p. 44) call 'the control paradigm [which ...] speaks in terms of slippery slopes, worst-case scenarios and ... conflates risks with harm, operating as if negative consequences are inevitable'. In characterizing the 'control paradigm' as a deficit theory, Third et al. (2019) highlight how adults think of children as either *at risk*, or as the risk. In either case, this seems to call for adult monitoring, evaluation and intervention and in neither case are children's perspectives – or agency – granted much consideration.

The popular metaphor of 'policing' your child's screen time exemplifies this dual lens perfectly, for whether policing is required to protect one's child from criminals or to treat them as the criminal, the parent is positioned as the clear authority and the child's voice plays no role in the exercise of parental power. Although supposedly the beneficiaries of regulation, in practice, children are positioned as the object of regulation; it is their thoughts and behaviours that rules about screen time seek to bring into line. It is children who become the problem when the rules prove to be unachievable given the multiplicity of digital devices and contents, not to mention the diversity of purposes for which they are used in a digital world. As Third et al. (2019, pp. 222–3) conclude, 'one of the control paradigm's most powerful and detrimental effects is its myopia, its foreclosure of the possibilities of the digital well before they have been fully probed or tested'. It may be objected that the alternative is to treat today's children as the canaries in the coalmine, or as lab rats in the huge experiment that is society's adoption of all things digital.

So, what would be a better alternative? Marsh et al. found that parents of under-fives identified the following motivations for using digital apps:

> Children: (i) found them fun to use; (ii) found interactive apps particularly engaging; (iii) enjoyed learning new skills and acquiring knowledge; (iv) liked apps that related to their popular cultural interests; (v) enjoyed practising skills

and achieving a sense of mastery; (vi) liked the positive feedback and rewards they received when they achieved goals; (vii) liked to play the apps that siblings and parents used; (viii) enjoying watching videos and more passive experiences when they wanted to wind down.

(2015, p. 21)

Rather than concluding that the problems of safety, security, privacy and commercialization associated with digital technologies are reason enough to limit, restrict and police children's digital engagement, it would be preferable to resolve such hygiene factors through better regulation, the widespread adoption of safety-, security- and privacy-by-design and by rethinking the business model that commodifies attention at the cost of human (including children's) rights. This would ensure attention also to the motivational factors that policymakers, designers and digital providers could support, thereby benefitting children's needs, interests and rights (Livingstone & Pothong, 2021). Summarizing a considerable body of research for the UK's Digital Futures Commission, Colvert advocates the practice of playful-by-design to promote the positives as well as address the negatives. She observed:

> Play with digital technologies provides myriad opportunities for imaginative play ... Children regularly integrate and transform narratives, characters and themes from computer games in their offline play ... However, opportunities for adaption and imaginative transformations of meanings can be limited by product designs and broader commercial strategies.

(2021, pp. 36–7)

Unfortunately, the problems with the digital environment and the consequent need for protection, significant and urgent though these are, are more vivid and concrete for adults than the benefits. Knowing what 'good' looks like for children's digital engagement is a struggle even for experts dedicated to children's rights. For example, identifying which digital games to recommend to children of different ages seems much harder than knowing which books to recommend for them. Moreover, adults can be puzzled by young children's digital activities. They may not realize that it takes time and patient attention to recognize the creativity, experimentation and imagination that makes these activities meaningful. In relation to a digital puppetry app, Wohlwend (2015, p. 154) showed how 'many hands all busy dragging, resizing and animating puppet characters and many voices making sound effects, narrating, directing and objecting' constitute a form of collaborative digital engagement that enables valuable storytelling practices. But to an outside eye, such activities may appear chaotic or aimless. It is also the case that some of the benefits of digital engagement are too new to be well known. For example, not many professionals who work with children are aware of recent developments with augmented and virtual reality technologies designed to enable children's involvement in narrative (Yamada-Rice, 2021). The DigiLitEY project explored how digital and nondigital resources could be imaginatively integrated within the Early Years' classroom:

> The children watched a professional puppet show based on the Moomin stories and then created their own illuminated shoebox puppet theatres, writing play scripts to be used with these. The children also created their own clay models of the characters. These were imported into the Qlone screening app so that they became 3D digital models. This allowed the models to be 3D printed and also taken into the VR app Google Tilt Brush. The children then donned a VR headset and used the app to create a VR version of the Moomin valley.
>
> (2018, p. 3)

These are multi-layered activities that require hardware, software and digital literacy to ensure their success. Finally, reflecting on the role of technologies in early years settings, Scott observes:

> With increasing pressure for formal pedagogies in early childhood classrooms, certain essential forms of play are becoming neglected, particularly solo and peer fantasy play … rather than restricting play, digital devices and texts may provide young children with precisely the opportunities for free (uninterrupted) peer fantasy play that are increasingly missing in other realms of their lives.
>
> (2018, p. 244)

Scott echoes widespread concerns that the offline realm is itself becoming impoverished as children's freedoms are increasingly constrained, while the Digital Futures Commission is exploring how established ideas of free play can be extended from the offline to online realms to expand and refresh society's expectations of the digital world:

> Children's free time and freedom of movement in the physical environment has been increasingly eroded. Children are spending less time outside and offline for multiple reasons to do with increased traffic, reduced public transport, cuts to community support for children's play, building over sports fields and green spaces and actual or feared threats to children's safety outside the home.
>
> (Livingstone & Pothong, 2021, p. 11)

Consequently, it is also worth considering how children's new freedoms online can be extended offline, expanding and refreshing their opportunities for imaginative, open-ended play, learning and sociability in all realms.

The challenges for parents, however, may seem never-ending. Barron et al. identified seven 'scaffolding' actions for parents in relation to digital media learning: 'teaching, collaborating on projects with, providing nontechnical support to, brokering learning opportunities for, providing learning resources for, learning from and employing children to assist with technical projects' (2009, p. 71). Observing the roles parents played in a digital makerspace for preschoolers, Blum-Ross and Livingstone (2019) confirmed these observations and added that parents could also be seen supervising, cheerleading, engaging in parallel play and using children's digital engagement for babysitting. While outsiders can disparage some of these roles, especially that of babysitting, parents themselves offer reasons for their activities that deserve to be heard. For instance, in the makerspaces, some less-privileged parents felt they did not understand the activities and themselves lacked the necessary skills, but they were nonetheless proud to offer their child the opportunity for something 'better' than they as a parent could provide at home (which might be 'just more screen time'); so, while they sat back and did not get involved, it was significant for them and their child that they had made an effort to bring their child and, though comparatively modest, their scaffolding intentions were good ones.

The UN Committee on the Rights of the Child, which recently adopted its 'General Comment 25 on children's rights in relation to the digital environment' (2021), offers some guiding principles which can help resolve the inevitable dilemmas that arise as society – including parents, educators, professionals who work with children and children themselves – engage with rapidly changing technologies (Livingstone & Third, 2017). The first is to consult children in age-appropriate ways and listen to their voices and experiences – and yes, this applies even to young children who can indeed express themselves on matters that affect them, as well as to parents and other caregivers (Crowley, Larkins & Pinto, 2021). As subsequent chapters show, the authors of this book have taken this principle very much to heart. The second is to ensure that policy decisions and advice to the public based on those decisions are robustly grounded in evidence, eschewing myths or partisan views and that, where possible, children should be involved in generating and deliberating on the evidence; this book contributes to this effort. The third draws on the 'best interests' principle of the UN Convention on the Rights of the Child and its article on 'evolving capacity' to argue that while it is likely to be in the best interests of the child to be protected up to the age of eighteen, it is also in their best interests to participate as early as they can and as much as they choose (Lansdown, 2005). In other words, rather than seeking a single age for children to go online (as with the popular idea of a digital age of consent), we should recognize that children may be ready to participate earlier than they are fully capable of protecting themselves. To facilitate their early participation while also protecting them, a mix of enabling parental mediation and child-rights-respecting service design would be optimal.

Parents need the support and guidance of governments and professionals in this task. In relation to the digital environment, these professionals include those responsible for designing, promoting and profiting from digital technologies (United Nations, 2011). However, in this regard, parents do not always receive the support they need for multiple reasons. Businesses can be reluctant to acknowledge that children use their services, neither designing for them nor providing family-friendly information about how services work. This means that parents are often faced with an impossible choice architecture that even experts cannot understand, evaluate or navigate effectively. Even when businesses do provide support for children or families, it tends to be generic, with little information tailored to children of different ages. Such support is even less likely to acknowledge the cultural diversity or socioeconomic realities of family life, nor that some children have special educational needs and disabilities. On the plus side, it seems that change is in the air. There are growing calls for better service design that respects child users' needs and rights, along with heightened public expectations for the government regulation of digital providers, while professionals who work with children are becoming more attuned to the digital dimension of family life.

4

Parenting and Digital Media

Introduction

This chapter examines parents' understanding of their role in relation to their children's digital media use and how they manage that in practice. But to understand research on parents' approaches to their children's digital experience, it is first worth considering a broader picture of claims about the way family life is changing. Some writings on the de-traditionalization of the family (reviewed in Williams & Williams, 2005) suggest that parenthood itself has been changing for some time. Parents are increasingly expected to be attentive to more aspects of their children's development and to negotiate with them, although a Spanish study of parents of young children suggested that such negotiations may be more of an aspiration than a reality (López de Ayala López & Haddon, 2018). However, this still raises the question of whether contemporary parents engage more with and invest more time in their children than some earlier generations of parents. Although it is beyond the scope of this current research to explore these developments, such changes in parenthood can be viewed as a backdrop to understanding some of the more specific parent-child interactions explored both in the earlier literature and the current Toddler and Tablets research reported in this book.

The chapter first gives a brief outline of prior research about digital media more generally and children and touchscreens specifically to provide a general context to the current research and because some studies cast doubt on the moral panics around these technologies. Next, there is an overview of the literatures on parental management of children's digital media use, initially covering the parents of older children but nowadays applied to the parents of younger ones as well. Those literatures give rise to the first more substantive theme of the review and the chapter: how parents develop their ideas about parenting, and childhood more generally, and specifically in relation to technology. The second issue addressed is the nature of parental concerns that lead parents to mediate their children's touchscreen experiences and how other contingencies can also influence this process. Finally, the chapter looks at the specific case of using touchscreens to occupy children since this can counter parental mediation policies and evoke mixed evaluations.

Literature review: Parenting and digital media

Various terms are used in the research on young children and technologies – ICTs and digital technology, for example – but for the purposes of this and other chapters, the term 'digital media' will be used. Some scholars involved in this work have observed that the study of early childhood and digital media has been a niche area compared to studies of older children (Stephens & Edwards, 2018). This research on digital media[1] covered both the home (e.g. Plowman et al., 2008; Stephen et al., 2008; Plowman et al., 2010; McPake et al., 2012.; Plowman et al., 2012; Plowman & Stevenson, 2013; Stephen et al., 2013; Chaudron et al., 2018) and preschool settings (e.g. Stephen & Plowman, 2003; Plowman, & Stephen, 2003; Plowman & Stephen, 2005; Stephen & Plowman, 2008; Wolfe & Flewitt, 2010; Spink et al., 2010; Roberts-Holmes, 2014; Vidal-Hall et al., 2020; Schriever, 2021) and the latter will be used to provide some context in the later chapter on preschool educators.

Stephens and Edwards (2018) noted that the introduction of the iPad in 2010 both contributed to moral panics and stimulated research on these devices, later covering other touchscreens, such as smartphones. From this time, studies emerged on issues such as children's access to these technologies (e.g. Marsh et al., 2015), what children do with touchscreens (e.g. Given et al., 2014; Chaudron, 2015), the total time spent using the devices and how different digital activities may be distributed across the day (Marsh et al., 2015), what children can do with touchscreens at different ages (e.g. Marsh et al., 2015; Neumann & Neumann, 2017), whether this affects their literacy (e.g. Neumann, 2018), what factors predict children's different use of these technologies (e.g. Lauricella et al., 2015) and how children learn to use touchscreens and who they learn from (Chaudron, 2015).

Although these lines of enquiry are not developed in this study, there are several findings of more direct relevance to the key themes of this book. One common observation is that, in contrast to fears about how these digital media might be changing childhood, digital technologies may be important but they do not dominate children's lives (Stephen et al., 2008; Plowman et al., 2010a; Neumann, 2014; Chaudron, 2015; Tőkés, 2016). Given concerns about technologies simply displacing other activities, another finding is that children often mix digital and non-digital play (e.g. Verenikina & Kervin, 2011); for a typology of this see Marsh et al. (2016). In relation to fears about children engaging with technologies in isolation, some of that research has drawn attention to how parents actually interact with children while they play with their touchscreens (e.g. Danby et al., 2013; a range of studies with this focus is reviewed in Marsh et al., 2018). Other researchers have noted that parents sometimes utilize these technologies to occupy children (Nevski & Siibak, 2016). Describing smartphone use and summarizing a European project, Chaudron added: 'In most cases, children use their parents' device in different contexts and different activities but recurrently across the different groups for filling gaps in the day, to get the children occupied in waiting time or when parents need to retrieve time for themselves' (2015, p. 8).

Turning to research specifically focused on parenting and digital media, there is now a substantial literature on how parents influence their older children's use of digital technologies under the broad heading, 'parental mediation'. This first emerged in relation to parents' approach to the children's TV viewing (e.g. Desmond et al., 1985; Austin, 1993; Valkenburg et al., 1999) but was subsequently developed to address the way parents manage their children's experience of the internet (Eastin et al., 2006; Livingstone & Helsper, 2008). There are some commonalities in these typologies of parental mediation, for example, active mediation capturing how parents engage with their children's digital media use and restrictive mediation referring to how parents impose rules about children's use. But the differences between typologies have also reflected how many and which factors were taken into account (Haddon, 2015). As noted, the focus of much of this literature was originally on the mediation of adolescents' digital technology experiences, although some researchers have applied that framework to parents of young children (e.g. Chaudron, 2015; Marsh et al., 2015; Zaman et al., 2016; Beyens & Beullens, 2017; Chaudron et al., 2018; López de Ayala López & Haddon, 2018).

Then there is an adjacent literature on how parents' overall approach to parenting might have implications for the way they engage with their children's experiences of digital media. Again, initially developed in relation to the parenting of older children, this work looks at 'parenting styles', including typologies (perhaps the most well-known of which is Baumrind, 1991) and 'parental practices' (Spera, 2005). For example, Baumrind built up her model according to the dimensions of how demanding parents are and how responsive they are to their children, producing the typology of authoritative parents (demanding, with high expectations of children but also warm and responsive to them), authoritarian (demanding but not responsive, associated with being more disciplinary), permissive (not demanding but highly responsive, making them inclined to be indulgent) and neglectful (not demanding, not responsive, so they tend to be uninvolved with their children). Subsequent writers have explored whether parental styles lead to different approaches to parental mediation (e.g. Valcke et al., 2010; Chaudron et al., 2018).

The question of what parents do in relation to children's use of digital media in the above literature suggests a prior question of how parents develop their ideas about how to parent (and about approaches to mediation and parenting) but also questions about how parents value play, how they think children learn and (of interest here) their views about the role of technologies in childhood. These were the 'ethnotheories' studied by Plowman (2015), a concept developed earlier by Harkness & Super (1992). In Plowman's (2015) research, parents were equally divided between those who encouraged technology use ('well disposed') and those who encouraged non-technology activities (that is, were 'guarded' in relation to technology). While their own childhood experiences influenced parents' rules about aspects of child-rearing, such as pocket money, bedtimes and eating habits, the researchers noted that it was more difficult for parents to build ethnotheories relating to those technologies that they had not experienced in their own youth – hence they expressed a good deal of uncertainty about how to manage these.

While there has been some work on the process of developing these ethnotheories, the context in which an adult learns to be a parent is itself changing. There is now a proliferation of sources of information and views that parents can draw upon, including lifestyle magazines, television programmes, books, parenting classes and courses and also a range of online options including parent advice websites and parent support groups (or equivalent spaces like chatrooms) (Plantin & Daneback, 2009; Doty & Dworkin, 2014). Such online advice may be gaining greater importance than traditional sources of advice such as family and friends because of a reduction in daily support from the latter and because parents have become more risk-aware (Beck-Gernsheim, 2002, discussed in Plantin & Daneback, 2009). Reviews of parents' use of these online sources suggest parents are positive about them, but they can also be critical (Plantin & Daneback, 2009; Doty & Dworkin, 2014).

Although the views expressed and information available online cover multiple topics (the most important of which is child health), the overall impression emerging from those reviews is that, for parents, other strategies take precedence over searching online for information about children's experience of digital media. One UK survey confirmed that while parents often search online, it is more for education purposes or looking up local activities (Livingstone et al., 2018). This research found that a third of parents had looked for advice online about digital media issues (with just over 10 per cent engaging with parent support blogs). This is a little more common than turning to friends and relatives, who appear to be consulted more about general issues than challenges around technology. Hence, another aim of this chapter is to use the empirical data reported here to reflect upon the use of these various sources of support, including more traditional face-to-face ones.

A second question that arises from the parental mediation material is why parents act as they do – what worries them? Past research has generally noted that, while any such concerns reflect broader discussions about digital media's implications for social, health and physical development (for example, whether they lead to lack of social interaction or exposure to inappropriate content), parents also express reservations and uncertainty about all this advice: 'studies say contradictory things' (Plowman et al., 2010a, p. 69). In fact, as in research on parents of older children (Livingstone, 2002), studies have shown that parents of younger children also want a 'balance' (to use the diet metaphor), rather than simply being opposed to digital media. Rules reflect this – children were allowed to use digital media but with some time limits (Chaudron et al., 2018). Most parents do not see technology as a risk if it is used in moderation and under supervision and most parents think they have got the balanced 'diet' right (Plowman et al., 2010b).

While parents may have concerns, they also make adjustments to how they handle children's experience of technologies. For example, one study observed how parents adapt to the changing nature of the internet and mobile technologies and household circumstances more generally (López-de-Ayala-López & Haddon, 2018). But parents also respond to the particularities and actions of the child – hence, the shift in the general parent-child interaction literature to consider bidirectional influences (e.g. Kuczynski & De Moi, 2015) along with attention to parent-child dialogue about media use (Clarke, 2011). That said, there is not much research on this adaptation process. Hence, a section of this chapter considers examples of how different forms of child agency have a bearing on parents' approach to mediation.

Finally, while it is important to understand parents' beliefs about parenting, such ethnotheories are not the only factor influencing how parents deal with their children's technologies. For example, the domestication literature draws attention to how the social context in which people live has a bearing on how they deal with technologies (the classic text is Silverstone et al., 1992; for a more recent review, see Haddon, 2017). By extension, that context of parents' lives – parents' routines, their commitments, their goals, the non-child parts of their life – means that, as noted above, sometimes they use digital media to occupy children. This use has been described in various ways, such as 'electronic babysitter' (Haddon & Vincent, 2015)[2] as the 'new pacifier' (Holloway et al., 2014) and as a response to 'parental needs' (Elias & Sulkin, 2017). Previous researchers found that parents often introduce technologies to children not so much for learning but for this purpose (Stephen et al., 2013), teaching them to use technologies such as DVDs so that the children subsequently do not disturb the parents (Plowman et al., 2010a). Some studies measure the frequency of this practice, ranging from 45 per cent of parents in Rideout et al. (2003) to 90 per cent in Vittrup et al. (2016), while others have examined which parents do this more or less (Chen et al., 2020). However, there is little material that explores when this occupying of children with digital media takes place and how parents feel about it. The last section of this chapter aims to shed light on this process.

Toddlers and Tablets findings

Developing ethnotheories

The process of imagining parenthood could start before the first child was born, sometimes long before. Of the parents in the *Toddlers and Tablets* research given voice in this research, the Bernards[3] (AU) and Stella Kramer (UK) had developed ideas of how to parent through their experience of being responsible for their own younger siblings when they were themselves children, while Angie Govender (AU) had learnt much from babysitting her nieces and nephews. Subsequently, Stella also worked in a nursery before her child was born. Meanwhile, Karla Spinner (UK) studied child development as part of her degree. But not all new parents had such a background. As Claire Petersen (AU) noted: 'I never really wanted to be a parent and so babies were like foreign territory to me, [I had] never even changed a nappy.'

Other parents had first considered the role of parenthood nearer the birth of their first child, for example, talking to their own parents, aunts (more than uncles), adult siblings with children, best friends with children, reflecting the more traditional sources of advice. At this stage, the Greenfields (UK) attended a formal training course on parenthood and several parents read books on the subject, whereas Jenna Campbell (AU) bought an app based on a popular baby book.

Once the children had arrived and were growing up, many parents sought advice from their own parents and siblings with children. However, previous research had noted that sometimes parents were critical of their own parents' advice and perspectives about child-rearing as being from a previous era and outdated (O'Connor & Madge, 2004). The *Toddlers and Tablets* project found examples of this, as well as the observation that their own parents sometimes said comforting things rather than being honest, as Denise in a UK focus group highlighted: 'They might tell you what you want to hear sometimes.' Moreover, as in the Livingstone et al. (2018) survey, while general advice from family, especially their own parents, was still important for many, new grandparents had themselves not had the experience of the variety of current digital media when they had been parents, even if they now had opinions about these technologies.

Other sources of advice included comparing notes with other parents at work and meeting other parents through preschool locations such as toddlers groups. Notably, Linda Palmer (UK) had had two daughters a decade apart and noticed the vastly greater number of local preschool options that had emerged during that period. This meant, in principle, that there were more places to meet other parents, though in practice, some parents, such as the Lawe-Tammell (AU) and Lim-Parks (AU), knew of no other parents to consult at that time.

Several parents in this study had been on parenting courses after their children were born. Although these were often more about parenting in general, some courses had started to address digital media, often in relation to risk and safety on the internet (the risk agenda, noted in Mascheroni & Haddon, 2015). Lastly, parents in both the UK and Australia still read about particular issues as their children were growing up or followed TV coverage, as when Angie Govender (AU) referred to a programme about screen time limits that she had watched a week before the interview.

The changing range of online options was reflected in this study. In addition to websites and groups specifically focusing on parenting/child issues, such as Mumsnet in the UK, some of these parents belonged to parenting WhatsApp groups, looked for advice on non-parent centric forums (e.g. a Slovak language forum in London) or took part in preschool-related parent discussion groups. Some, like Rita Chen (AU), regularly resorted to online options such as Google, while others, like Angie Govender (AU), were critical of such sources. She was especially critical of the information on 'Dr Google' and mummy bloggers: 'I don't like it when they start doling out health advice which they're not qualified to do and can be very dangerous to people.'

The parents had mixed evaluations of parent forums, especially, but many found them useful and interesting. This was partly because of the varied views and advice and, as Amanda noted in a UK focus group, because the forums had helped her feel that she was not alone in facing some child-related issue. In that group, Kath added a word of caution that there was so much variation that it was easy to seek advice that fitted with one's pre-existing views about parenting. Meanwhile, Helen (UK) observed that timing sometimes affected the decision to go online; if it was night-time and there was no one to talk to, she might look up online advice but then talk to someone about that same issue when they were available the next day. Kate Andrews-White (AU) regularly read parenting blogs but added 'you take it all with a grain of salt'. Nevertheless, she would still turn to Google if there was a problem because she was 'not very good at asking for help'.

Other online interactions were significant over and above motivations for looking up information online, as revealed by one particular parent from a UK focus group. Liza first explained that she did not commonly use digital support groups (or social media) in life and did not use parent ones either. Nevertheless, she had checked them out but regarded them as a 'big waste of time … and dominated by stay-at-home parenting concerns about cooking, health food and exercising'. She was an example of a parent preferring to go to expert websites (e.g. *Choice on health*) or academic blogs (e.g. *Parenting for a Digital Future*). Hence, we see someone who preferred some online sources to others. Meanwhile, Liza was particularly critical of a recent trend on Facebook, even in emails she had received from parents talking about the fact that 'high tech execs (in America) do not allow screen time at their homes'.

> Liza: This news is very, very popular among parents now. They think that (these CEOs) are specialists in parenting and we ought to follow their advice because they know about technology … It has a lot of power. Now things like that are very difficult to talk about in the *WhatsApp* parents' group … I notice something that parents, the so-called Millennial generation, think they are experts in digital technology … so they are not prepared to question or to think critically. I sent that to the group and she sent back to me a huge response saying but … quoting the American Psych … you know the old advice of the American whatever … She sent me a number of links and then I didn't have the time to really respond and I would sound very patronizing and then I gave up … you know. I just stopped.

The above example most clearly shows that seeking specific advice or developing ethnotheories in general was not simply a matter of gathering or being exposed to information on parenthood but often involved a critical evaluation. Several parents talked about '*unwanted*' tips from various offline sources. For example, the Tosettis (UK) avoided advice from their own parents because they were critical of the older generation's overprotective approach and thought many of their ideas were '*outmoded*'. Meanwhile, after their own research effort involving reading books and looking at online sources, the Greenfields (UK) concluded there is no one right way to raise a child because all children are different. The Cheun-Yeos (AU) found a parental approach that suited their situation while acknowledging that other parents might make different decisions in different circumstances. Karla Spinner (UK) decided to take elements from different sources. And specifically, as regards online advice, the Ross (UK) parents were appalled by normative judgement about children's appropriate behaviour and parenting genres that they had read on a parents' online forum and vowed never to consult them again.

Apart from developing ethnotheories about children's experience of digital media, parents also decided how to approach parenting in ways pertinent to the parental mediation of touchscreens. Some parents were more articulate about forms of parenting than others in this respect. The Browns (UK) had quite a few parenting principles, such as avoiding saying 'no' to their child by finding more constructive ways to respond to an issue and supporting their child whenever something caught his interest (during the visit, ranging from an electric drill to apps on a tablet). The Tosettis (UK) preferred their child to try something independently (e.g. using a key to open a door), only intervening if he got stuck. Even then, they tried to encourage him to solve the problem for himself, an approach they also applied to their son's digital media experiences. Apart from these decisions or feelings about how to approach parenting, more specific parenting practices appeared to carry over from the non-digital world. Observations made during the interview visit and videos made of the families interacting also showed many instances of parents engaging with children's use of technologies. In relation to apps on a tablet, this involved asking the children what they thought was happening, what they wanted to do, what they liked, or just using the opportunity to talk about any other issue (elaborated in the parents and learning chapter). In this sense, the interaction did not seem vastly different from comments a parent may make when reading a book to a child or asking about their play or other non-digital activities.

Finally, in line with much other research, the parents in this study also referred to the desire to find a balance. Over and above evaluating the pros and cons of digital media, this overarching principle often guided parental evaluations and hence their interventions. Moreover, most parents stopped worrying about the overuse of digital devices because the children simply did not use digital media very much and were at least equally interested in a range of non-digital activities.

Parental concerns and unanticipated digital media uses

Parental worries about the consequences of touchscreen technology for younger children overlap with but are not identical to parental concerns about older children. Fears about a potential lack of balance were evident, with Louisa Langridge (AU) commenting: 'There's just too much stuff out there, really and it's very tempting for them to just get sucked into it.' As noted above, several parents observed that if their child had been using digital media 'too much', they would have intervened; however, it turned out this was not an issue because the children simply did other things. Others were apprehensive that touchscreen use was already out of balance, as when Linda Palmer (UK) thought her daughter was overusing the tablet. Yet other parents tried to avoid getting to that potential stage by encouraging alternative activities. For example, Kate Andrews-White (AU) explained: 'I've had to put down some rules with him now about watching videos on YouTube because he was getting really obsessed about it and wanting to watch them all the time and not wanting to read, not making anything, not doing anything.'

Sometimes parents faced a dilemma because such concerns conflicted with wanting their child to become familiar with the technology, as noted by Jenna Campbell (AU), who commented on the future of her twelve-month-old daughter: 'I want her to be able to be at the forefront but I don't want her to be a screen-playing kid ... I'm terrified of her having too much screen time and not being able to be at the same level as her friends at school as well.' Meanwhile, Stella Kramer (UK) allowed five-year-old Libby to use the tablet and indeed supported that use when her child could not progress in an app. But Stella did not actually promote its use because she worried her daughter might become 'dependent' on the technology. However, this changed when her daughter went to nursery and Stella discovered that digital media were on the curriculum and Libby was behind peers in computer skills; at this point, Stella encouraged more use of the tablet.

Some concerns seemed more specific to younger children, with a few parents, in particular, referring to what they had read about good parenting practices. Rohan Mansi (UK) had read that technology was bad for brain development because the interaction was relatively passive. Klara Brown (UK) was a little apprehensive after coming across an article suggesting that children might become less able to entertain themselves if they relied on digital stimuli too much and that the structured digital world might also restrict the development of imagination compared to free play. This worry about the kinds of play children experience in digital contexts and its implications for mental development was also expressed in Australian interviews: 'I think it actually stifles creativity' (Kate Andrews-White).

Parents sometimes develop a more nuanced understanding of different digital media by comparing screen technologies (e.g. TV versus tablets). Francoise Jameson (UK) was another parent worried about tablets limiting children's imagination; however, she was even more critical of TV having this effect. Francoise's husband Craig followed up Francoise's discussion about some people using tablets as electronic babysitters by pointing out that older generations had used TVs for the same purpose. Linda Palmer (UK) may have had a few reservations about tablets but thought they were much better than TV because they were interactive. Klara Brown (UK) was also far more critical of TV, observing that two-year-old Simon could not turn away when watching TV and became irritated after a while. Meantime, in the Cheung-Yeo family (AU), dad Jo talked about a spectrum: TV watching was the most passive; games on the tablet afforded some interactivity, though within set rules, while human interaction provided the richest experience.

Regarding the physical consequences of using tablets and smartphones, like the parents of older children (Haddon & Livingstone, 2014), some parents in this study feared that using these technologies might lead to eyestrain. These worries about physical development seemed more acute with children of this young age, the most striking example being Lorenzo Tosetti's (UK) concern that his son Leopoldo might not develop as much physical dexterity by using apps compared with offline activities. Meanwhile, Daniel Spinner (UK) expressed some reservations about the radiation his daughters might be exposed to long-term with all the Wi-Fi boosters in the house.

Various worries about online risks identified in research on older children (Mascheroni & Haddon, 2015) were less apparent in the *Toddler and Tablets* study. For example, possible exposure to adult content was only mentioned by the Davis family (AU). This may partly be because these young children could not usually access the digital world, or the internet in particular, without parents' help, or else because there were parental settings that meant 'On the iPad, there's nothing going to harm him' (Kate Andrews-White, AU). Moreover, some parents in both countries made sure they were always around when the child used apps such as YouTube and many parents ensured that only YouTube Kids could be accessed.

Where there was a concern about content, some of the same themes as with older children emerged – for example, 'shoot 'em up' games on the devices were seen as a form of exposure to violence – although sometimes there was a different emphasis compared to adult content for older children. For the Ross family (UK), one danger for their young child, which first emerged in relation to a music channel on the TV rather than the tablet, was sexualization when a girl band of eighteen-year-olds wore revealing clothing and danced in a sexual fashion. Linda Palmer (UK) was concerned about an animation on YouTube that showed stealing, indicating an issue of the moral principles being communicated to young children. Even though it was in a cartoon, she was not sure if the depiction of the birth of the baby was age-appropriate for her four-year-old. Meanwhile, the Petersens (AU) observed that YouTube videos taught young children consumerist values.

The Lim-Park family (AU) illustrates the complexity of concerns and related strategies. Mi Na had initially allowed her children to have iPads, although even this had been strictly controlled like other routines in their lives, so they could only be accessed during snack times. The iPads had been used in part for watching educational videos in the case of her son Michael but also initially to calm down her daughter Emily. But Mi Na had started to feel that the iPad programmes were making her son more aggressive and her daughter less patient. She finally decided to withdraw the iPads because of events in preschool. Staff there had recommended that children should not have digital technologies like iPads until after children were ten years old and showed a video claiming that constant exposure to digital images made children restless in class. Finally, there was one incident where staff pointed out that after Michael had watched Spiderman on the iPad, he had become quite aggressive towards classmates. At that point, Mi Na stopped the children from using iPads. The preschool teacher had also noted that just seeing the hero character might be a problem prompt. So, Mi Ni also removed all related merchandising (e.g. Michael's superhero lunchbox).

To put this discussion of concerns into perspective, it should be added that there were more positive evaluations of touchscreens, some of which will be discussed in the later chapter on parents and learning. And even parents with some apprehensions often acknowledge that children have to know something about technologies as 'part of the modern world' (Mirabella Tosetti, UK). The Tosettis, in particular, were among the parents who were quite proud of their child's digital skills and they were also positive about the digital world in general.

> Mirabella Tosetti: I think we are trying to expose him to lots of different foods and languages and people and things ... because I grew up in a small town, I was really bored, it was pre-internet and I always desired to have something like this, but it didn't exist ... so I thought what a wonderful thing for him to have access to, all these marvellous things.

Sometimes the positive evaluations were also based on the bearing these technologies could have on interaction amongst family members. The most unproblematic use of touchscreens was videochat apps like Skype and Facetime, discussed in previous research (e.g. Kelly, 2015; McClure et al., 2015), used to keep in touch with grandparents and also parents when they were away. These were far more common in the Australian sample, perhaps reflecting the longer distances involved and less face-to-face contact, but it was also used by the UK participants who had relatives abroad. Only Jenna Campbell (AU) had some reservations about her husband, Adam, FaceTiming twelve-month-old daughter Julia at bedtime since this appeared to upset Julia: 'I assume she didn't get the cuddle and the warmth that comes with bedtime; she just saw Dad on a screen and then: "Where'd he go"?' Sometimes, benefits were tinged with regret about the growing constraints on children's lives. Claire Petersen (AU) noted early in her interview that her children were potentially 'missing out on their childhood' compared to her memories of her own childhood spent in independent activities outdoors: 'Our generation of parents feel guilty like we have to spend all this time with our kids or we're not doing a good job whereas our parents' generation were like: "We'll see you at 6:00 p.m."' Husband Jeff later added that this was one of the benefits of digital technology:

> Jeff: They have a measure of independence there that I guess is possibly not open to them given that ... you know, we've got a great park down there, but we can't put them on their bikes and send them down there on their own. So, I guess (the online world is) one of the spaces that they can have a degree of independence in.

Lastly, whatever the ethnotheories about digital media and the broader styles, practices and principles of parenting, sometimes other factors had a bearing on how parents actually used these technologies. One significant factor was the non-technological experiences of the children themselves. For example, when twenty-three-month-old Sergei was upset or ill, parents Rohan and Nadia Mansi (UK) sometimes allowed their son to play on the tablet. Two-year-old Leopoldo Tosetti (UK) sometimes had nightmares and his parents allowed him to look at pictures of the family on the smartphone while still semi-asleep as a way to calm him down. Simon Brown (UK) had a genetic disorder that meant he did not want to eat. Hence, as part of the major effort at mealtimes, his parents found it was useful to let Simon watch the tablet since it distracted him while they fed him. Similarly, Ellen Brent (UK) suffered from constipation, so mother Elisabeth let her watch the tablet, once again as a distraction, while she gave Ellen some medicine for this condition hidden in fruit puree. In fact, her mother Elisabeth was also happy to let Ellen take the tablet to the toilet because 'as long as she's got that with her, she'll sit there quite happily and not try and get off'. Ellen also had special needs[4] and her language learning difficulties meant that she received much more parental dispensation to use her tablet than her two older brothers had been given at her age. Further highlighting its use as a helpful distraction, when Elsa Petersen (AU) had to have stitches in her head at the doctor's after an accident, mother Claire persuaded her to play her favourite game on the iPad during the process to take her mind off it.

Lastly, parents' decisions to allow children to use digital media did not always arise from a need to solve a problem related to challenging or bad experiences. More mundanely, Marie Cheun-Yeo (AU) let twenty-month-old Samuel watch YouTube when she wanted to cut his fingernails. And Stella Kramer (UK) had not planned to teach Libby to read at five, but when Libby herself expressed an interest in learning to read, Stella acquired relevant apps for her tablet to support that.

Occupying children with touchscreens

The last section shows how the problems faced by, or demands of, children themselves sometimes led parents to allow them to use technologies in ways they would, ideally, not have preferred. Some other practicalities had the same effect. As parents, or just as adults, they had other goals to achieve besides interacting with the child, or they faced time demands that meant they occasionally granted children access to and time with touchscreens, even when this went against their own general rules or parenting policies.

Perhaps the most commonly cited case in both countries was letting children access tablets or smartphones to occupy them on long journeys. In fact, Jo and Marie Chuen-Yeo (AU), who usually tried to limit twenty-month-old Samuel's use of the touchscreen, intended to occupy him with an iPad on the flight from Australia to Singapore. However, it did not work since Samuel lost interest after five minutes.

The Mansis (UK) carried an old smartphone in the pram in case they needed to occupy Sergei and the Greenfields (UK) were willing to let one-year-old Andrew use their phones when they were 'out'. Sometimes the aim was to occupy children at particular times or in particular spaces, such as when a relative was visiting, cooking a meal, or at the hairdresser or the doctor. Stella Kramer (UK) even downloaded extra apps in preparation for some of these occasions, while Sherryl Cullen (AU) sought apps to 'entertain' her young son while her older daughter was having treatment for a long-term medical condition. And while the Campbells (AU) would not ordinarily dream of using technology for this purpose, when at a restaurant during vacation: 'Our approach for the holiday was a bit ... whatever we can do to keep her happy for those long nights and stuff ... and that's why we downloaded it.'

As Elisabeth Brent (UK) pointed out, whereas she might sometimes occupy her older children by giving them something to read on such occasions; since the youngest child, Ellen, could not yet read, letting her use the tablet was the alternative. Elisabeth added that she now had less time for parenting four-year-old Ellen compared to when her other children were younger because she now had to attend to Ellen's older siblings. For this additional reason, Ellen was once again allowed more time to use the technology than her siblings had been at that age. Even Mi Na Lim-Park (AU), who had withdrawn her children's iPad use, sometimes allowed Michael to watch YouTube videos on her smartphone when she needed to engage with other activities.

When evaluating the role of touchscreens for occupying children, Kate Andrews-White (AU) cited this practice as one of the benefits of touchscreens, adding 'it gives me a bit of peace and quiet', Isabelle Davis (AU) described it as being 'convenient' while Rosalie Lawe (AU) noted this also could be good for five-year-old son Ben: 'He is Mr Active and he can get a bit fired up. It does help him relax and have some quiet time.' In both countries, parents acknowledged the practicality of occupying the child. This could also benefit the parents, giving them a break to get on with other things as Kate Andrews-White noted of two-and-a-half-year-old Scott: 'Because he's started to use the tablet and watch television independently, I can sneak away and do a tiny bit of study whereas I couldn't do that before. So, it does give you that bit of time.'

However, sometimes parents had reservations about occupying the children with touchscreens as Claire Petersen (AU) observed: 'I think I've let them watch too much during the week because it's been ... it's helpful to me at times.' Nadia Mansi (UK) referred to other people's perception of this practice, admitting that she felt guilty about occupying Sergei in this way, for there was some stigma attached to it. Then there were some public spaces where parents had differing views about resorting to these technologies. The Spinners (UK) took the tablet with them when they occasionally went to a restaurant, 'in case of an emergency', for example, if daughter Imelda suddenly wanted to go home. Usually, Imelda would be offered some alternative first, like something to colour in, which would suffice. But the tablet was the backup. However, other parents, such as Stella Kramer (UK), said they would never use digital media in this way in spaces where they were publicly on show to others as a parent. Reflecting on this, Denise noted in one UK focus group:

> Denise: [Parents in that situation] automatically assume that people are going to think that they don't pay their children any attention … And they don't interact with them; they don't get their imagination going. They don't get their creative sides up; they just automatically plonk them in front of a TV or in front of a tablet or something like that and then … I think they feel a bit guilty because it makes them look bad. I think that's what it's more about, is making the parent look bad.

The suggestion here is that over and above occupying children at times, which all the parents did at some point (sometimes with non-technological options), the use of technology to achieve this had a particular resonance, symbolizing the failure to be an engaging parent.

Conclusion

Given that many of the parents in this study had relatively recently become parents, the chapter first explored how the process of learning to be a parent is changing, especially since this is relevant for the development of approaches to parenting and, more specifically, mediation of digital media. Of course, there were continuities from previous eras with the influence of family and friends. However, new parents can have reservations about these sources or simply not have them available at this stage in their life. But becoming a parent is also changing, both through the availability of more non-digital sources, such as the proliferation of written material, courses, more preschool options and the availability of different types of online feedback. The overall impression is that parents make an effort to construct their ethnotheories of parenting and childhood from various sources and can think critically about these, including evaluating online advice.

The next focus was on parental evaluations of digital media since these would have a bearing on their mediation practices. While from the literature, there appears to be overlaps with the goals of parents of older children, for example, in terms of finding a balance in children's lives and concerns about overuse of digital media, the risk agenda is less prevalent than a developmental one. Here there is more emphasis on how technologies might have a bearing on how their child learns, develops their creativity, becomes more independent and enjoys themselves in these (more) formative years. Enabling this is made easier by the degree of dependency of younger children, meaning that, when they wish, parents can relatively easily monitor and, if necessary, control their children's digital media use. However, whatever the overarching parental strategies, contingencies mean the parents find themselves giving children access to digital media in ways that they had not planned.

This discrepancy between parental mediation intentions and actual practices becomes even more visible in the case of using digital media to occupy children. This is a coping strategy when parents need to do other things, such as focus on other children in the family, attend to other tasks or simply have a rest from the demands of being a parent. It is a common, practical solution in response to these other demands, one that is valued, but one which at the same time runs the most risk of creating guilt, especially through a sense of being judged as not sufficiently performing the parental role.

5

Grandparents

Introduction

In order to understand grandparents' types of engagement, or lack of it, in their grandchildren's interactions with digital technologies, it is first useful to identify three things. One is grandparents' perspectives on the influences shaping modern parenting that were explored in the preceding chapter. These can inform grandparents' understanding of why their children, as parents, act in certain ways, including how they try to manage their children's technological experiences. Second, it is important to appreciate grandparents' own understanding of their grandparenting role and its limits. These possibilities are initially outlined in the literature review and then explored further in reporting the *Toddlers and Tablets* findings. And third, while acknowledging the range and diversity of grandparenting, it is necessary to examine grandparents' own perceptions of the place of touchscreens in children's lives. In the light of these three factors, it is easier to understand any grandparent interventions. Lastly, interview material from the parents also provides some clues to how parents evaluate grandparents' actions.

Literature review: Grandparenting

In general, grandparenting was neglected in family studies for many years but has seen a renewed interest in the past four decades (Bates & Taylor, 2013). Even then, only some of that literature refers to grandparents of young children, compared to a greater amount of material on grandparents' relation with older, especially adolescent grandchildren. Before considering technology, it is worth setting the scene with some observations about grandparenting in general. Some of this literature notes that grandparent-grandchild interaction is not just about 'being there' for the grandchild; it can reflect an attempt to reposition grandparents' relationship with their own adult children, the new parents. When children leave home and form relationships, being independent can mean a period of far less interaction between the (now) grandparents and adult child. Hence, the arrival of grandchildren provides a legitimate basis for greater contact with adult children, the new parents (Breheny et al., 2013). At the same time, grandparenting can be a new role for people in mid- and later life, which can have a bearing on their sense of identity and worth, even if, compared to parenting, it has been argued that the role lacks explicit functions and clear rights and responsibilities (Thiele & Whelan, 2006). Thiele and Whelan note a further question of how central that grandparent role is in their lives (for example, this may be less so if they are working, spending time with friends or have community roles). Lastly, these authors note that the role is a highly contingent one, with grandparents often having little control over the timing of grandparenthood, how many grandchildren they have, how close they live to them and how often they see them.

There is a great variety of grandparenting styles,[1] just as there are variations in parenting styles (Valcke et al., 2010). Some grandparents are a source of advice and wisdom, others are fun-seeking companions, some serve more as surrogate parents, while yet others are distant and uninvolved[2] (Bangerter & Waldron, 2014). To put this *Toddlers and Tablets* AU/UK research into perspective, there can be cross-cultural variation in grandparenting roles (Thiele & Whelan, 2006). This review also found evidence of change over time, with 26 per cent of grandparents feeling that having fun was the most appropriate style in a 1964 study, that figure rising to 50 per cent in 1981. Moreover, the grandparenting role changes over the life course of the child, typically with more involvement with young grandchildren and less involvement as the grandchildren enter adolescence (see also Dunifon et al., 2018).

Generally, grandparents' roles may also be changing in other ways than the forms of grandparenting noted above. In one study, a number of grandparents observed that nowadays there was actually a higher expectation for them to help out, especially in terms of providing childcare (Breheny et al., 2013). In earlier generations, when more mothers had stayed out of work to bring up children, some current grandparents reflected on the fact that, when they were young, their own grandparents had been less involved in taking responsibility for them as grandchildren. In fact, some interviewees in that study observed that being a grandparent now was more burdensome, while the researchers themselves thought that the grandparent literature showed grandparents were increasingly filling the 'parent gap' due to social and demographic changes. Some studies pointed out how this expectation was gendered, with particular pressures on grandmothers (Horsfall & Dempsey, 2015).

One theme that is especially relevant for *Toddlers and Tablets* findings is that the literature has described how many grandparents are careful not to 'overstep their bounds and infringe on the parenting styles of their children' (Forghani & Neustaedter, 2014, p. 4182). The grandparents did not want to be seen to be interfering or criticizing the parent (and indeed, in that same study the parents interviewed did not want the grandparents to influence their children's behaviour in certain ways). Other studies have also referred to these different 'interfering' practices, such as offering unsolicited advice, or offering opinions on appropriate parenting behaviours (Breheny et al., 2013) and how this sometimes leads to conflicts. In fact, one study of 'grandparenting norms' showed that the two most important rules were 'not interfering' and 'being there', but in practice there was sometimes ambivalence about both of these rules (Mason et al., 2007).

Turning to the place of technologies in grandparents-grandchild interaction, although there is some work on the media channels through which grandparents and grandchildren communicate (Quadrello et al., 2005; Petrovčič et al., 2015), videochat such as Skype has received most research attention. Some of that material examines the difficulties very young children face in managing video when trying to communicate (Balagas et al., 2009; Kelly, 2015), the problems grandparents can face when using the technology (Forghani & Neustaedter, 2014; Share et al., 2018) and the limitations experienced and effort required to manage video communication (Kelly, 2015; Share et al., 2018). Once such difficulties have been overcome, various other studies show how some form of video connection was often felt to be better than the phone since young children could more easily show their grandparents objects and grandparents could see how the grandchildren looked, how they were growing up, or see the children demonstrate a new skill (Forgahni & Neustaedter, 2014).

One quantitative and qualitative Israeli study covered issues nearer to the concerns of this chapter: grandparents' familiarity with and perceptions of digital media and, of particular interest here, their mediation of their grandchildren's technology use (Elias et al., 2021). Overall, the researchers thought the grandparents in this study had relatively poor media literacy and the grandparents were somewhat critical of overuse of smartphones and content on TV, although they appreciated the educational value of some material. Many respected and followed the rules laid down by the parents, although some decided not to implement those (restrictive) rules, considering this to be the parents' responsibility. However, comparing the parents' own childhood with that of the grandchildren, some observed that there was now a richer media environment and so nowadays more mediation was needed.

Toddlers and Tablets findings

Diversity of grandparents' experiences

Although the study of grandparents was limited to one focus group in the UK and two in Australia and all but one participant was female, this material provided enough examples to demonstrate the diversity of grandparent experiences. Reflecting broader emerging family structures impacted by divorce and re-marrying trends, the focus groups included grandparents with step-grandchildren and those who had their own under-eighteen children at home while being grandparents to others. Many had multiple grandchildren from their own different children, with teenage grandchildren as well as the age group birth to six (which meant that in the focus groups the grandparents sometimes reflected on when their older grandchildren were younger). Some grandparents were still working, which had a bearing on how much time they had available to be involved with grandchildren, including time for babysitting. Lastly, the grandparents had contact with the grandchildren to different degrees, from several times a week to more irregularly. In the case of the families interviewed, in both the UK and Australia, a number of parents were originally from other countries and so face-to-face contact with the grandparents living abroad was rarer, often limited to Skype or other forms of videochat. Likewise, the involvement in grandchild care varied – the most extreme cases being in the Zhang/Chen (AU) family, where the grandparents had moved from China to Australia to look after the grandchild during the week and the Petersen (AU) family where the grandmother lived with them in a granny flat and dropped off and picked up the two children from preschool and school.

In the interviews with parents, there were occasional glimpses of less technologically versatile grandparents. However, the opposite end of the scale was best demonstrated in the UK focus group where all of the grandmothers commented on their years of dealing with computers during their working lives, dating from programmable devices and punch cards in the 1970s, to their later use of PCs. In fact, before the interview started, these grandmothers were showing each other pictures of their grandchildren on their smartphones and discussing the pros and cons of putting those images on the Cloud. Similarly, in the Australian focus groups, some commented on how they had experienced technology throughout their lives:

> Marcy (AU): Well for me I've been using (them) over 30 years – Oh, not the smartphones but from computers … we've always had a computer at home. Then as technology's progressed then I've progressed with it like using maybe an iPad and then a laptop as opposed to the old computer in the study and then the phone has now started to take over everything pretty much.

Moreover, some grandparents who were still working used a variety of technologies in their job, with Dee (AU) commenting that she needed to use the smartphone to access her work computer. But apart from biographies that involved encountering technologies over time, several grandparents could point to their own feelings about those experiences, as when Dee was not alone in expressing the sentiment that she sometimes found the technologies too tempting:

> Dee (AU): I'm guilty of it, I can see it happening … something that just eats into your time. You go to do something for one minute and all of a sudden you look at the clock and go: 'Oh forty minutes ago I was supposed to start doing something else and I've been here for forty minutes' … and it's gone like a flash.

Marcy (AU) was an example of a grandparent who had tried reducing her own smartphone use but who found responding to messages on her phone difficult to resist: 'It's about putting up rules for ourselves.'

In the broader literature of older people's experience of technology, there is often still a focus on 'older older people', aged eighty and above and corresponding comments about their lack of technological competence and even resistance to newer technologies. However, there is a generational effect whereby many people moving into retirement nowadays are 'younger older people' in their sixties and seventies who had experienced the digital world earlier in their lives, especially their working lives. This frames their responses to technology at this stage in life. The same is true for grandparents and since this includes grandparents of younger grandchildren, some of these belong to an even younger age cohort in their fifties.

Comparing parents' and grandparents' views on digital media

Sometimes, the grandparents thought that they had a particular vantage point from which to comment on their grandchildren's upbringing, by virtue of being in a stage in life where they felt under less pressure than their own children. Delia (AU): 'We are maybe a little bit more distanced, (the parents) have got that pressure of: "We've only got so many hours in the day" ... and they're working and they've got mortgages ... and we remember what that was like.'

Specifically, as regards technology, some grandparents noted the benefits of being in the 'digital immigrant'[3] position of having lived throughout an earlier stage in technological development, with more distance to reflect on the consequences of the digital world.

> Dee (AU): We've had years and years and years with no (technology) and doing the physical things as children. Then we've been able to grow up and grow into the technology as adults and raise our children in that technology and then watch their children. So, we've got a really unique perspective 'cause there'll be no other generation that's ever not had the technology.

That said, in practice, many grandparents had equivalent concerns to those of parents, for example, about how the time young children spent using touchscreens might inhibit the development of social skills and displace time for learning other non-digital skills. In addition, the grandparents also referred to benefits similar to those mentioned by parents, for example, that it was important for children to engage early with technologies that will be a part of their life and that children learn dispositions like concentration. Some apps were positively valued because of their educational potential and some grandparents believed that children learn about the world through these devices or else use of the devices reinforces that understanding. Lenka (AU): 'Because you can use the technology to teach the nursery rhymes so you can still have the same thing but it's an enriched experience.'

Sometimes grandparents were critical of using digital media to distract children, as when Claire (UK) complained about her daughter-in-law's nanny using the tablet to get her grandchildren to eat breakfast more quickly in order to send them off to school. But others, such as Jackie (UK), saw it as being legitimate to use touchscreens as a distraction 'if all else fails' or else some grandparents approved of their adult children's actions, as in the case of Erin (AU): 'My son has actually downloaded an app that (the granddaughter) plays while ... 'cause otherwise she just has an absolute horror of having her nappy changed.' Similarly and like parents, sometimes grandparents were critical of their adult children using touchscreens to occupy the grandchildren (or children in general, as when they are at restaurants). But Claire (UK) also recognized that grandparents themselves sometimes used technologies to occupy children; it was just that the devices and the extent had changed: 'I suppose what we did, we sat them down in front of the telly. Because you had half an hour to do a job or something. But now iPads and phones are portable and so they can give them anywhere.' In fact, some grandparents still used technologies to occupy grandchildren, as Delia (AU) noted: 'I must admit I was babysitting yesterday and I did give my great-grandnephew my phone at one stage just to distract him while I wanted something done.' Even Claire (UK), who was generally very critical of children using ubiquitous touchscreens, thought that the technologies had a role in occupying grandchildren on long journeys and Lucy (UK) added: 'When you're out in a restaurant, it's going to keep them quiet. That's when their attention span is short and adults want to stay there, I mean … in some ways it's quite nice.'

The grandparents could also be reflective, for example, about the dilemmas facing parents. Dee (AU) noted that on the one hand more and more technology is being used in preschools and indeed children will be disadvantaged if they had not experienced these at an earlier age. Yet, on the other hand, this seemed to be at odds with the advice to parents to try to control their children's use of devices at home. Also, the grandparents referred to how childhood was having to change because the world was a more dangerous place:

> Elaine (UK): Well, I can remember going outside (as a child), nobody worried about you. No, but as children get older … in a way is it the world we live in, it's almost safer to keep them inside doing …
> Sarah (UK): Yes, they don't go outside and play.

Overall, the grandparents thought that their children as parents experienced more pressures than they themselves had at that life stage, as was discussed at length in the UK focus group. This included women being more likely nowadays to have careers, the higher expense of childcare, pressures to have more material possessions and generally having more things to worry about. As in the Elias et al. (2021) study, this included having to manage the vast increase in the technologies that their children might now encounter. Karen (UK): 'All we had to worry about really was, were they watching too much telly? Were they watching too many videos repetitively? And then when they got a bit older, should they be allowed to have a phone or a telly in their own room? That was about the sum of decision-making.'

Moreover, there were more pressures to parent in certain ways and this did not simply reflect a progression from more stricter ways of parenting in the past, as suggested in some academic discussions.[4]

> Claire (UK): Because they have high expectations of themselves, because they read a lot of books, they consult a lot of reference points like the internet

and all that sort of thing and I just did what my mum did. And I took my lead from her, more or less, I think and I think now it's almost like a competition.

Karen (UK): And they seem to have gone backwards. Like in our day we were sort of quite laissez faire [let it be] I think with our children ... whereas Heather's much more rigid with John than I was with my kids in terms of routine and things, really.

Lucy (UK): Absolutely.

Claire (UK): They watch Supernanny[5] and if their child doesn't do the right thing, doesn't achieve the right milestone at the right time, there's a bit of angst about why that is, what are they doing wrong? And you think: 'Well kids are just different', you know.

A similar point was raised in the Australian focus group where one grandmother was critical of the pressure on parents to make sure that the child was developing at the right pace and was not below average, arguing that this does not do justice to the variety of childhood experiences. Lenka (AU) was also critical of the sheer variation in advice: 'Like every couple of months, the way you bring up a child or a baby and their sleep patterns and whatever changes.' Meanwhile, Erin (AU) was critical of her daughter-in-law's rigid ideas about absolutely keeping to routines for the sake of the child, even when it was an inconvenience because child bedtimes required any engagement with the grandparents to take place earlier. She argued that parents should be more flexible and that the child has to learn to adapt when something disrupts routines.

In sum, despite some grandparents' perception that their longer life and technological experiences gave them a different perspective to their children, the actual range of assessments of touchscreens, their evaluation of the practice of using devices to distract and occupy children and their own activities in this respect were not so different from those of the parents. However, their own experiences of parenting, not necessarily stricter than their children's later parental styles, led some grandparents to be critical of the sources of parenting advice noted in our earlier discussion of how contemporary parents learn parenthood.[6]

Grandparents' actions and digital media rules

As in the literature reviewed, grandparents in the UK and Australia were wary of being seen to interfere in the children's parenting. Dee (AU): 'I have a personal opinion about that ... but that was what was in their household ... so obviously

I didn't interfere, that was what they were allowed to do.' This had a bearing upon what grandparents would say about their own adult children's parental mediation rules. That said, there was one case when Lucy (UK) did not think so much screen time was good for her grandchildren and had shown the parents newspaper articles about this issue. Things came to head when the grandchild went to hospital because of neck pains.

> Lucy (UK): And it was purely because he spent so much time with his head like this [gestures that it is bent forward at an angle]. They took (the screen) away completely for nine weeks maybe … and then he was just allowed so much per day. I think it's all now been forgotten and it's sort of slowly creeping back up … but no, we [Lucy and her husband] both felt very, very strongly about the fact that they were using them so much.

Apart from this case being unusual in showing how grandparents could research parenting issues and in this case the parents followed Lucy's advice (for a while), what was noteworthy was that in the focus group all the other grandparents were amazed that Lucy had been willing to intervene in this way. They commented that it was 'brave' and asked how she managed to persuade the parents. It became apparent that while many of them had views on their grandchildren's use of digital devices, they would not dream of publicly questioning their own children's approach to parental mediation.

However, there are some complications. As regards following the parents' rules, it is first worth noting that grandparents are sometimes privy to the rule systems of more than one family and so different grandchildren can experience very different rules. For example, Dee (AU) observed that one of her daughters who had younger children maintained tight control over technology use, whereas the one with the older children gave them more free range.

Second, those rules could be more or less explicit, as Elaine (UK) indicated: 'Oh God, the first time my daughter left her little one with me, I had three foolscap pages of notes.' However, sometimes grandparents had to work harder to find out what the rules were. Dee (AU): 'It wasn't explicit, it was more about picking up on implicit cues … so for me it wasn't necessary for either of my daughters to tell me, I very much could take the cues.'

Later during the focus group she added:

> Dee (UK): I probably want to have the conversation with my daughter and with my stepdaughter if I'm babysitting hers. I need to ask those questions; I need to actually find out what their thoughts are and what their requirements are for me if I'm looking after those children 'cause I haven't done that and it's something that I've not thought to do.

Meanwhile, Erin (AU) gave an example of her son saying something for the first time that revealed the implicit parental rule system that was in place:

> Erin (AU): But he did make the comment about the television: 'Oh it might be time now that she can ... we can put it on' ... which was sort of later in the day which I thought: 'Oh okay, he obviously has got some rules or restrictions in place of when the telly's on' ... and that sort of thing actually pleased me.

One response of grandparents was to apply different rules to those of the parents and engage in different activities when the grandchildren were alone and based at the grandparents' house. For example, when the granddaughter visits, Delia (AU) removes the keyboard and mouse, while Marcy (AU) does not use the iPad when looking after her granddaughter; instead, the children play with other toys. Amongst the grandmothers who attended the UK focus group, there was unanimity about this approach, where these grandparents had similar views about their homes being havens from the technology in part because it was felt that digital media were undermining sociability. Elaine (UK): 'I don't think any of us are anti all this new stuff for the children. I think what worries us is that they spend too much time and not enough time actually talking to each other.'

The point Elaine makes about not rejecting a place for technology *per se* in the lives of young is not based on grandparents' ignorance about the digital world. These grandparents, mostly grandmothers, actually knew how to use technology. It was more an issue of feeling that digital media were becoming too dominant in their children's lives.

> Lucy (UK): Our house is a total free zone as far as the grandchildren. No, we ... they never bring them. We say we don't want them and we never have the television on when they come, we are just totally free from that sort of technology ... 'cause they are immersed in it in their own house'.

In the focus group, Sarah (UK) also noted how she turned the TV off when grandchildren visited and engaged them in non-technological activities such as cards and Ludo, while Claire (UK) also offered alternatives to technology. The grandchildren seemed to accept this.

> Claire (UK): And the only time this summer that they wanted their iPad was when their mum walked through the door ... and OK, (my granddaughter) was tired, she was a bit crotchety ... she was coming towards the end of her day and she was a bit grumpy and she saw her mother and she said: 'Mummy, Mummy, I want my iPad' ... you know, it was like ... you know: 'Hang on a minute, Mae, you haven't had it for two and a half weeks!'

Overall, these grandmothers felt that the haven approach worked: Elaine (UK): 'I think they're much more talkative when they come to my house ... whereas when I go there, they sort of look up: "Oh God, it's the grandparents ... I've got to speak to (them)." [The other grandparents laughed, knowingly]. They do speak ... but not much.'

While they could create such havens in their own house, the UK grandmothers acknowledged that this was not possible in the grandchildren's house. Claire (UK): 'If their parents are there, it's different because it's their parents' turf and not yours. I think you have to respect that ... whereas when they come to your house, it's my house, it's my rules.'

And Helen (UK) added: 'Well you can't do anything with them because you're in their territory. But it's different than when you've got them in your house.'

While the picture painted of grandchildren being less willing to engage with grandparents when they are in their family home may be partly true, further discussion showed the situation was more complicated. When visiting their adult children, rather than babysitting for them, the grandparents were often more engaged in talking to the parents, while children were (literally) left to their own devices. And indeed, Lenka (AU) commented that she could understand why the parents were happy to occupy children with technology because they wanted to talk about 'adult' subjects with the grandparents.

The other observation to make about the grandparents' 'haven' strategy, including planning activities for when the grandchildren visited and setting aside blocks of time to play with them, is that sometimes they could only manage to do this because some had retired and hence had more disposable time. Helen (UK): You think: 'Oh they're coming on Tuesday, so I'll cook something so it's ready for them ... this and that and "We'll do such-and-such" ... and you have spent the time. You never have the time like this with your own children.'

To summarize this section, although there was an example of one grandparent questioning her adult children's handling of the grandchildren's access to touchscreens, on the whole – and in keeping with the literature on 'interference' – those in the focus groups were wary of such interventions. There were more examples of trying to follow their children's parental guidelines, although these rules were not always totally clear. That said, one strategy[7] most explicit in the UK focus group was for the grandparent to make their own home a haven free of technology for the grandchildren, even if they could not have much influence in the grandchildren's home in this respect.

Parents' observations and perspectives

Although in the family interviews and in the focus groups parents had a limited amount to say about the grandparents, there are some observations that complement the material from the grandparent focus groups. In those focus group grandparents had referred to grandchildren occasionally trying to involve them in their technological experiences, as in grandchildren asking grandparents how a game worked or wanting to show them their progress. However, the family interviews provided more examples of grandparents taking the initiative. This included letting grandchildren use their own touchscreens, as when Rita's mother in the Zhang/Chen family (AU) let her granddaughter watch YouTube on her smartphone. In the Petersen family (AU), the grandmother spent more time engaging with the granddaughter's digital media use than the parents did, as Claire explained: 'But one thing we haven't done which Mum does … and so this has skipped a generation. Mum will sit and play the game with them on the iPad. We don't very often at all. So, she has the time and the patience to sit there and do silly hairdos with you, doesn't she?'

In the Tosetti family (UK), the grandmother learnt from the grandson.

> Mirabella (UK): One thing I should mention that really impressed me is that my mum is not very technological. She can send emails; she can go on eBay and YouTube. But she's not very technological and she's seventy-one. And when she came here and they were watching the iPad together, I realised my mum was starting to use the iPad. And I asked how can she do that? 'Cause she was really one of those people who are scared to touch anything. And she said: 'I just did what he was doing'. And that really made me think … She learnt to use the iPad from just watching Leopoldo, which is really weird … I'm trying to convince her to get a smartphone finally. And, you know, that made her more confident 'cause she said: 'If he's using it and he's actually teaching me just by showing me then I can use a smartphone too.'

In line with the literature reviewed, using videochat facilities like Skype or Facetime was one of the more common and acceptable ways for grandchildren and grandparents to interact through technologies. Even in the grandparent focus group, Claire (UK) noted that Facetime and Skype were particularly useful when the grandparents did not see young grandchildren often because it meant the grandchildren remained familiar with the grandparents. At the other extreme, some parents like the Campbells (AU) sometimes used Facetime to show the grandparents to their one-year-old daughter even though the grandparents lived just further up the same street. These grandparents looked after granddaughter Julia three times a week. Jenna (AU): 'If she hasn't seen her for a few days ... 'cause she has so much contact that it's a bit weird ... if she has a few days not seeing them ... she looks really lost afterwards, she's like: "Where are they?"' However, not all grandparents could manage to use the technology and sometimes the grandchildren did not go along with this desire for interaction. Claire Petersen (AU) noted that she had to settle for simply showing the grandparents, via Skype, how the children were playing.

That desire to keep informed about grandchildren was sometimes itself an impetus for the grandparents to engage with technology, as when Trish Greenfield (UK) downloaded Facebook software so that her divorced mother could use the videochat facility on Facebook Messenger to see her grandson. That point had also been made in the focus groups. Karen (UK): 'And you think about Women's Institute (WI) members who wouldn't have touched technology, they are actually driven by wanting to keep in touch with their families.'

Returning to the theme of interfering that had been discussed by the grandparents, Francoise Jameson's (UK) own mother had made a comment about Craig's and Francoise's frequent checking of their smartphones: 'You don't even notice but you're constantly on your machines and it's not very nice for the boys 'cause they probably would want to play a game instead.' In this instance Francoise accepted that her mother had a point, adding: 'We've tried ... I've ... mostly me ... to have a sort of detox, digital detox.' Clearly in this case Francoise accepted the intervention. But others, like Angie Govender (AU), were clearly not going to accept any advice: 'My mother-in-law has a very different way of parenting ... so I say: "Mum, we're doing it my way, if you don't like it, leave". [The grandmother normally replies]: "Okay, we'll do it your way. Okay, tell me what I'm doing."'

At times, there were negative feelings about the grandparents' own engagement with the grandchildren's touchscreens as when, in one parents' focus group, Tang (AU) commented: 'I know sometimes she like to show him little funny video clip on her phones. Then I thought that's bad idea 'cause ... it's very hard to get them away from the phone.' Meanwhile, Claire (AU) had some reservations: 'Grandma has let her have the iPad in her room from time to time ... but I don't like that, I like that to be within visibility.' Perhaps the strongest reaction came in the Davis family (AU) when Malcom's parents unexpectedly bought an iPad for grandson Jacob without asking Isabelle or Malcolm first. While acknowledging their generosity, Isabelle thought this over-stepped a boundary: 'I was more amazed that permission wasn't sought to say: "Should we buy him his own device" ... I would have thought that would be something you ask a parent.'

Overall, the parent interviews, in contrast to some of the grandparents' comments in the focus groups, provided examples of grandparents engaging with grandchildren's use of touchscreens. The most popular technology, as captured in the literature review, was videochat to keep in touch with grandchildren and be aware of their development, which could even be a catalyst for some grandparents to use technological facilities that they might not have used otherwise. But we also see examples of parents commenting on grandparent interventions, sometimes accepting their observations and sometimes being critical of these actions.

Conclusion

Clearly grandparents can reflect critically upon processes, identified in the parent chapter, that are shaping the current social construction of parenthood and, in doing so, they are by no means simply 'conservative', referring to a time in the past when parents were stricter. Many appreciated the factors that created pressures on their adult children in their role as parents. As might be expected, in many ways the grandparents' views were as nuanced as those of the parents, sometimes appreciating parental dilemmas. This chapter has demonstrated how grandparents can have their own views on the place of technologies in young children's lives, even if many choose not to voice them in the presence of their own adult children, itself reflecting the concern about interfering identified in the existing literature. Some engage with their grandchildren's digital experiences, some try to work out and follow the parents' guidelines (as exemplified in the Elias et al., 2021 study), but some also implement their own strategies, for example, by creating a 'haven from technology' for grandchildren visiting their own homes. But as that case also illustrates, even when grandparents are critical of technology being too prominent in children's lives, this is not necessarily a judgement from a position of ignorance about new media given that, in contrast to the Elias et al. study (2021), many of the interviewees in this study had considerable familiarity with the digital world.

6

Digital Media in Preschool Settings

Introduction

This chapter aims to further our understanding of the processes affecting the degree to which preschool use of digital media has changed, ways in which preschool staff (and children) do or do not engage with these technologies and staff and parent perceptions of the place of touchscreens in children's lives more generally as well as in this setting.

Literature review: Preschool and digital media

As noted earlier, Stephen and Edwards (2018) describe the boom in research on tablets in preschool settings (e.g. Couse & Chen, 2010; Verenikina, & Kervin, 2011; Flewitt et al., 2015; for a review see Kucirkova, 2017). However, this chapter reviews studies of digital media more generally in preschool as well as considering a range of technologies discussed in the focus group material from the *Toddlers and Tablets* project, since these provide insights into the settings in which touchscreen technologies may or may not be adopted.

To put the history of research on preschool and technology into context, it is useful to bear in mind the various ways in which the world has changed since some of the earliest literature. Not only do we have new technologies, like the tablet and smartphone, but the 'digital landscape' more generally that children inhabit has evolved (Kontovourki et al., 2017). Children now grow up in a more media saturated environment, which has led some more enthusiastic researchers to ask what happens when 'digital natives'[1] come to preschool (Zevenbergen, 2007).

While in both the UK and Australia digital media have for many years been part of the preschool curriculum, various studies have examined what place digital technologies actually have in day-to-day activities. Even in the pre-curriculum era when most adult intervention in the child's use of digital media was 'reactive' rather than proactive – for example, making sure children took turns to use the technology – staff occasionally engaged in 'guided interaction' in terms of explaining to children how to use the software, suggesting alternative actions, demonstrating how to use a tool, offering remedial help when an error occurred, providing positive feedback on a task completed and moving children to an appropriate level of difficulty (Plowman & Stephen, 2005). Subsequent research in nurseries where there were initiatives to promote digital media showed staff were becoming more positive about their use of technology in preschool (Stephen & Plowman, 2008; Roberts-Holmes, 2014). This included taking a broader view of what was being learnt by children. Stephen and Plowman (2008) noted the practitioners in their study reported an improvement in children's 'positive learning dispositions'[2] (e.g. confidence, self-esteem, sense of security, perseverance, playing cooperatively, taking turns), in 'extending knowledge' (e.g. more competence linking spoken and written language, ability to retell stories, use of language) and in improved 'operational knowledge' (e.g. how to log on, mouse control). A range of later studies have shown the different ways in which preschool staff use digital media more creatively (summarized in Neumann & Neumann, 2017; see also Marsh et al., 2018; Jack & Higgins, 2019). That said even one more recent Australian study showed a mixed picture, with some staff still resisting or constraining the use of ICTs in their preschool settings (Schriever, 2021).

If we turn to the question of what influences staff's use of ICTs in preschool, one candidate noted since the earliest studies is practitioners' own lack of confidence in using digital media (Marsh et al., 2005; Plowman & Stephen, 2005; Roberts-Holmes, 2014). This latter research noted that many nursery staff referred to the children in such a way as to portray them as the 'digital natives' (i.e. competent through having been brought up with digital media); yet, by contrast, the staff felt they were like the 'digital immigrants' (people who had encountered digital media later in life).[3] But now there is evidence that this is changing, this particular consideration is less important, at least for younger preschool staff (Palaiologou, 2016; Hatzigianni & Kalaitzidis, 2018)

One issue identified is simply the lack of new technologies available in preschool settings (Fenty and McKendry Anderson, 2014). Another, again observed since the earliest studies, is whether staff in preschool settings have a pedagogical understanding of the benefits of digital media to frame their interventions, that is an understanding of how children could learn through technologies, not just learn about them (Stephen & Plowman, 2003). This is captured in studies showing preschool staff noting that their own teacher training does not prepare them to incorporate technology in their practices (Fenty & McKendry Anderson, 2014).[4] However, although these practitioners cannot see how technology can support certain learning outcomes, some studies showed how that understanding can change, especially by observing what children actually do with technology (Flewitt et al., 2015; Vidal-Hall et al., 2020).

Edwards (2016) argues that the problem really lies in the fact that the key conceptual frameworks in the field of early childhood learning were formulated in an era before children's lives were immersed in digital media. In particular, their 'theories of play' do not take into account how children now play in the digital world, or develop 'converged play' combining digital and non-digital elements.[5] This can lead to practitioners being critical of the place of new technologies in preschool, as they contrast their use with (more highly valued) traditional play (as demonstrated in the study by Schriever et al., 2020). However, Edwards indicates how practitioners can develop a broader understanding of children's play outside of the preschool setting that includes children's engagement with both digital devices and the popular culture they sometimes mediate, and build on that in preschool.

Apart from the influence of early learning pedagogy, there are lastly the various senses in which practices in preschool should not be seen in isolation from wider society. First, over and above their training and day-to-day experiences, preschool staff themselves live in a social world encountering discourses about technologies, including moral panics about adverse effects on children (Plowman, McPake, & Stephen, 2010). Hence, there is a question of the extent to which practitioners' own specific beliefs in part reflect these wider societal representations, including, for example, the screen time advice described in an early chapter of this book. For instance, in the particular UK nursery they studied, Wolfe and Flewitt (2010) found the staff were very critical of what they saw as technology-dominated childhood. Aubrey and Dahl (2008) also noted that while staff were positive about digital media in general, their main concern was about children using technologies too much. That uncertainty continued to be reflected in later research (e.g. Palaiologou, 2016; Schriever et al., 2020) as some staff said they had to 'find a balance' (Hatzigianni & Kalaitzidis, 2018).

If children are growing up immersed in a more mediated environment at home, how much do preschool staff take into account what children bring to preschool? This line of thought prompted one review to comment: 'Young children were portrayed as entering educational settings with specific dispositions as literate beings, that might differ from those identified in the literacy curriculum' (Kontovourki et al., 2017, pp. 11–12). At a general level, the relationship between home and preschool has occasionally been examined. Various researchers (e.g. Plowman, Stephen & McPake, 2010a) have referred to the fact that there is often little continuity between home and preschool institutions. Children do not have the chance to demonstrate their technological competencies in preschool, so staff do not appreciate these skills. Practitioners may have a limited knowledge of what children do with their technologies in the home, sometimes from what the children tell them (Schriever et al., 2020). In one small-scale study, where the staff did not know about the children's use at home, the majority of parents said they had never discussed this aspect with the nursery staff (Aubrey & Dahl, 2014).

The literature review conveyed the sense of some variation between preschool settings. In building on that, in the *Toddlers and Tablets* research we can also ask whether particular preschool institutions have policies and priorities (and more or less funds, training and IT support options) that can have a bearing on what teachers within them do with digital media. In addition, as noted, the curriculum in the UK and Australia requires preschool institutions to promote some understanding of digital media in principle. But, to what extent does this influence staff decisions in reality? And how are digital technologies used in practice?

We can also ask a second set of questions concerning that link between the home and school. What type of knowledge of, but also expectations about, digital media do these young children bring to preschool and how are these managed by staff? How much do staff know about their children's home lives nowadays, how did they build up this picture and how do they evaluate children's experiences of technology at home? Lastly, there is less research on parents' understanding of what goes on in preschool, so we will conclude this chapter with some reflections of parents' evaluations of digital media in preschool and how they interact with nursery staff.

Toddlers and Tablets findings

Use of digital media in preschool

The two UK nurseries and the Australian nursery studied in the *Toddler and Tablets* project all had a tablet in the reception area showing pictures of the children for parents to see when they came to drop off and pick up their children. But that was the only tablet possessed by the UK Peter Pan Nursery.

Those working there made limited use of digital media. Some of their equipment (the PC, the iPod) was broken. The nursery had invested in some software for learning numbers but staff did not use this – they adopted other teaching approaches. The fact that even these staff occasionally showed the children material on their own personal laptops (e.g. about the planets, plants in Kew Gardens) suggested they were not averse to using technology. Ivanka and Maria had even been to an exhibition of educational software to see what was available for nurseries and subsequently talked about what might be interesting. But they would need to raise money for that, so it seemed a long way off. However, at least this showed some of the behind-the-scenes ('distal') activities related to digital media (discussed in Plowman, Stephen & McPake, 2010b; Stephen, 2010).

These Peter Pan Nursery staff pointed out that some wealthier nurseries had iPads that the children could use, whereas (despite getting top grades from the UK regulator, the Office for Standards in Education, Children's Services and Skills [Ofsted]) the Peter Pan Nursery was financially poor and the technologies they did have were sometimes second-hand. Despite her reservations about children's use of technology at home, even Bridget, one of the older members of staff who was somewhat critical of digital media, would have liked some more technology for children to use at their nursery. Meanwhile, Ivanka said that she had always wanted a white board. And the staff generally would be interested in a *CBeebies* programme[6] where the main character used sign language. Recently the staff had decided that they would teach the children to sign and so they had already been discussing the fact that they might watch this signing programme.

Sometimes, the staff appreciated not so much what could be done with technology but how, like non-technology activities, digital media could stimulate children's imagination, as in the following example of 'playing office':

> Maria (Peter Pan): We have one broken laptop which didn't work and they (the children) pretend that it's working. And it's much better because it works with their imagination. I don't want them to sit in front of the computer here because they do it at home ... but they [are] very happily playing office with computers.

Staff from the UK Pemberton Nursery reported more digital technology use than in the Peter Pan Nursery, although to put this into perspective, all three staff in the focus group noted that in the nurseries where they had previously worked, they had used technology even more. For example, Carmen's ex-workplace had possessed a number of tablets with rubber cases so they would bounce if children dropped them on the floor. Sita noted that in her last nursery the regime was different and the children had freer reign to use technologies and they would happily play educational games on their own. However, Carmen reflected from her previous workplace experience that it was also important to have support from those often still referred to as IT staff and that sometimes this did not exist – she had had access to computers and iPads before but they did not always work. Carmen added that there was no point in buying digital media if this support is not in place. In general, she thought staff in nurseries still had limited digital media skills, especially older staff, and there was a lack of training when newcomers started in the job – staff often had to work out for themselves how to use the equipment.

Pemberton nursery had a visiting teacher once a week who let the children take pictures with a camera. Leo had tried to get the children to try out a metal detector in the garden but its batteries had failed. And later he remembered that the children had used the microscope to look at plants in the garden; they had then taken photos of the plants, loaded the photos onto a computer and printed them out – one of the few examples where the children had produced something using digital tools. As in the Peter Pan Nursery, Pemberton staff used their own personal digital media. Leo sometimes plugged his iPad into a boom box for a children's singalong. Carmen let the children look up topics on her tablet (e.g. when one child was interested in China), also showing them the photos or the videos of the children that she had taken as part of the on-going assessment of their development. She had showed them the special effects options on the tablets to produce images (e.g. infra-red) and had let children use software on her iPad (e.g. matching image of jungle animals and the sounds they make). In sum, there was a mixture of exploring what could be done with technologies and using them to supplement traditional activities.

The Australian Play and Learn Nursery had ten iPads, one in reception and three in each of the rooms. They were mainly used as audio-visual aids, for example, in a ten- to fifteen-minute group session when the children were singing along to a song on the iPad, watching a slideshow display of the pictures they had taken, or watching a short film. One mother had taken photos of her son on holiday and had sent them on to the nursery, so on one occasion the children looked at these pictures on the iPad. And the tablet would be used to look up anything children spontaneously asked about, such as when one child wanted to find out something about Singapore because his friend was going there. For this purpose, using the iPad was more convenient than going to the nursery library. Staff had mixed feelings about using the iPad as a talking book – one older member said she always preferred to read a book, but another noted the iPad used in this way was more attractive to the children.

Cam: And so, I read the book and I said: 'OK, we've finished a book and then we can have a look to see it on the iPad'. Well halfway through reading the book … three or four kids had wandered off and then as soon as I got the iPad, they knew the book was finished, got the iPad, they came and sat back down and sat through the whole thing.

There were some basic educational apps (e.g. matching items) that staff sometimes used with children but they did not want to overuse the technology, partly from their own priorities but also taking into account the preferences of parents, as Dawn explained:

Dawn: We've got to be very careful with apps. In our industry we can link so much into technologies (…) you do have to minimize that … lots of parents tell us (their children) have a lot of screen time so they do like that minimized here. And children get lots done … not saying screen time isn't educational but the hands-on learning, old school way … there's so many things you can do with that.

Overall, although this nursery had used more technology, it was employed more for supplementing traditional practices.

Staff from all three nurseries raised a similar point about why they only allowed the children to use technologies under supervision rather than simply letting children play more freely with them (the exception being that the Australian Play and Learn staff sometimes allowed the children to take selfies with the tablets):

Bridget (Peter Pan): When you've got too many children swiping, swiping, swiping, nothing, it's not … nothing gets learned like that.
Carmen (Pemberton): I don't let them play (on my iPad) very often 'cause it gets swamped, everybody wants to play it.
Ivanka (Peter Pan): (The children say) 'I want to see *Peppa Pig*', 'I want that'. Yeah, they will shout at each other like that. 'I want it', 'I want it', 'I want it'. And you say: 'No, no, no'. But it's on us to make it more interesting. 'Come on, I would like to show you something really cool.'

In this latter example, staff at the Peter Pan Nursery wanted to use the computer for different purposes compared with what the children would have liked, preferably linking its use with some activity such as creating images on screen, where children could develop their imagination. Ivanka added that if staff could persuade the children to try out something new, the children were usually not bothered that they had missed what they originally requested. These three examples suggest some effects of home experiences of digital media: the children are familiar with and eager to use the technology; they know about practices such as swiping; and they have expectations about what they would like to do with the technology. But then staff have to manage the demand this creates – and hence they choose to allow only supervised access and persuade the children to try out other activities.

There were other considerations shaping the form of access permitted to children. At Pemberton, the children were given some choices (e.g. about what music was played) but they were not allowed to click on links to flit between different videos on YouTube, so that they did not encounter 'the dark side of YouTube' (Leo). Time was another issue:

> Ivanka (Peter Pan): I grab the computer, call a couple of children, two, three older ones and say: 'Would you like to help me type labels or notes for our display?' And they said: 'Yeah'. One by one, each of them types one or two words you know … which takes them ages to find the letters!

Time issues arose in other ways. The week before the focus group, the Pemberton staff had received training on how to create animations with the help of digital media, so they thought that there was clearly an expectation that they should find ways to use technologies like tablets in a creative way. Leo had even thought about how to role play with the children, video the outcome and edit that video on the iPad in order to then show it to the children. However, Leo also noted that one barrier to achieving more with digital media was that the innovations needed staff planning and, once again, time was a consideration because time was a 'precious resource'. In addition, these larger projects with animations need much more preparation and sometimes teamwork on the part of the children. Leo observed that if a project took twenty minutes, the children started to lose interest; they could not concentrate for that long – they liked to see relatively more short-term cause and effect, receive instant rewards, which, he thought, is why gaming was probably more appealing. That said, both Carmen and Leo appreciated that if the children could be persuaded to persevere, they could learn that there is a longer-term reward and change their behaviour in the future. Just as they had learnt sharing and turn-taking, they could learn to be patient and increase their attention span. In other words, the children could learn new dispositions through technology use as well as through other activities.

Although there is now more academic interest in digital learning and digital play, there had been a battle nearly twenty years ago to establish ICTs on the curriculum, in terms of children's operational knowledge. In fact, staff from neither UK nursery prioritized teaching children how to use the technologies, reflecting the fact that the regulator, Ofsted, had other priorities (e.g. Carmen pointed to maths, Ivanka to anti-radicalism). In fact, during their last inspection at Peter Pan, Ofsted staff had not asked any questions about digital media. A few years previously, when digital technologies had been more of a priority, the Pemberton nursery staff had bought a range of equipment that were now used less, which they lamented. This shows how wider policy, or in this case the implementation of policy, can have a bearing on practices in the nursery.

The other factor was that the curriculum ICT skill requirements at different ages were quite low. Carmen, from Pemberton, cited some of the objectives in the focus group meeting, adding that by the time children were in nursery, they could already meet those (very simple) targets because of their experiences at home (also noted by Ivanka from Peter Pan).

> Carmen: As soon as you sit them at a game on the iPad and they start playing the game then you can say they've achieved 'Using ICT hardware to interact with age appropriate' software.' So, it's quite easy to find evidence.

That prior home experience also contributed to the fact that both sets of nursery staff did not have to invest a great deal of time in teaching children how to use digital media and focused more on how to teach children about other things through using digital media. Meanwhile, Leo from Pemberton said that he made the assumption that digital media were already 'covered' at home, whereby the children were already experiencing them and learning how to use them at home, so that he did not have to make such an effort to teach that skill at the nursery.[7] Of course, that assumes that all children have such experiences at home but, as Australian Play and Learn staff observed, that's not always the case:

> Abbey: Then there's a couple of kids that say 'I don't have an iPad' or 'I don't use Mummy's phone or whatever' ... and when you've got the iPad out you can see them just sort of standing watching because it's all a bit new for them and ... you know ... that they're just specific families that don't have a lot to do with that technology.

Lastly, Leo drew attention to the fact that priorities depended on the ethos of different institutions and that Pemberton was very 'outdoor oriented'. He referred to a study showing that children lacked outdoor activity; hence, he appreciated the emphasis on engaging the children in activities they encountered more rarely outside the nursery. That reflected a broader desire to expose children to new experiences that they were less likely to encounter in the home. This is important because it shows how the general priorities, rather than views on digital media *per se*, may lead to a non-technology focus.

Relationship between home and school

Staff knowledge of children's use of technologies at home varied. The staff at the Australian Play and Learn Nursery described how in both formal and informal meetings, parents and staff mainly talked more generally about what development stage the child had reached and what the child was doing in the nursery. Thus, it appears these staff still had a limited knowledge of children's home-based use of digital media from speaking to parents (as noted in Plowman, Stephen & McPake, 2010b), even if they can get some impression of domestic digital media use from the relevant technology competencies that children displayed in the nursery.

Meanwhile, at the UK Pemberton Nursery staff described how parents were kept informed about their children's life in the nursery (although this was more general, not specifically referring to digital media):

> Carmen: We take lots of photos of the children doing their learning and we upload them to *Tapestry*[8] *and* we assess the children against the curriculum and write a description of what they were doing ... the parents have a look in so parents can see images and comments about what the children have been doing as well as being able to visit there as well and talk to us.
> Sita: When they come to pick children up, we usually give them feedback.
> Leo: Yeah, see what they might have been doing, who they've been playing with, if they've made any friends ... like, if they're just settling and they don't know anyone.

Some parents did ask what their children did in nursery and the parents were entitled to come and see and join in, with a few doing so occasionally. The parents sometimes added photos to the *Tapestry* system (e.g. of holidays) so this was one way that staff had some ideas about what children were doing outside of preschool. Some parents had asked what items the children used at nursery in order to arrange for an equivalent version for the home (e.g. a toy kitchen). But that did not necessarily work out; in this case, the kitchen was less interesting to play with at home when the child was without peers. Mimicking the nursery in the home was not straightforward because the setting was different, with different expectations; preschool was a space to play at carrying out adult activities, a space to be with peers of the same age which was different than being at home with an older or younger sibling.

As regards digital media, staff knowledge of children's experiences outside the nursery often came from moments of observation.

> Sita (Pemberton): And when we go on a home visit (before the children first come to the nursery) I've seen most of the children with their own iPad (…) I've been to so many and I've seen all the mums just give them iPad or a phone to keep them quiet.[9]
>
> Leo: I do see some of them when they get collected, they're just like going for their parents' phone, they're like: 'Okay, I'll have this now … You've had it all day, now it's my time.'

Ivanka and Bridget from Peter Pan had seen the same type of interactions and were very critical of parents using digital media to occupy children. Although Ivanka said she could understand parents doing this when under pressure, she was worried that the child would expect to have access to these technologies all the time. In addition, she was critical of parents who were 'too involved' in using their own technologies rather than interacting with their children.

> Ivanka: And also, the parents do it as well. We've got signs on the door: 'Please do not use your mobile phones during the nursery pickup and drop-off' … and we've got a picture there of a mother typing on the phone and child standing there and crying. Yeah, we don't want those parents to come to the nursery with … they just came, talking to somebody, didn't even look at the child, didn't even speak to the child and we don't want that.

One particular case illustrated how staff sometimes asked parents about their children's technology use if there was a perceived problem. In this instance, they may well be right about the child's 'overuse' of digital media, but it also revealed wider, common views about the potentially anti-social consequences of technologies that were documented in the literature review.

> Bridget: We've all had meetings recently asking what the children are currently doing at home. I mean, one child in particular spends a lot of time on an iPad and I think it has impacted on his social skills to the extent that he's …
> Ivanka: He's a little bit lost. Doesn't speak because nobody talks …
> Bridget: Yeah, but his dad says that on the iPad he's very capable.
> Ivanka: Oh, I bet he is.
> Bridget: So sometimes I think … well in my opinion these things can be quite anti-social … and the children are very young … because it's such an

> isolating thing. It's ... you're not involving ... you're not interacting with other children.
> Maria: Definitely.
> Ivanka: You know, he will be maybe able to complete his programs, but he doesn't know how to put his shoes on, he doesn't even like ... he will be standing like that [holds out her arms] waiting 'til somebody will dress him.

Moreover, at least some of these staff, like many commenters, make the assumption that technology use is inevitably isolating. For example, later in the interview Bridget said that 'you can't replace human interaction and you cannot substitute that with machines', which falsely assumes human interaction is never taking place when a machine is being used at home.[10]

Parents' view of children's learning in preschool

Last, there are the perspectives of parents, from the individual family interviews, focus groups and, in the Australian case, from staff reporting what parents had said. In general, the parents were very positive about preschool (both nurseries and toddlers groups) for a variety of reasons: because they thought they were richer environments, materially and in terms of activities; staff gave their children sensory stimulation; the parents valued their children being in a structured environment; many parents thought the staff were more aware of learning principles than they were themselves; and it enabled their children to socialize with people their own age. However, several parents noted that staff had limited time to interact with parents because they were very busy.

There was a mixed picture as regards the use of digital media in preschool. Some UK and Australian parents talked of nurseries where they had seen many screens and were aware of software being used in their own children's preschool institutions (e.g. Mathletics, Alphablocks). They also reported activities such as singing along to YouTube songs and where nursery staff encouraged the children to try out things in the home (e.g. using Google map). Other parents reported nurseries where not many digital media were used, or only staff used them and made the same point as Carmen about the limited technological qualifications of those staff.

However, the parents still had some reservations. For example, when encouraging children to try using digital media in the home, parent Liza (UK) noted that the teachers made assumptions about what type of technology is available in the home and a lack of the right level of digital media might disadvantage some children.

Liza: I try not to ask too much, not question the place of technology ... so for example when I asked the teacher: 'What if a child doesn't have ... ?' I said: 'What sort of screen do we need for that?' And she looked at me like ... the assumption was ... this was an irrelevant question because she hadn't thought of that ... and I didn't want to come across as the annoying parent.

Parent Helen (UK) worried that when digital media were used in nurseries it was because the teachers were being a bit lazy and then the technologies were too tempting, creating a problem for the parents when they went to pick the children up.

Helen: I think teachers must also use it as a prop ... 'cause as soon as they're doing something like with an iPad or computer, they've got that child's attention ... because they love absorbing that information, they love seeing it in that format. [Then] at the end of the day when you go to collect them, they're always watching Alphablocks ... and they're all just there kind of mesmerized by it. As you come to collect them, they don't want to leave, they want to carry on watching it even though you're desperate to get home.
(...)
Claire: If they do their music in school and if they're watching a screen just before you pick them up and that behaviour change that you said after they've been removed from the technology ... it's actually quite difficult for you then ... you've got the whole way home having that removal.

The other problem was when parents felt that nursery staff used digital media to distract or occupy the children, especially when the parents dropped them off at nursery. The parents wondered what type of message this was giving to the children and whether that could create problems in the future.

Helen: When the [children] have trouble with being dropped off or don't want their parents to leave [the staff] will get an iPad out and put on like Fireman Sam or whatever to distract them so that the mum can leave, or the dad can drop them. Because they are suddenly occupied by watching something on an iPad ... which is really young straight away to be like: 'Here you go, here's a treat, watch this, don't worry about your mum leaving.'
Claire: Yeah, there should be other sort of tools that they possibly use first ... like when I had all the problems dropping off Harry at South Harrogate, they didn't take very long to distract him with a book or with a pen ... but then the problem is if they use the TV then every day [the children] are going to be like: 'If I make a fuss I get to watch TV so I'll make a fuss every day' ... it's difficult to know when you're creating a behaviour and solving a behaviour.

> Kath: If you're distracting children just with a screen, it doesn't kind of quite feel right. If you're like: 'Hi, I don't want the teachers doing it, that's my laziness, (Other parents laugh, as if knowing what she means) [so], don't you do it as well.'

In fact, there is another issue where parents' concerns about what they themselves should be doing as parents spill over into their reflections on preschool: screen time. The Australian Play and Learn Nursery staff noted that some parents had, in their view, misleading perceptions that the children spent too much time watching the iPad:

> Carey: I did have one time, [when a parent said] 'Are they watching the iPad the whole day?' And I say: 'No, we just started now because I want to get everyone's attention before they go home, I want to prepare [them all to be] ready for home'. But the parent is thinking we put it on all day 'cause it was on at the end of the day.

Trisha, also from the Play and Learn Nursery, later clarified how the iPad use was limited and educational:

> Trisha: I think initially you do get the odd families that are just like … they do not want any screen time but generally by the time they're in this room I think they've understood that what we use them for is for education, it's not babysitting, it's not the TV in the living room and they're not … going hours and hours and hours of time watching screens … you know, they might get a three or four-minute story and that might be it for the entire day.

But sometimes the parents' reactions were more subtle when they became aware of their children using screens at school, as this UK mother explained.

> Chloe: Cole, my son, woke up this morning said: 'Oh Mummy, when I come back from school, I know you don't let me use your phone but Mummy, could I watch something about the *Blue Planet*? We watched it yesterday at school'. I was just like 'Oh, oh okay, that's fine.' (…) But I was so surprised when he said: 'Mummy, I was on YouTube' and I was like: 'What … I'm trying to limit you at home and then they watch … ' I felt so like … not betrayed but I thought like: 'Oh like, I would have liked to be informed' … I would have never said 'if you're watching it take Cole out of the class' … I would have never said that … but just to be informed.
>
> (…)
>
> Claire: Because if you are limiting how much screen time they have and they've had, I don't know, for argument's sake not very long but probably like 20 minutes at school … do you then include that in your allowance of screen time in a day if you are controlling that? I don't know.

Finally, Chloe's comment that she would have liked to have been informed about digital media use in preschool underlies the fact that the home and preschool can be two separate social worlds with limited communication between them.

> Claire: There's an assumption that we're all very comfortable with the amount ... the technology as a learning tool. There's never been a conversation, you know: 'Are we okay with us showing YouTube.'

Conclusion

Although only based on material from a small study, covering several nurseries, this chapter provided some idea of the variation and also the nuances of digital media use within different institutions. In the UK, Peter Pan Nursery made more limited use of digital technologies, but staff still had some ambitions and even used their own equipment. The UK Pemberton nursery staff had used digital media more in the past, including when the technology was more in vogue with the regulator, but their prioritization of outdoor orientation limited time for children's digital engagement, as did time constraints more generally when some uses of technology demanded substantial preparation. However, these staff engaged in a certain number of activities with a range of devices. Like the Peter Pan staff, they sometimes made use of their personal equipment and there was one example of allowing the children to produce material in a digital form. These staff had even more ambitions and at the end of the focus group they continued to talk amongst themselves about what they might do with digital media in the future. While the Australian Play and Learn Nursery had more tablets and used them for a range of purposes, the activities were not ones where the children engaged with these devices creatively. Staff also limited digital media use because they were concerned about over-use of screens.

In these three particular settings, unlike some nurseries, children did not have free reign to play with technologies and use was very much supervised. This in part arose from the experiences, knowledge and expectations the children brought from home – staff thought these would lead children to replicate what they did with digital media at home if the staff did not try to persuade them to try out new things.

Generally, staff used digital media to achieve certain learning goals. For the most part staff still did not prioritize teaching children about using digital media (although Leo from Pemberton had shown the children how to upload and print and had aspirations to teach video editing). This in part reflected the fact that, because of staff perceptions of the knowledge children brought from home, it was easier to achieve the rather low curriculum targets and the digital technology section of the curriculum seemed itself to be less prioritized nowadays. Besides, the emphasis was on teaching children about what they did not do at home, exposing the children to new experiences and in this respect learning about digital media was already perceived to be 'covered' in the children's home life.

As regards the relations between the home and preschool, parents and staff did have some communication, staff made gestures to engage with parents and some parents followed this up. But contact was often limited and, in the UK studies, discussions between parents and staff were more general, rather than talking about the children's digital media experiences. Therefore, in many ways the situation was still similar to what was reported in the literature review. However, more specific issues now exist in part reflecting wider social discourses but also based on staff observations about digital media use. Staff were sometimes critical of parents occupying children with technologies. Or they felt that some parents themselves were too pre-occupied with devices. And sometimes staff were concerned the children's digital media use outside the preschool could have negative consequences for their sociability.

The UK parents' view seemed to be that preschool was still a separate world. They were in general positive about their children's experiences in preschool settings but were sometimes surprised to find out about children's digital media use in that setting. In part, they brought their own concerns about how they as parents should manage their children's engagement with technology to their evaluations of digital media use in preschool, as illustrated in the case of perceptions of staff using digital content to occupy or distract children and the issue of screen time.

7

Infants

Introduction

The Infants chapter investigates the digital practices of very young children (aged from birth to twenty-three months), as observed by researchers and as discussed by their parents and siblings. Responding to Nevski and Siibak's (2016, p. 228) agenda around exploring parents' 'justifications for making these [smart] devices available to infants and toddlers', the chapter asks, 'What factors do parents consider when enabling digital media use by infants up to two?' Nine of the children in the ethnographic study were in this age group: six in Australia, three in the UK. Table 7.1 (overleaf) shows participant children, ordered in terms of the child's age.

The pages that follow consider parents' and families' different digital media engagement strategies with respect to infants' agentic tech use and reflect upon the attitudes shared by participant parents. It does not consider 'babies under the data gaze' or some parents' use of 'a variety of intimate surveillance apps and devices' (Mascheroni & Siibak, 2021, p. 65; see also Leaver, 2017).

Reflecting a lack of scholarly literature focusing on digital media use by under-twos, and acknowledging the influence upon this of perceived rules against screen-use by that age group (see Chapters 2 and 3), few studies include children of below twelve months. This project contains two children in that age group, and seven in the twelve- to twenty-three-month range, although that gap around babies is addressed in part by the recollections of some parents when talking about older children. Many infants enjoy digital engagement. Challenged as they are by less-developed motor skills and an absence of formal language, infants' use of touchscreens can nonetheless offer an experience of self-directed activity and freedom (YouTube, 2011).

Table 7.1 Infant participants

Family	Name	Birth Order	Group	Age	M/F	AU/UK
Govender	Eliza	1	Infant	4 mths	F	AU
Campbell	Julia	1	Infant	11 mths	F	AU
Cullen	Finn	4	Infant	14 mths	M	AU
Langridge	Cecilia	2	Infant	19 mths	F	AU
Kramer	Owen	2	Infant	19 mths	M	UK
Cheung-Yeo	Samuel	1	Infant	20 mths	M	AU
Greenfield	Andrew	1	Infant	21 mths	M	UK
Lim-Park	Emily	2	Infant	23 mths	F	AU
Mansi	Sergei	1	Infant	23 mths	M	UK

In terms of research approaches, capturing the purposive and tactile elements of very young children's digital activities in interviews sometimes prompted the inclusion of a second researcher. Prior to each parent-based interview, it was arranged that the youngest child in the family would be with that parent. In almost every case where this strategy was adopted, the child paid attention for a while before getting bored, as young children often do when parents are chatting with other adults. Where the second investigator was available, that was the point at which their role became more important. Sitting in on the parent conversation, as if interested but not involved, the second researcher paid attention to the child and their activities. In search of something interesting to do while the adults were busy, the child would often seek to use the parent's phone or other digital device, which had been left by the parent in a customary place. Sometimes the child's request for device access was necessarily delivered with gestures and pre-verbal sound.

Assuming the child gained access to the media device, sometimes handing it to their parent to insert a password or PIN number, the second researcher began to show an interest in what the child was doing. If that interest was demonstrated too early, it risked making the child shy. Properly timed and with the parents' acceptance of the researchers and their presence, most children were keen to demonstrate what they were doing and why they enjoyed it, while the secondary researcher noted the skills each child displayed and their capacity to negotiate digital environments. Using this approach, researchers could collect data with pre-verbal children, as well as older children who more readily displayed their abilities.

These research approaches were written up in a blog post framed around the co-opting of parents as field collaborators (Holloway & Stevenson, 2017). The innovations around research practice varied a little with country, context and age of the child. It was not always possible to use two researchers, however, particularly in the UK. In those situations, the sole researcher (typically Leslie) would improvise, sometimes returning on a subsequent day to video the child's digital activities. This was the situation with the three case studies that examine parental support for children's learning with digital media (see Chapter 11: Parents' evaluation of children's learning through digital media). Where there were two researchers in an interview, Kylie was supported by Kelly in Australia, and Leslie had help from Svenja in the UK. (See Acknowledgements for further details.)

Having briefly addressed methodological issues, this chapter now considers each of the nine infant participant families in turn before exploring similarities and differences across the cohort while seeking to understand the factors that parents consider when enabling digital media use by infants up to two. The chapter concludes with a policy-engaged discussion, but first, an introduction to the youngest members of the *Toddlers and Tablets* cohort, noting that the Appendix includes additional summary information.

Eliza Govender, four months, northern Perth suburbs

Angie (forty) and Yussef (forty-one) experienced difficulties conceiving and were married for many years their daughter Eliza was born. Eliza arrived prematurely and spent a short period in a neonatal care unit before her parents could take her home. A few months later, Angie maintains contact with her midwives and her GP, using a range of apps recommended by her private health care provider to monitor Eliza's progress.

At this stage of their parenting journey and with Angie at home and Yussef working long shifts in a refinery, Angie makes a point of sending him regular pictures and videos of Eliza's daily activities: 'and now, if it doesn't come, he's: "So where is it? Where's my video?"' Angie uses WhatsApp for this, since she believes the images are better protected than those uploaded to Facebook or Messenger: 'I'll only Facebook images of her when I think it's the right time 'cos I'm very wary about putting pictures of a baby online.'

Angie has set up the front room 'like a bit of a gymbaroo' because Eliza gets bored if she's doing the same thing for too long ('about ten minutes'). Angie personally likes children's television, 'I love the fact that I get to watch it and have an excuse', but it's only Angie that's doing the watching because all the play equipment is turned to face away from the television screen '"cos I don't want her looking at screens just yet … because of blue light and all that sort of stuff'. Angie is aware of guidelines that suggest no screen time for under-twos 'which I don't think is possible for most people'. 'I know she's interested', notes Angie, because Eliza will 'arch her back and go that way [demonstrates trying to turn in her seat] so she can actually [try to] see'.

Because Eliza was born prematurely and with IUGR (Intra-Uterine Growth Restriction), she was 'perfectly formed but just very little'. Angie felt 'she was just this tiny little potato that scared me. Pretty much. That I just tried not to drop every day'. Angie's first focus was on feeding Eliza who 'could suck on a bottle but she didn't have the power to breastfeed'. Once that was sorted out, Angie moved onto a sleep app: 'There's no website that tells you, you know, "New mum, by the way, when she's four months she won't be sleeping at all."' Angie has several older sisters and sisters-in-law and a mother, mother-in-law and stepmother, who all 'want to give me as much advice as possible'. Instead, Angie 'bought a [sleep] program off a bunch of strangers because it's much easier for me to do that … I just trusted them that they knew what they were talking about. And it just made sense'.

Soon after Eliza's birth, Angie sensed she was suffering from postnatal depression and referred herself for additional midwife support: 'I wanted more health professional help at that point, rather than mother help, if you know what I mean … Really, to be fair, I haven't really enjoyed being a mother until just recently.'

In terms of her vision for Eliza's future technology use, Angie describes herself as being 'in the middle' of a continuum between 'laid back' and 'anxious': 'I'm definitely not laid back, but I don't want to be at the other end either because I know I have tendency to go that way'. She is concerned about the 'addictive' aspects of technology use: 'I think you spend more of your life looking at a phone than actually looking at your child's face and that has happened to my husband because he's so focused on taking … photos of the baby he forgets that that takes ten minutes out of his very limited time with the baby.'

Asked about her vision for Eliza's technology-based future, Angie says, 'I hope that she's not part of a generation that are forever taking pictures of themselves. I just don't like it!' Angie adds: 'Saying all that, she will be on the internet by the time she's three because it's just part of our life, but I will be very careful about what I let her do.'

Julia Campbell, eleven months, inner city Perth

Like Eliza, Julia is an only child. On the cusp of her first birthday, she loves the TV remote for its effect but isn't fooled by a play version.

As an older first-time mum in her late thirties, Jenna has heard a range of 'snippets' that she adopts in her parenting. For example, she'd heard that a child that had three books a day read to them from birth starts school a year ahead; so, every day Julia is read three books a day and loves them. Julia already has clear preferences and chooses the books she wants read.

Julia's parents use the Wiggles on an iPad or via Netflix to support them getting on with their everyday tasks and for when Julia might be getting fractious. The Wiggles come in handy when Julia becomes 'ratty' for about fifteen minutes in the afternoon and Jenna and dad Adam also downloaded the show to their iPads before going on a twelve-day holiday. Even so, Jenna wouldn't use an iPad to distract Julia in a café: she'd prefer to talk to Julia or take her for a walk. Julia's extended family knows her love for the Wiggles and Dora the Explorer and Jenna expects a range of brand-linked merchandise for Julia's first birthday.

Working in sales, Adam sometimes spends periods of time away from home. Jenna notes, 'When we're Facetiming, she'll go to touch Adam's face and stuff … I never did a selfie before I had a baby, but she loves it, she points at her own face and stuff like that.' Co-present digital play and the creation of shared selfies with Julia is fun for them both.

According to Jenna, Julia can occasionally 'fluke' unlocking a phone via a swipe, but only if it's already activated since 'all the devices are password-protected' (Adam). Julia understands that some screens are interactive and tests all screens to see if they are touchscreens. Adam also notes that Julia plays with 'a learning app' that requires her to touch the screen for effect. However, Jenna doesn't want her daughter 'to feel connected to her device all the time' and that's something that also worries Adam: 'Like before I go to bed, I'll check for emails and I check as soon as I get up in the morning. I don't think I'd want that for Julia.'

Jenna is concerned that excessive screen time 'might make kids more hyperactive or anxious and things like that' so she wants to avoid digital overuse while also acknowledging 'the benefits with the learning, learning all the time'. Adam has concerns about individual privacy and technology's intrusion into everyday life but also sees advantages in embracing innovation. '[Technology] makes your life a fair bit easier, introduces perhaps a little bit of complexity but it makes it a lot easier.'

Finn Cullen, fourteen months, multi-generational household, north-eastern Perth outskirts

At fourteen months, Finn is the youngest of four children in his family. His older siblings Elle (sixteen), Adam (twelve) and Alexa (nine) are confident IT users and Finn was born into a family with a relaxed approach to digital parenting. It's a very different approach from the one that seems to characterize first-time parents and mum Sherryl acknowledges that she parents Finn very differently from the ways in which she parented her first-born, Elle.

Given that her digital media rules have changed over time, Sherryl is also aware that they are, to some extent, child-specific: 'I do restrict to a certain degree the bigger kids; [Finn] not so much … it has evolved over time, you know.' Even while expressing concerns about her children's technology use, Sherryl adopts a relaxed manner: 'Elle is terrible, she's on the computer like I'm on my phone … she would admit as well that she's on it too much.' But Sherryl acknowledges her own IT use doesn't set the best example: 'I try and convey that to the kids, that "I know that I'm not doing the right thing, so don't follow my example!"' She has decided against intervening in a determined way, however: 'I know that the backlash from stopping it [children's digital media use] will be worse than the actual doing it in the first place.'

Sherryl's view is that Finn 'was always a bit of a sook when he was little so it was kind of "What can we do just to keep him quiet for the next five minutes?"' She thinks Finn has probably been using her phone since he was ten months old: 'Half the time I don't even know what he's doing on it … and I find that he's sent a text message to my friends.' Although he's only fourteen months old, Sherryl recalls Finn as having been semi-competent before he turned one: 'I have to open the app and press the start button 'cause he hasn't figured that bit out but yeah, once he's actually in there he's got it all sussed out.'

The family has a busy start to the school day, made more complex by Sherryl's own university studies. By the time Sherryl and Finn have returned from the school run, 'he, nine times out of ten, will fall asleep … if I put him down on his little couch, he'll sleep for an hour. If I take him to bed with me and I have a nap too, he'll sleep for two or three hours. He's very attached to me … ' Sherryl tends to follow a parenting path of least resistance, fitting in with Finn's own preferences: 'We sleep with the TV on because it's … like, I used to turn it off but then when he got a little bit bigger as soon as I turned it off, he would wake straight up!'

Cecilia Langridge, nineteen months, Perth hills

With a drive-in, drive-out remote-working dad Dean (fifty-one) and one set of grandparents living nearby, Cecilia enjoys a rich variety of caregiving including at home, by neighbouring extended family and in the childcare centre at the university where mum, Louisa (forty-one), works. Louisa notes it was a big decision to have formal childcare some twenty kilometres away from where they live, but 'I know if something happens, I can quickly go down or see. If I get stuck at work, I know I don't have to race home …' ' Even though she doesn't want her children 'to be in childcare for more than three days [per week]', Louisa's glass half-full approach sees many advantages to the paid-care arrangement: 'I don't do glitter, that's what they go to childcare for, so it's those kinds of things plus interaction … '

Like many second siblings, Cecilia is so focused on keeping up with older brother Jasper (three years, five months; see Toddlers chapter) that there are instances where she almost overtakes him. Louisa comments that Jasper's 'not a particularly independent child so I will help him with most stuff', contrasting that with Cecilia who 'had a big drama this morning. She refused all her t-shirts until she got the one she wanted'. Louisa worries about the 'second child' syndrome: 'I really feel for her [Cecilia …] I didn't actually persevere with a mothers' group; I probably should have 'cause she hasn't really got any little people of her own age around'.

At the same time, some parental strategies that worked well for Jasper continue to pay dividends in Cecilia's life too. There's 'a baby karaoke app and someone got us onto that very, very early and they both love it'. It's been part of the children's lives since they were 'two, three, months' and is the go-to salve for when 'everything goes pear-shaped'. 'Give them that and it's designed in a way that they just love [… Cecilia] will have the phone and she, you know, just sways along with the phone.' One of the advantages of this app, from Louisa's viewpoint, is that it is audible, rather than visual, so it offers engagement that's quite different from conventional touchscreen interaction.

Whether audio or video, Cecilia is very intrigued by digital media. While people might assume that older brother Jasper has better motor skills, Cecilia 'just observes and then copies, so she is very persistent. She's the one who accidentally calls people or locks my [Louisa's] phone for fifteen minutes'. A few minutes later, Cecilia demonstrates her prowess to the research team at a point where Kylie asked Jasper to show them how he uses an app: [researcher Kylie, to

Cecilia] 'Oh, you're wanting to have a go, are you?'; [to Louisa] 'So she obviously knows that that button does something 'cause she keeps going to touch that button'; [To Cecilia] 'Hold onto that one, thank you. Wow! It's making a noise!'

Owen Kramer, nineteen months, commuter town, north of London

Like Cecilia Langridge, Owen tends to take his technology cues from his older sibling Libby (four years, one month; Preschooler chapter). Mum Stella (thirty-one) notes that Owen doesn't really use the tablet: 'He's interested, like, if Libby's playing on it, he'll have a look and he'll, you know, hit the screen and stuff, but … he doesn't ever really sit and play with it like Libby does.' The smartphone is a more accessible device, however: 'He likes to play with the Duplo apps, anything with trains or animals … and Owen knows how to hold it, how to talk [on Facetime] and how to turn it off.'

It's Stella's perception that Owen gets the knowledge he has from a combination of observation and trial and error:

> Even if he just hits the screen, after a while he seems to get what he wants so he's quite happy about that. He does learn a lot from Libby, from sitting and watching her do it … she does try to show him how to do some things but I don't think that makes much difference. I think it's mainly he sees what she does and then tries to do it himself.

Stella's major concern around technology is that 'it's really hard to balance it … I was worried about it displacing other things, about both of them really, not playing with toys properly or … yeah, not reading, not playing outside … '. Her issue was less that the children would be 'addicted' and more that 'it'd be easier to have a child that can entertain themselves by colouring or by playing with toys … I didn't want them to be dependent and I didn't want to be dependent on it'.

Later in his interview with Stella and the children, Leslie videoed older sister Libby using a tablet. He recorded what happened next between Libby and Owen:

> At this point, Owen tries to take the reindeer soft toy she [Libby] was holding. She does not let him, moving it out of his reach. A few seconds later, he crawls onto the table between us and tries to take my glass of orange squash. Libby immediately gives him the reindeer to distract him. This may have been because I was her audience and she did not want her brother disturbing the fact that I was giving her attention and videoing her.

(Leslie's notes)

Leslie subsequently reflected on this vignette, suggesting that Libby's use of a limited digital resource, the tablet, initiated a competition over resources with Owen that resulted in him trying to secure the reindeer toy, prompting Libby to give it to him to stop him distracting Leslie from recording. 'Even at that time', says Leslie, 'it struck me as a major social and quick decision about what was more important [to Libby] and how to manage her brother, by making a sacrifice'. This recounting of an interplay between the siblings around technology use highlights how children's everyday digital media activities teach more than straightforward technology skills.

Samuel Cheung-Yeo, twenty months, southern Perth suburb

Marie (thirty-seven) and Jo (thirty-eight) believe in a strong routine for themselves and for Samuel: 'He goes to bed between 7.00 to 7.30 p.m. and then it's "us" time as a couple.' That routine extends to zones for technology access. Phone use tends to be in the living and dining area, while Marie's tablet is in the bedroom since 'I hardly [ever] carry my tablet out'. Samuel's parents aim to have one of them sitting with him when he uses apps or watches television (Nick Junior). 'TV screen time is five o'clock, so after the afternoon snack', but Samuel also dances along with music in the morning played via the 'blank screen' TV. Marie works from home on some days and will occasionally have Samuel on her lap: 'That would be in the study ... we have a PC that's never on so I would actually just let him sit there and he can just touch the keyboard while I work ... from my laptop.'

Samuel's routine includes engaging with his grandparents and other overseas relatives via Skype 'when he is eating, so in his high-chair ... at breakfast or after afternoon nap during snack time'. This helps entertain him while his parents are preparing or eating meals and Marie says it also helps Jo and herself 'keep in touch with our families ... either the Singaporean or Vietnamese grandparents and sometimes both [sets of] grandparents in one day'. Marie first included Samuel in Skype calls when he was about seven months 'but he wasn't really interacting until he was ten [months ...]'. Samuel 'gets excited' by the Skype dial tone and recognizes that a call on Jo's phone is ' ... his parents and my [Marie's] phone is my parents'. He responds 'differently to grandma's and grandpa's voice'. Over time Samuel has met in person all the relatives he Skypes with.

At twenty months, Samuel has clear ideas about the apps and digital activities he likes, even though he can quickly find them boring. Marie helps him navigate through screens by finding his favourite icons, which she enlarges as 'he knows that he can swipe'. Even with his mum on hand as facilitator, Samuel will sometimes 'actually grab my fingers. For some reason, sometimes he thinks that is more effective' than doing the actions himself. Although dad Jo says 'we try to limit him', he and Marie are pragmatic around screen-based activities. From when he was about seven months, Samuel's parents would turn on YouTube 'so that he would sit still enough for us to cut his fingernails'. Jo recounts how they 'started letting him play games because we were going on a trip back home'. The five-hour plane journey didn't work out as planned, however, since Samuel 'was more interested in walking along the aisle than playing [on tablets and] things like that' (Jo).

Jo notes a general Australian concern about young children's digital media use: 'Child health nurses here actually encourage us not to expose them to screens until later' and contrast that approach with Singapore where digital media is often used as an apt distraction: 'Back home it's just the way to occupy them when having meals, at the mall, when crying.'

Andrew Greenfield, twenty-one months, south London flat

At twenty-one months Andrew is in full-time childcare with both parents, Trish (thirty-five) and Danny (forty-one), working in professional roles. His parents trust that the nursery is supporting appropriate social and educational activities: 'To be honest, half the time I don't really actually know what they are doing with them' (Trish). This suggests that the parents are quite relaxed about Andrew's possible digital technology exposure, given that Trish is not anxious for Andrew to engage too greatly at this point: 'I don't think they get them to do activities or do anything on the iPads.' Even so, she notes that the childcare centre uses iPads to send photos home, complementing Andrew's 'homework book'. Danny uses digital media with his son on an occasional basis: 'I was on a train journey back from central London with [Andrew] and I put it [mobile-delivered video] on for a bit to … make the journey pass a bit quicker.'

Trish will sometimes show Andrew digital family photos, but without actually allowing him to access her device: 'I worry about him deleting stuff on my phone or messing things up. Don't really want him to have a free for all.' When they go out 'to a pub or somewhere', 'I'll put in a couple of books, or I'll bring a few of the crayons and maybe the odd little toy or whatever'. That's her preferred strategy, but if 'he's, like, getting a bit grumpy, I'll just get the [phone] and show him some photos'. With both the TV and Trish's phone Andrew is exposed to digital media but not allowed to access the technology for himself.

Trish's primary worry is that Andrew would 'watch [YouTube] all the time. That's why we kind of try to just keep it off … In the weekdays, it's probably [on] about an hour a day'. Andrew particularly engages with bus and balloon videos and animations, with a parent operating the TV controller. His parents got 'a toy controller that replicated the one we had, … [then] he realized it wasn't the real one and [lost interest]'. Trish worries that this kind of engagement is reinforcing a short attention span: 'He'll be watching it [YouTube on TV] a little bit and then he'll be like: "No, no, change … " and we'll be like: "No." He'll sit there and go: "Please" and we just keep changing it.'

Trish later videoed one such TV-YouTube session. The video demonstrated extensive negotiation between herself and Andrew, showcasing Andrew's strong motivation to develop clear communication in the absence of good language skills. Leslie notes that Andrew 'goes to the TV and puts his hand on the option he wants (which he recognizes even though he cannot read the words)'. In subsequent written analysis, Leslie speculates that 'despite Trish's complaints and concerns about Andrew wanting to watch too much of this type of material, one could view this kind of interactive content as providing a level of stimulation that a parent might find hard to match if left to their own initiative'.

Emily Lim-Park, twenty-three months, multi-generational household, northern Perth suburb

Mi Na (forty), Emily's mum, has ambivalent views about digital media. She limited Emily's older brother Michael's digital access till he was two, but allowed Emily to use touchscreens before she was one, since that was what Michael was doing. Emily's parents initially used digital media as a distraction 'when she started screaming and crying and we couldn't control her and we showed her iPad just for a temporary fix and it worked'.

But then the family noticed that Emily's iPad access seemed to act as a mood destabilizer: 'After a while [when] she was exposed to iPad, she was a bit less than patient … [and] she gets really frustrated in short period of time.' After he turned three, Michael started at a local Montessori school and teachers there suggested the family restrict digital media until he was ten. Following this change, Emily also lost digital access, although Mi Na notes that the children 'didn't notice they didn't have iPads, they didn't even realize that iPads had gone ... [but] if she sees it, she likes it'. Even so, Emily predominantly thinks of iPads as 'oh iPad, I can watch cartoon'. Mi Na adds that Emily 'knows how to switch on TV but she will do that then she walks away. She switches on TV just for the sake of [using the remote]'.

In contrast to their success in weaning Emily off iPads, the family goes to great lengths, unsuccessfully, to stop her climbing: 'She's so quiet but she climbs ... she'll climb our fridge, our freezer – she will step on the lower fridge doors and then climb up.' Even though the fridge is now locked to stop Emily opening it, she can climb the outside 'so that [lock] doesn't stop her from climbing'. Mi Na adds, 'She can climb out of high-chair when it's – with the belt on ... And we have the lock on the chairs 'cause she carries them round and climbs.'

Mi Na perceives the family as balanced ('middle') between being strict and easy going: 'I give my son, my daughter freedom in terms of how they want to play, what they want to do, but when it comes to bedtime and, you know, study times or something like that, they have to [follow the rules].' This is easier with Michael than with Emily. Michael started at a Montessori school while he was three but 'Michael was a very mature child; when he was two and three, we could reason, we could negotiate ... but with Emily, I think we're thinking when she turns four'.

Given the many differences between her son and her daughter, Mi Na wonders how much these reflect differences in early exposure to media: 'My son was never exposed to TV and any technology until he was two and he never drew on the wall. I'm not sure, it's just my observation, [but] my daughter was exposed to iPad when she turned one and she's drawing everywhere on the wall. I'm not sure if there [is] any correlation between them?'

Sergei Mansi, twenty-three months, Camden apartment, inner-city London

Nadia (thirty-eight) and Rohan (thirty-four), living in a wealthy locale of inner-London, had an agreed evidence-based approach to child-rearing prior to Sergei's arrival. Nadia notes: 'I was going to be very strict ... to leave him to cry a little bit, absolutely, you know, he should learn.' Once Sergei arrived, however: 'None of it's actually valid' (Rohan); 'It just went against my very instinct' (Nadia). Instead, Sergei's parents found 'attachment parenting' (Nadia). Rohan contacted people with 'a similar parenting ethos to what we had kind of developed' and they did further research that suggests: 'For cognitive development, it [attachment parenting] is a more kind of sound way of parenting and in terms of developing their emotional intelligence as well' (Rohan); 'strangely enough, we didn't read about it before' (Nadia).

When Sergei was 'two and a bit' months, full-time parent Nadia began structured engagement for herself and Sergei in groups/classes with other mums and babies. Termed 'mum and baby yoga', the first group 'was literally 30 minutes of mum holding him essentially the whole time' (Rohan), 'and we would kind of move their arms and legs' (Nadia). Sergei's parents differentiated the yoga class from Sergei's 'activity' groups, starting at six-months old, when he could 'sit and touch things ... Baby Sensory'. At twenty-three months, Sergei still attends three or four activity groups per week. Nadia notes that 'each child is with a parent or with a carer'.

With his mum as full-time caregiver and with input from his (visiting) grandmothers, Sergei doesn't require professional childcare but Nadia needs help to get things done. Once her son was about six months, Nadia started using digital media 'so he would just look and be mesmerized, kind of focus for five minutes whilst I did what I needed to'. Noting that she 'was kind of ashamed about it', Nadia says:

> If it's just me and we need to get ready quickly, I give him an iPad or [show him a cartoon on] a laptop so that I can quickly get everything done in 5, 10 minutes and we go ... because there's a little [bit] of a stigma attached to it. When I talk about it – 'It's very educational for him and he's learned from it' – I do feel like, 'Do I sound like I'm making up an excuse?' But in our case, it's already showing results.
>
> (Nadia)

Nadia recalls that 'we never really showed him how to use it [touchscreens] ... He doesn't really care so much where he's going as long as there's activity on the screen'. Supporting this, Rohan's view is that, once he or Nadia have unlocked the device, Sergei 'does it all on his own'. In the research team's video of Sergei interacting with a smartphone, however, when Sergei doesn't know what to do, he 'gives the smartphone to Rohan to sort out' [Leslie's description]. The same interview notes chart Sergei's repeated desire to show Leslie the videos and photos which feature him.

What factors do parents consider when enabling digital media use by infants up to two?

The nine infants participating in the project are mainly pre- or early-verbal and have developing motor skills. All but Eliza, the youngest at four months old, have some experience with touchscreens but the children's digital media experiences and parental expectations around these are widely varied. The family-based infants' vignettes aim to capture 'stories about individuals, situations and structures which can make reference to important points in the study of perceptions, beliefs and attitudes' (Hughes, 1998, p. 382) relating to children's use of digital media. It is possible to examine these vignettes for commonalities and differences regarding parents' statements and actions in relation to their choices around their infant's digital media use. Comparisons are explored below, starting with comments around the family context for the child, then parents' attitudes, followed by a focus on what we can learn from the vignettes about children's own agentic digital media use. Having considered these various aspects of the data, the chapter moves on to consider the implications of our observations for policy and practice.

Parents begin their parenting journey with a range of attitudes and expectations but seem readily able to adapt as they (with their child) develop shared family ethnotheories (Plowman, 2015) and parenting styles (Baumrind, 1991) that contextualize their approach to their child's digital engagement – sometimes the plans that parents make progress as expected. This is the case with the Campbells, whose first aim was to prioritize reading as a child-focussed activity. This worked well in practice, for them. In the example of the Mansi family, in contrast, Nadia and Rohan had imagined that they would be 'strict' parents but found themselves much more flexible, subscribing instead to an attachment style of parenting and discovering, retrospectively, a range of evidence-based research that supports this developmental approach. A third example was offered in the Cheung-Yeo's commitment to routine, with Marie and Jo supporting time-based structuring of Samuel's activities and also having designated spaces and times in the home for various aspects of play and learning. These three families are each first-time parents raising their one child. The Cullen family, with participant child Finn the fourth-born, presents a very different picture. In that case, Finn is being raised within an established pattern of family media use and mum Sherryl appears happy to adopt a strategy of 'whatever seems to work best' for Finn. At the same time, she acknowledges that her approach with her fourth child is very different from the principles she used with her firstborn, Elle.

Where there is more than one child in a family, parents will often note children's collaboration, engagement and contestation around access to digital media and the transfer of digital skills (Houen et al., 2021). This was the case with two of the three families where the infant has an older participant sibling: the Kramers and the Langridges. In both cases, parents indicated that the older child had helped teach technology skills to the younger child and they noted the younger child had learned, in part, from watching the older one. In Owen Kramer's case, researcher Leslie watched older sister Libby 'negotiate' with younger sibling Owen using a soft reindeer toy (that Owen had previously revealed he wanted) as a trade for her continuing access to digital media and her monopolization of adult (Leslie's) attention. Here, as elsewhere, these children demonstrate that they learn far more than the motor and technical skills associated with digital media use once they engage in social bartering around access to technology as a limited resource (Dunfield et al., 2011). As well as socio-emotional skills, as Bazalgette persuasively suggests in her meticulous investigation of young children's viewing of moving images, children are also actively learning when they are 'just' watching videos: 'Toddlers' instinctive responses to movies [should be seen] as meaningful and important, rather than trivial and transient' (2022, p. 8).

Emily Lim-Park is the third child in the Infant cohort with an older participant sibling: Michael (four, Preschool). Mum Mi Na didn't share her views about sibling engagement in technology use, instead talking about sibling differences. Unlike her brother, Emily is a fearless and inveterate climber. This appears to be far removed from Emily's digital media experiences, but Mi Na worries that Emily's climbing and her habit of drawing on walls might be an indirect effect of her early (but interrupted) touchscreen interactions, which started before her first birthday but stopped when Michael joined a Montessori school. Although parents are sometimes concerned that digital media use might trigger inattention and hyperactivity, no causal link for this has been found (Corkin, 2021).

Some parents find that monitoring their children's technology use places their personal media habits in critical focus (Lauricella et al., 2015). This is an issue highlighted by both Sherryl Cullen and Adam Campbell. Sherryl appears ruefully resigned to her digital shortcomings, expressing the hope that her failings will prove an object lesson for her children. Immersed in a media-saturated world, families can feel challenged by balancing adult media practices with the laying down of child-specific media rules. This mismatch may be particularly amplified when parents do or say things they believe they 'ought' to do or say, rather than what seems to them to be practical or justifiable. Thus, Nadia Mansi talks about 'making excuses' and feeling there is a stigma attached to child digital media practices that, in her experience, are commonly adopted by parents of young children and which she sees as having identifiable educational benefits. This may reflect the dominant public discourse in Anglosphere contexts (Jaunzems et al., 2019) around limiting screen time for young children (see Chapter 3). Parents with additional cultural contexts, such as Samuel Cheung-Yeo's dad Jo, note that other societies perceive technology differently. Jo's perception is that Singaporean parents, for example, happily rely on screens to distract young children when that's what seems to be useful.

Parents have a complex range of attitudes and concerns when it comes to their use of digital media as 'a babysitter', or as a distraction (Haddon & Holloway, 2018). In Samuel Cheung-Yeo's case, for example, his parents readily resorted to YouTube content to allow them to cut his nails. Julia Campbell's mum is happy to use digital media to support her daughter over a 'ratty' fifteen minutes when she is tiring in the afternoon, but she prefers not to use it when she and Julia are in a café. Other parents might plan upon digital distractions to help them manage a long journey. In the Greenfield's case, with twenty-one-month Andrew, this works reasonably well, while the Cheung-Yeos soon realized that digital media would not distract twenty-month-old Samuel from the excitement of air travel and walking up and down the plane's passenger aisles.

Parents note some reasons why they might use digital media in relation to their child, in addition to supporting their child's use of that media. Some principal caregivers use digital media to keep an absent parent up to date on their child's activities: this was the case with the Govender family, for example, with mum Angie sending dad Yussef videos of baby Eliza's daily activities. In his turn, Yussef prioritizes making his own photographic record of his daughter's development. The Campbell, Mansi and Greenfield families all note how much their child enjoys looking at photos of themselves. Other families talk about how FaceTime, Skype and other forms of digital visual engagement are used to connect their child with distant relatives (McClure et al., 2015). In Samuel Cheung-Yeo's case, for example, Samuel has daily Skype access to talk with grandparents in Vietnam or Singapore, or both. Such conversations keep him alert and engaged, while helping him attune to his cultural and linguistic heritage. In this case, Samuel's media integrates him within his extended family while also supporting his parents at a busy time of day, preparing family meals or finalizing other activities such as getting ready for work.

Parents' use of formal childcare services also reflects their perceptions of what is important for their child, in addition to supporting adults' work and study commitments (e.g. Rouse & Hadley, 2018; Garvis & Phillipson, 2019). Louisa Langridge notes that she doesn't 'do glitter' and is glad that daughter Cecilia can access that kind of messy art and craft play via her childcare centre. The Greenfield family, with parents Trish and Danny both in paid work, has enrolled twenty-one-month-old Andrew in full-time childcare. They are somewhat uncertain as to what Andrew does in his inner-city nursery centre, but they don't think it involves much digital media use. Sergei Mansi's mum Nadia is similarly unsure but speculates that early years' childcare services 'probably wouldn't [use digital media] because part of the reason parents [use childcare is] because all of us at this point [use digital media] at home [as a distraction]'. This latter construction of childcare centres as eschewing digital media use so that parents can feel relaxed about using it in family settings tends to minimize the possible educational motives and curriculum imperatives underpinning early childhood educators' support for children's digital media use. Instead, it prioritizes Nadia's view of the value of digital media as a just-in-time distraction that parents can rely upon.

The ubiquitousness of digital media in the everyday helps reinforce a general parental perception that even very young children have a natural facility with touchscreens (Plowman et al., 2008). This was asserted by several families, including the Cullens and the Mansis, with Rohan Mansi suggesting that Sergei's skill is 'partly through kind of intuitively understanding how these things work which I don't understand how they know, but they do know'. As the video of Sergei Mansi's digital media use makes clear, however, Sergei hands the phone to his dad whenever he gets stuck. Parents' perceptions may consequently reflect a lack of awareness of their own offers of support, input and step-by-step demonstration and teaching.

In the Greenfield family, mum Trish worries that, if it were up to him Andrew would watch YouTube 'all the time' while the Mansis talk about Sergei being 'mesmerized' by video content. Bazalgette's (2022) research findings might offer them reassurance as to just how much very young children are learning when they watch moving images. In line with the WHO guidance in this area (World Health Organisation, 2019), while possibly not knowing about such guidelines, Owen Kramer's mum Stella is challenged by 'finding a balance' between digital engagement and other activities. As we note in Chapter 3, the WHO findings suggest, 'While sitting still for extended periods is not advised, it is more critical that positive activities known to contribute to wellbeing are not displaced.'

According to their parents, many children are entranced by videos of vehicles, especially buses and trains, with dad Rohan noting that Sergei will enjoy 'a stationary camera at a tube station. He'll watch that'. Other parents make a conscious point of using digital media in ways that divorce content from visuals, possibly to disrupt the dominant connection with screens. Thus, the Cheung-Yeos encourage Samuel to enjoy dancing to music with the TV screen off, while mum Louisa Langridge loves the 'baby karaoke app' that daughter Cecilia and older brother Jasper (around three and a half) both enjoy, even though (or partly because) it is purely audio.

There's no question that children enjoy the sense of skilfulness and control conferred by digital technology use. This is clearly demonstrated in the viral video of an under-one-year-old pressing her knee to check that her finger still 'works' when it fails to impact a magazine but has a significant impact on a touchscreen (YouTube, 2011). This pleasure in control is evident across the age range (see Third et al. (2019) for discussion of this in older children and young adults), but is also clear to parents. Julia Campbell's parents and Andrew Greenfield's parents both experimented with toy controllers to distract their child from using the actual remote control. The strategy failed, with their children soon tiring of the game when they realized the remote didn't work. In Emily Lim-Park's case, mum Mi Na allows her to access the controller but once Emily switches on the TV, she ignores it, indicating that it may be the power to activate digital content that is exciting, rather than the content itself.

The perspectives shared by participating families demonstrate how parents' motivations for providing access to digital media by under-twos are varied and multi-faceted. Parents might celebrate their own or their child's engagement with media, providing examples of their child's technological prowess and family connection, or worrying that they use digital technology as a babysitter and that their child might grow up to be dependent on digital media. What is particularly notable is that parents only mentioned policy settings in terms of their failure to follow the policies as they understood them and their willingness to make assumptions about what children were doing in relation to digital media access when they were enrolled in formal childcare, for example. None of the parents interviewed suggested that families had been short-changed by a lack of policy intervention or support. Nor did they argue that industry, technology manufacturers and software designers should take responsibility for creating products that addressed the possible disadvantages they perceived. While parents were predisposed to assume that any digital-parenting shortcomings were related to their parenting, or their child's behaviour, it is to the matter of policy that this chapter now turns.

Infants' media use: Policy considerations

Moving from a child and family focus to consider the policies designed to support children's digital engagement, it is interesting to note the extent to which families have incorporated wider policy discourses on themes such as screen time and safety and privacy implications of digital technologies into their everyday discussion and practices as parents. Screen time stands out as the dominant trope in this regard with each of the families exhibiting some awareness of the issues surrounding levels of exposure to screens for younger children (see Chapter 3). Parents also display some tacit knowledge about issues of privacy arising from their own use of technologies as well as the more specific risks related to 'sharenting' (Siibak & Traks, 2019). Similarly, parents reference debates about technology's 'addictiveness' and reflect somewhat self-consciously on their own use of digital devices as an important factor in digital parenting. First-time parents appear to be cautious in this regard when it comes to digital technologies in the home environment. A more relaxed approach to digital parenting is exhibited by parents of more than one child suggesting that, as children grow and develop, parents accommodate the presence of digital technologies in their children's lives to a greater extent and adapt their approach to parenting accordingly. Yet, a more general ambivalence towards the digital environment is also evident, with parents noting the challenges they experience in seeking to achieve what is best for their child against the backdrop of an all-pervasive but not always developmentally appropriate digital sphere.

In this early years' context, what is interesting from a policy point of view is the question of where parents get their information from and what sources of guidance may be available to parents of very young children to support them in their nurturing and caring roles. Parents, it would appear, receive information in diverse and sometimes ad hoc ways. However, the discourses of professional groups such as clinicians, health professionals and, to a certain extent, educators stand out as important influences particularly when parents come to consider the potential risks of too much screen time, the impact on sleep patterns or the lack of physical play opportunities that arise from over reliance on digital devices. In addressing these challenges, parents appear to lack knowledge of all but the more general and widely circulated guidance and this points to the need for much greater investment in the development of educational resources about digital media for parents of this age group. Additionally, there is also a striking absence of digital solutions designed with very young children in mind. That the infants in the study adapt so easily to touchscreens and appear to effortlessly learn how to navigate apps highlights the dilemma experienced by so many parents: such convenient access to entertainment and stimulation promises enormous opportunities, yet the modalities of access are rarely designed with children in mind, highlighting significant gaps in digital design and provision for this age cohort.

8

Toddlers

Introduction

This chapter addresses the digital engagements of children in the two- to three-year-old age range, as volunteered by parents and as observed by the project's researchers. The research question is, 'How do parents perceive their toddler's digital media use as creating, or constraining, possibilities for the future?' As with the infants (aged birth to twenty-three months), this slightly older group comprises nine children in the ethnographic study: five in Australia, four in the UK. Five of the nine children have siblings in other age groups. Jasper Langridge has a younger sister, Cecilia, while Emma Davis, Scott Andrews-White, William Bernard and Evan Jameson all have elder siblings. Table 8.1 (overleaf) shows the children contributing to this chapter, in rough age order.

Whereas the last chapter investigates a variety of factors, both positive and negative, that parents consider when enabling digital media use by infants up to two, this chapter explores parents' perceptions of how their toddler's media might open (or close) future possibilities. In doing this, we reference an early output of this research which notes: 'Parents of children in this age group [under six] are less concerned about inappropriate content and contact [but ...] tend to reflect more on the learning or developmental benefits or detriments of touchscreen use' (Haddon & Holloway, 2018, p. 113). Before considering the research contributions of our toddler participants and their parents, we will briefly situate this cohort in terms of their developmental stage (Piaget & Cook, 1952; but see Chapter 11 for a nuanced critique) and note aspects of our research methodology that are particularly relevant to this age group.

As the vignettes below demonstrate, toddlers are more able than infants to use language to express themselves and better able to communicate specific reactions and feelings. They are increasingly independent and may have opinions about what they want to do and wear. This age group is likely to be advancing in

Table 8.1 Toddler participants

Family	Name	Birth Order	Group	Age	M/F	AU/UK
Tosetti	Leopoldo	1	Toddler	2 yrs	M	UK
Davis	Emma	3	Toddler	2 yrs	F	AU
Brown	Simon	1	Toddler	2 yrs	M	UK
Zhang/Chen	Lavinia	1	Toddler	2 yrs 4 mths	F	AU
Andrews-White	Scott	3	Toddler	2 yrs 6 mths	M	AU
Ross	Penny	2	Toddler	3 yrs 3 mths	F	UK
Langridge	Jasper	1	Toddler	3 yrs 5 mths	M	AU
Jameson	Evan	2	Toddler	3 yrs 6 mths	M	UK
Bernard	William	5	Toddler	3 yrs 6 mths	M	AU

their toilet training. Digital media can help with this, as the Tosetti family notes: '[Leopoldo] just sits there on his potty with the iPad which is quite funny to see. There are apps for potty training ... there are rewards and, you know, puzzles and all sorts of things he can do, songs.' These children are, however, at the stage sometimes termed the 'terrible twos' and toddler behaviour may be punctuated by tantrums and a rebellion against rules and restrictions. This tendency may be especially prevalent in contests around toddler's access to digital media.

Reflecting their better command of language, toddlers are often able to indicate what they like and don't like, sharing their opinions about everyday activities, including playing with digital media. Both the Australian and British research teams collected information using three hula-hoops with different smiley faces to indicate like, neutral and dislike. The children in this group generally accepted an invitation to play a game around the child's activity preferences, placing cards to indicate whether toys, technologies and pastimes fitted into one or other of the hoops. The game is explained using an introduction like this one, where Kylie tells William Bernard how the game works:

> Over here we have some big hoops. ... On these cards are some things lots of kids like to do, don't like to do, sometimes do; and we're going to decide whether you like them a lot, you really don't like doing them, or you're just not sure. So, where do we put the things we really like doing? Where would you put them?

[Kylie affirms the child's response] Here? With the smiley face, yeah! Where would you put the things you just don't like? Beautiful! And in the middle go the things that you don't really care about, you don't do, or you're not sure.

As the game progresses, the researcher discusses the child's activity choices and later asks the child to walk them through a show-and-tell exploration of digital media used in the home by the family. Where the child remains interested, they are then invited to share their favourite digital activities, which also indicate their digital skills and competencies. (See the William Bernard vignette that follows.) In the infants' age group, this data was generally collected from parents about their children (Holloway & Stevenson, 2017).

Having considered some characteristics of the toddler age and stage and addressed the research methodology, this chapter moves onto toddlers' family-based vignettes before considering what the data collected reveal about parents' perceptions of how their toddler's digital media use might create or constrain possibilities for the future. The chapter concludes with some reflections upon the policy settings applicable to children aged two and three years old.

Leopoldo Tosetti, two years, north-west London

Leopoldo lives in north-west London and attends a nearby nursery. His parents are happy with the care he receives and have recently increased his time in care to five days a week. Mum Mirabella (forty-one) enthuses about the space and the experiences offered: 'Things that I would never even think about … I'm surprised how well they structure these activities, how cleverly organized they are … Leopoldo is made to feel like he's part of something.' Dad Lorenzo (forty-one) works full time; Mirabella stopped paid work when Leopoldo was born. Leopoldo's parents are both Italian-born and bred. Their son has limited language skills but speaks Italian at home, English elsewhere. Since commencing nursery, his parents explain that there have been positive changes in Leopoldo's behaviour over the past 'month, month and a half' and give the example of how he no longer tries to break their spectacles: 'If he finds my glasses, you know, on the sofa and he wants to put them on me … he's very careful to, you know, align them' (Mirabella).

Leopoldo's Italy-based paternal grandparents keep in touch with their grandson using Skype, accessed via an iPad: 'So obviously he got used to the idea of seeing images on it', says Lorenzo, who subsequently remembers that 'at the beginning, the very beginning', Leopoldo would look behind the iPad for his grandparents. Mirabella takes up the story: 'It lasted maybe a few weeks, he was looking at the back thinking, you know, ... "Where are they?" Yeah. He did that for a while but then he stopped and now he doesn't do it anymore.' Mirabella began using apps with Leopoldo from 'a few months old [... also reading him books but,] for him; it was easier to relate to the images and music [of apps].' She talks about the initial barriers: 'He wasn't even able to close his hands yet or to point with one finger ... he can use it [touchscreen tech] really, really well now ... and, you know, eye-hand co-ordination.' One thing that hasn't improved, however, is Leopoldo's impatience and Mirabella wishes she could make the responsiveness of digital apps 'quicker for that kind of age because they have no concept of waiting for something – so they get really frustrated'.

One day, Mirabella realized that Leopoldo could do virtual jigsaw puzzles on the iPad 'but he was struggling with real puzzles, real, you know, made of cardboard [... he couldn't] pick it up and yeah. But when I saw that, I thought "Hmm, we have to do real life things more!"' Despite this concern, Mirabella says they give Leopoldo unrestricted access to digital media: 'I never thought it's good to be restrictive because I don't see the point, really.' Lorenzo adds a caveat about lack of restrictions being balanced by Leopoldo's more complex interactivity with technology: 'I think we rely a little bit on the iPad in the evenings [... but] he's not passively watching the videos.' Lorenzo goes on to explain Leopoldo's particular skill in managing his screen viewing: 'He has a video on a smaller setting like – I can show you, basically like a quarter of the screen and he keeps browsing all the other videos until he finds one which he likes ... and he basically skips advertising; he knows where the button is, he presses it after five seconds.'

Emma Davis, two years, semi-rural Perth outskirts

Like the parents of some of the infant participants, Emma's mum Isabelle (forty-one) comments on toddler Emma's ease with technology, speculating that 'they watch us as parents do [it] or it's just intuitive'. Isabelle is concerned that Emma's capacity to follow links on YouTube, selecting content that interests her, might leave her vulnerable to inappropriate content: 'You get to Barbie dolls and then Barbie inflatable dolls and then seedy-kind-of-men-dolls and things like that' that are, even so, 'recommended' in the YouTube selection panel. Although she has concerns, Isabelle sees consuming internet-delivered content as being more active than watching television programming, since the child navigates and selects the videos/images they want to see. At the same time, she worries that it's 'not really teaching them patience or anything like that, is it? "I want it now; I will be satisfied".' (This notion of a developing disposition such as patience is discussed further in the children's learning through digital media chapter.) Isabelle adds, 'The picture here [on the YouTube trailer] is not necessarily the first picture you see when you open the movie ... and she'll get annoyed because she's like "No, I wanted that one" and you've got to wait a little while for "that one" to appear.'

Isabelle notes that Emma particularly enjoys looking at family photos and pictures of herself as a baby, but a favourite pastime is role-playing 'mums and babies' with her dolls and toy prams. She seems most interested in using digital media when other people, such as her siblings, are online. When her brother Jacob (ten) is playing videogames, Emma will sometimes sit next to him using a games controller that is not connected, pretending to be doing what he's doing. In similar imitative style, Emma knows how to find Phoebe's (five) *Reading Eggs* app:

Isabelle [to Emma]: [Is that] Phoebe's *Reading Eggs*?
Emma: Yeah. Me [... but then Emma can't open the app because she's been sucking her fingers and can't click enter.] 'Mum?'
Isabelle [to Emma]: Do you want to try and press it again? ... You're like me, we just press until it works, don't we?

A minute or two later, Isabelle [to Emma]: 'You press *Reading Eggs* ... oops, I don't know how to get back' [To Kylie]: 'See, this is where I need the [older] kids.' [To herself]: 'Why won't it let us ... maybe that takes us home? ... '

Isabelle [much later in the interview, to Kylie]: 'Oh, look at that, she's got to *Reading Eggs* ... And now she's going to enter it a different way.' [To Emma]: 'You want to read a book?'

When Emma successfully navigates an animal-focused app, naming frog, duck, rooster, sheep, puppy dog, pig, horse and calling the cow 'moo', Isabelle notes: 'Malcolm deliberately loaded this app because he thought this is something that's worth putting on.' Adding to Kylie, in a whisper, 'normally she doesn't like playing with it much. So, it's interesting that today she wants to show you.' Asked about her parenting approach in relation to Emma's digital media use, Isabelle says she has no fixed views but bases decisions on experience: 'If it's working for me and it's working for them, they do it. If I think it's affecting them, we stop.'

Simon Brown, two years, inner London

Jerry (thirty-eight) and Klara (thirty-seven) have chosen to raise toddler Simon without formal care services. Clarifying that Simon might start at nursery when he's three, 'for a few hours ... to socialize and be with other children', Klara adds that 'we do go to playgroups ... we go to TumbleTots [baby gym], we go swimming [... but] I also spend like really lots of time, you know, trying to get him to eat and stuff'. Simon's parents are constantly on the look-out for when 'he sees something that interests him – and we really, like, try and let him, like, interact with it as much as possible', says Jerry. Klara adds: 'We want to let him be a child and make a mess.'

Simon's mother tongue is Slovak but he is being raised bilingual, as Dad Jerry is British and speaks to Simon in English. Although he doesn't speak much at present, Simon learned counting and alphabet songs on YouTube, which taught him his ABCs and to count to ten in English and Slovak before he turned two. Even though Klara and Jerry hadn't intended for Simon to practise his alphabets and numbers at such a young age, Jerry explains they kept 'encouraging him'. But, says Klara,

> children need to learn to entertain themselves ... If I just don't put [the smart TV] on, he just goes into that corner and picks up stuff and he plays happier there than if he was, like, having the television on as well ... Running between the two, he gets somehow more frustrated [... and] irritated and just try[ing] to ask for this and that and, hey, [then] you can't please him anymore.
>
> (Klara)

Noting that her smartphone is 'a good babysitter at times', Klara adds: 'I don't try to restrict him too much when he asks for it – but, yeah, I don't just give it to him and let him play with it.' The exception is at night-time when Simon sometimes wants to watch videos of songs. 'We try not to give it to him', says Klara, explaining that there can be a 'big scene' when it's time for bed: 'He just doesn't want to switch it off in the evening ... when he's tired and grumpy.'

Jerry notes how Simon can operate the phone when it's on standby and 'turn it on and start [his favourite] app'. Klara shares how Simon 'can call my parents [in Slovakia ... with] the other person, like, "Hello, hello?" ... he will be just like smiling and listening, but not saying anything'. Simon also performs for selfie videos. Jerry explains: 'I left him with the phone, like, facing him – and it's recording and he was like doing all these funny faces.' In addition, Simon uses the phone to take photos, which Klara speculates may be accidental since 'there is a big button that he – it's, like, attracting the finger!'

Lavinia Zhang/Chen, two years four months, suburban Perth

Lavinia's weekday routine is located in her maternal grandparents' home, five minutes' drive from her own parental home. Accepted as Australian permanent residents soon after Lavinia's birth, the grandparents are Lavinia's work-day caregivers. Every morning, Monday to Friday, grandma Lily takes Lavinia to a swimming class, library story time or playgroup. These activities all involve Lavinia connecting with other children using English and Lily sends photos of Lavinia's excursions 'to all of us', says mum, Rita (thirty-three), 'my dad, me and hubby'. Lavinia's extended family were born in China and her grandparents are mainly Mandarin speaking. Rita and Lavinia's dad Stanley (thirty-six) are bilingual and both work in the Australian business community. They want Lavinia to grow up fluent in English, even though they speak Mandarin at home. Lavinia's parents and grandparents have a regular routine. 'Every single day we go out, we make sure we come back by 12:00 p.m. so she can have her afternoon nap', says Rita, adding that Lavinia is already 'fully trained on toilet training'. Lavinia's parents join her grandparents after work and the three generations dine together before Lavinia's parents take her home.

Rita and Stanley value education and have a clearly mapped pathway for Lavinia:

> Maybe from second half of the year to, like, a drop-in, like, we can put her in about three hours in a child centre and just get her ready to pre-kindy next year and kindy the following year ... I don't want to put her in a girls' school ... that's get rid of lot of good school from my list ... She got enrolled already in at a private school near our home .... I've done two tours in the school and, as soon as I told them 'I haven't seen many of the kids with similar background, there's not many', then they say 'yeah, no, there's not many' ... Interview happened last month, was a good one.
>
> (Rita)

Rita believes video games 'are just addiction, those ones they can just open and [get] so addicted' but she has positive views about some cartoons: 'You know *Peppa Pig* program, I just find that cartoon is teaching a lot of things ... They teach what Christmas is about, they teach, you know, how to do a teapot.' (Such immersion in new cultural practices through technology is further discussed in the children's learning through digital media chapter.) Rita explains her rationale: 'So when she [Lavinia] goes to kindy or pre-kindy and other kids talk about it *[Peppa Pig]*, I hope she knows about it too. I don't want, you know, [that] she feel, you know, lonely and then there's no socializing with the other kids.'

One of Lavinia's personal reasons for enjoying *Peppa Pig* seems to be her access to (the same) episodes in both English and Mandarin. While Rita was being interviewed in English, Lavinia set up a *Peppa Pig* episode on her iPad in English and then streamed, by herself, the identical episode dubbed in Mandarin from her mum's phone to the smart TV. (Diverse characteristics of children and their parents' technological orientations, approaches to parenting and aspirations are discussed further in the Diversity among Children chapter). While adults were talking about the importance of bilingual skills, Lavinia[1] convincingly demonstrated her own bilingual prowess and her digital competencies.

Scott Andrews-White, two years six months, southwest of Perth

Dad Richard (forty-eight) often works a long way from home leaving mum Kate (forty) in sole caregiver mode for the three boys: Ben (eight), Liam (four years, eleven months) and Scott (two and a half). Scott is a regular dummy-user and 'hasn't even started' toilet training, but he's fascinated by 'soccer balls, footballs, tennis balls … hitting a ball with a bat or a racquet; he'll practise and practise and practise until he gets it. He gave himself a blister [once]'. Scott also has a range of digital media skills, including screen navigating, opening and closing apps and managing to close pop-up advertisements. He will use an ABC Kids' iView app to 'find his particular cartoons that he wants to watch and watch episodes. … Because he's started to use the tablet and watch television independently, I can sneak away and do a tiny bit of study … I mean, it gives me a bit of peace and quiet' (Kate). When she was providing additional data for the project by videoing Scott's media use, Kate said: 'I came out of the shower and he had three screens going at once and I thought "Oh my God, I've got to get this [on video]".'

Kate describes her parenting style as 'laissez-faire': 'Whatever works for you and your family, just go with it and don't worry about what other people say.' She sees her role, in part, as a facilitator of her children's activities. She describes how the three children might be 'sitting on the couch, one will be on the Xbox, the other two will be on touchscreens … and you look up and you're just like "what are we doing?", but we do it, we all get involved … and I'm not prepared to give up my technology either'. Kate sometimes helps Scott when he gets stuck, saying that he can become lost when navigating the phone. At present, Scott doesn't know the password that unlocks Kate's phone and iPad, but the two older children, Liam (Preschooler chapter) and Ben, do. Kate can't remember the age at which Scott first accessed digital technology, but it was 'as soon as he could reach out and do it 'cause it is, it's so instinctive for them. They just know exactly what they're doing'.

Kate's approach to digital parenting includes flexible time limits: '[We] say "half an hour" but it never is … after a while, whatever time it is, we say, "that's enough"'. That's especially the case at weekends and during school holidays. There is one very firm rule, however: 'After they've had their bath and had dinner [about 6.00 p.m.], there's no more screens because we have had it in the past and they'll just lie there and not sleep.' In terms of her concerns around children's media use, Kate says: 'I don't want them to see pornography. I don't want them to see extreme violence. And I worry about shoot-'em-up games.' She has downloaded a number of education-focused apps, 'all the *Reading Eggs* and stuff … ', but Kate notes, 'They hardly ever play them. They're not that interested.' (Further discussion of the Andrews-White family can be found in Green et al., 2019.)

Penny Ross, three years three months, outskirts of inner London

Mum Sandra (thirty) spends her mornings with toddler Penny but she's uncertain what Penny learns at nursery, apart from to 'socialize with children her own age, learn that important sharing role'. She adds: 'As long as she's come out and said, "We read a story, we did this, we did that" … I'm happy.' Sandra and dad Ron (thirty-one) have reservations about the quality of some digital content. They looked at *mumsnet* (n.d.) at one point: 'Worst thing ever', says Ron. Sandra says she'd never seek advice there: 'People are horrible to each other … everyone's just, "That's not right, you're bringing up your child wrong"'. (This is discussed further in the Parents chapter.) Sandra does respect some authorities, however, and read widely before Penny's older sibling Frankie (aged six) was born: 'I was anxious to get things right … like making sure I put him in the bath properly.' In retrospect, she sees these anxieties as 'silly things'.

The children have a dedicated tablet for their use. Initially, Frankie didn't allow Penny to share the tablet, 'so she took it off Frankie [… at] about eighteen months'. Sandra adds that Frankie 'was very good at the tablet at [Penny's] stage, he was scary good. Thankfully, she's not'. Penny is sometimes allowed to play with Sandra's phone, taking selfies, calling her dad and singing along with songs from a movie she likes for 'the next three weeks, if not longer, until she finds a new film'. Sandra has concerns about Penny watching music videos: 'The music's fine, just turn the video off.' Ron agrees: 'I'm disgusted. That's someone's daughter on the screen, with things hanging out, doing twerking and that – and I've got my three-year-old trying to copy.' 'You just go, "No!"', adds Sandra, 'You're three, you can't be dancing around like that!' She prefers it when Penny 'records herself on the [Nintendo] DS singing the alphabet and then plays it back to herself'.

Sandra takes responsibility for monitoring the content the children can access via the tablet: 'I can just restrict it all the way down to, … well, [when] it's pretty much safe, I think. Until I read something later and find out that it's not. And I'll have to redo it all again.' Adds Ron: 'You don't want your kids going on stuff what we look at, or I look at. … I have to have a fingerprint recognition now.' In contrast, Sandra hasn't put any security on her phone ('if they want my phone, they literally have to be sat next to me'). She has a health condition that might trigger an emergency and she wants the children to use her phone if they need to call for help. Sandra's contact list includes photos of key people the children might need to contact. When Penny calls her dad and sees his contact photo come up, says Sandra, Penny sometimes mistakenly thinks her dad can see her: 'Daddy, I've got a lolly, look!'

Jasper Langridge, three years five months, Perth Hills

Jasper's mum Louisa (forty-one) sometimes finds herself doing extended parenting for toddler Jasper and younger sister Cecilia (nineteen months; Infants) when their dad Dean (fifty-one) is working away from home. She says that, unlike his assertive sister, Jasper's comparatively dependent, 'very cuddly, he's very attached and he's very much focused on me'. One example: 'He's got no interest in toilet training …, he wants to keep his nappy, which is really interesting 'cause they push that at childcare … ; a lot of the kids haven't got nappies anymore but that doesn't bother him at all.' Louisa's grateful that Jasper is 'really good at entertaining himself' but notes that when he's with her, Jasper wants her attention, 'he wants one-on-one time all the time [… but] I go "No, I have to do the washing"'. In practice, she says, he gets her attention and it tends to be the household chores that end up not being done.

Belgian-born, Louisa keeps in daily touch with overseas family and friends using an app to send them photos of the children. She says the children know 'how to take photos [… and] access photos, 'cause they like looking at them'. Over time, however, she has become wary of allowing Jasper too much access to the iPad: 'Soon as you try to take it off him, it's just a huge drama. … I know the more he plays with it, the more he will want it, so it's a kind of a self-preservation kind of decision to say "no". [... The iPad habit] keeps on feeding itself.' After coming home from childcare, if he can't play with the iPad, Jasper wants to watch television. Louisa resists this: 'I really do struggle [as someone from Europe] with them wanting to sit down and watch the telly when the weather is nice.'

Later, when Jasper plays the three hoops research game that helps children identify their likes, dislikes and neutral attitudes towards a range of pastimes and technologies, Jasper repeats something he possibly hears Louisa saying to him, but which he also potentially identifies as a personal perspective. He correctly names the image of a television and says it makes him happy. After talking about the next prompt image (drawing and colouring), Jasper seems to say: 'Sometimes I get lots of telly ... and I get grumpy.'

This nuanced response is also evident in a verbal exchange at the end of his game with Kylie:

> Kylie: The last thing is an iPhone.
> Jasper: You put it there [neutral pile].
> Kylie: You put it there? It's just okay, is it?
> Jasper: Yeah.
> Kylie: It doesn't make you happy?
> Jasper: ... Maybe sometimes.
> Kylie: Maybe sometimes it's somewhere else?
> Jasper: Yeah.

In this snippet of conversation, Jasper mirrors the ambivalence towards digital media communicated by his mum, a sentiment expressed by many parent contributors to this research.

Evan Jameson, three years six months, inner city London

Thinking back to her preparations for starting a family, French-raised mum Francoise (forty-one) notes that, no matter how much someone reads, 'until the baby comes you don't really know what happens. They have their own personality ... and you're quite surprised at how much they absorb without you realizing'. Francoise takes toddler Evan and older brother Floyd (five, Preschooler) to sensory classes that introduce them to 'different textures and sounds to wake up their senses'. Her aim is for the boys to 'play without any TV or anything like that ... They can be for hours on their own playing – so much imagination!' Dad Craig (thirty-eight) adds: 'And then later in the afternoon, it's just – more peaceful, quite literally is more peaceful for us 'cause they're physically tired and they want to go to bed.'

Craig's aim around his sons' digital media use is to build a foundation 'where they can actually think and play without it. It matters not if they have some exposure to it, or a lot of exposure to it, as [long as] they have the ability to … disconnect. Something we have to force a point on'. He says Evan has 'only just started to properly talk – and communication, like, you know … they're too young to have a rational discussion. I think [they will be] once they're maybe ten and above … '. In terms of technology skills, Craig says: 'It takes two seconds to learn how to use the tools, right? … The longer you tend to delay it, I think, the better.' While some parents are happy, even impressed, when their children learn digital skills at a young age, Craig thinks this can wait and be learned quickly when children are older. Instead, he argues that the children benefit from real life 'exposure to blocks, puzzles and basic books' adding that Evan 'won't go to bed unless he's read his book'. Francoise says Evan is 'amazingly good at puzzles' and credits his nursery play leader for this: '[She] would set up puzzles and her groups playing puzzles. And Evan would come back just playing puzzles non-stop.'

Although Francoise sees advantages in limiting digital media, she describes herself as trying personally 'to have a sort of detox, digital detox. And the holidays [in the French countryside] are fantastic for that, when you don't have any signal; … we've come back very relaxed, we've read tons of books, the boys are relaxed as well [and] you've played games with them'. Craig, who was born in Australia, sees one clear positive for internet-connected media: 'Maybe a little bit of Facebook to see cousins in different countries.' Francoise's positive is: 'Skype, we use Skype … ' Craig adds: 'To see Nan and Pa and cousins, uncles and aunties'. Francoise clarifies that the use of Skype didn't come automatically to Evan: 'But Evan was very shy 'cause he didn't know who they were until we went to Australia … Since then, Skype sessions are a lot more interactive because he knows who he's talking to.' (Discussion of the Jameson family is included in Green et al. (2019), with Evan referred to as Owen.)

William Bernard, three years six months, Perth northern suburbs

Mum of five children Sarah, early forties, was helped in the joint interview of William and his brother, Connor (five, Preschool) by her eldest child, Xavier (thirteen), who is very much a hands-on big brother. Possibly because Sarah and Xavier were part of the interview discussion, the two younger children tended not to say much, although both happily engaged (separately) in the three hoops assessment. William was happier to display his digital skills than was Connor, but both boys can use volume controls on phones and tablets, take photos and videos (sometimes by accident) and exit apps. They ask for help from older siblings or parents when they need it.

Like many parents, Sarah says, 'It's amazing to watch [... children's digital activities]. When they're little and they just start flicking through photos and stuff that they like and you think "Oh my God".' At the same time, Sarah expresses some surprise that older son Sean (ten) likes to watch YouTube vloggers playing *Minecraft* even though Sean doesn't play the game himself.

As the youngest child, toddler William sometimes needs help with digital media and Sarah explains how preschooler Connor might offer to help: 'Yeah. [Connor says]: "Let me have it and I'll fix it. I can do it".' She implies that accepting such help can be inherently risky with similar-aged siblings since there can be arguments when William wants the tablet back, 'so we've got a couple of tablets that they can play with; there's not all the same games on them'.

Kylie prompted William to demonstrate his skills in using Sarah's phone. She started by asking:

> Kylie: What's that? Is that a lion?
> William: It's a tiger.
> Kylie: I couldn't tell!
> William: That's a tiger.
> Kylie: Can you make it bigger so I can see it? [William enlarges the image] It is too, there he is. Right, that's a lion and that's a tiger ...
> William: Smaller [demonstrating how he reduces the size back to normal].

Although Sarah sees the advantage of having a choice of devices for the children, she also has misgivings about the children's technology access: 'They've got tablets, they've got DSs, they've got PSPs, Xboxes and I just think it might be a little bit too much for the kids sometimes.' Sarah indicates that this level of choice might be more than she feels comfortable with, but she explains that her husband Scott has no such misgivings; he believes that 'kids need to have that exposure and they will have that exposure because, you know ... Scott is all about technology, so he wants the kids to be exposed to it and stuff'.

This vignette about William Bernard and his family concludes the precis of ethnographic data informing this chapter about toddlers. The discussion that follows aims to establish common threads amongst the families but also the families' different perspectives and experiences of opening up, or closing down, future digital possibilities. Having done that, this chapter then addresses the policy settings for toddlers' touchscreen activities.

How do parents perceive their toddler's digital media use as creating, or constraining, possibilities for the future?

Many of the issues identified by parents of toddlers as benefits, concerns or observations around their child's technology use are developments and continuations of those touched upon in the preceding Infants chapter. Thus, several toddlers are identified as particularly enjoying using technology to review photos of themselves. This is the case in the Zhang/Chen, Davis and Langridge families, for example. Within the toddler cohort, however, that enjoyment can be associated with displays of technology skills, with deliberate choice and with the collaborative engagement of a parent (Danby et al., 2013). The annotated transcript of the Brown family interview records how Simon's dad Jerry demonstrated his son's reaction to the opportunity to record a selfie. Jerry (to Leslie): 'You can see here, look. [Jerry shows Simon the video set to selfie mode and Simon immediately looks at it and makes faces.]' Simon's response may indicate his knowledge that recording his reaction offers him an opportunity for additional father-son engagement because, as Jerry notes, he can 'play it back to him [Simon] and he would find it funny'.

Penny Ross is a little older than Simon and has greater self-recording skills, capable of initiating the recording function on the Nintendo DS. Mum Sandra says of Penny's ability to record herself singing the alphabet and then replay it to herself: 'You've only got ten seconds to record [on the Nintendo DS], so she only gets to the letter M generally, every time.' Sandra hasn't shown Penny how to make recordings on the tablet because that would consume 'the storage in a heartbeat with the amount that she can sing!'

As in the infant cohort, a range of parents in this chapter acknowledge they sometimes use their child's digital media activities as 'time out' for themselves. (This notion of digital media being used to occupy children is further discussed in the Parenting and Digital Media chapter, Chapter 4.) Kate Andrews-White, for example, takes advantage of Scott's ability to access his favourite cartoons via the ABC iView app to 'sneak away' and do some studying for her university course. Lorenzo Tosetti implies a vestige of guilt when he notes the family may rely on the iPad 'too much' in the evening when he and his partner are tired. Lorenzo takes heart, however, that Leopoldo doesn't watch videos passively but instead browses actively, and simultaneously assesses alternative programming. For Klara Brown, Simon's tech-based play can sometimes act as 'a good babysitter', while Sandra Ross notes that, with respect to Penny, 'it does make sense sometimes to go, "You know what, you're going to be happy for five minutes; I'm going to be happy for five minutes. Yeah, why not?"' These responses are complicated by public health-model injunctions against young (zero to five) children's unsupervised use of digital media: 'Coview with your children, help children understand what they are seeing and help them apply what they learn to the world around them' (AAP, 2016). Such perspectives stoke debates in the public sphere that help fuel parental guilt (Jaunzems et al., 2019), since children's self-directed solo use of apps is relatively common and, to parents' minds, can have a range of benefits.

Toddlers' parents are as likely as the Infants' parent cohort to identify their child's skills as intuitive (Plowman et al., 2008). Sarah Bernard's 'Oh My God' reaction to some of her children's digital skills was quoted, while Sandra Ross compared the skills of her son Frankie (six) with those of her younger daughter Penny and sees a difference in these, noting that Frankie was 'scary good', recognizing that not all toddlers are equally capable. In her interview with Kylie, Isabelle Davis notes that Emma can't find her way back to where she was on her phone, saying 'this is where I need the [older] kids', implying that Emma's siblings have greater technology skills than she does. However, Kate Andrews-White, who notes her children's 'instinctive' technology skills and that they 'know exactly' how to use digital media, nonetheless recounts how son Scott will hand her the phone when he gets stuck, thus indicating an element of teaching and a reliance upon adult problem solving.

Alongside comments about their children's natural facility with digital media, parents offer alternative examples of how toddlers have a developing awareness of how digital media works. For example, in the early days of Skyping his grandparents in Italy, Leopoldo Tosetti would look behind the iPad hoping to see them. Similarly, Penny Ross thought the photographic image of her father in her mum's phone contacts that comes up when she is on a voice call with her dad might be able to see her eating her lolly. Such observations reference debates around the dual nature of screen-based media. As Shinskey (2021) notes, 'A symbolic artifact such as a video has a dual nature. It is a concrete thing itself and a symbol of something else (DeLoache, 1987). Infants struggle to hold two things in mind at once and it is easier to respond to a symbolic object's concrete nature than to see past it and respond to its symbolic function' (Shinskey, 2021, p. 7). These dynamics are evident to parents of very young digital media users. Toddlers' parents note that children's learning in this area is comparatively rapid, however, while Jenna Campbell, mother to infant Julia (eleven months), considers stopping Facetiming Julia's father during his time working away from home because it upsets Julia when the call ends and Julia responds '[with the pre-verbal equivalent of] Where'd he go?' (see Chapter 4).

The toddler vignettes offer ample indication of imitative play (Piaget, 1952), for instance, Emma Davis playing with an unconnected games controller when she watches brother Jacob gaming. Meanwhile, the research team were so intrigued by Lavinia Zhang/Chen's choice to simultaneously stream Mandarin and English versions of the same *Peppa Pig* episode on two devices, just as they were discussing the challenges of bilingual education with mum Rita Chen that they wrote it up as a case study (Stevenson et al., 2021).

As with Lavinia, a significant number of children in the toddler group are raised in bilingual and multicultural contexts. Interactive digital media appears to serve two specific functions in these circumstances, regardless of the detail of individual national and linguistic profiles. Firstly, it helps children keep in touch with families and friends overseas (Kelly, 2015) and, secondly, parents celebrate the value of accessible media in a language other than English to support alternative language acquisition and development when living in the dominant Anglosphere. We see this in the immersive accounts of infant Samuel Cheung-Yeo's Skype conversations with grandparents in Singapore and Vietnam and the Brown, Langridge and Tosetti accounts of their use of digital media to connect young children with relatives and friends elsewhere. Even the Jamesons, with their emphasis on sensory play and non-digital engagement, make an exception for Skype and Facebook contact with family in Australia and France. The Brown, Tosetti and Zhang/Chen families provide examples of how digital media supports their bilingual child in developing skills in more than one language, thereby creating positive family connections and bilingual possibilities for their future.

The Zhang/Chen family was unusual in the toddler cohort in sharing a clear step by step plan for Lavinia's educational future (see Green et al., 2019). Most interviewee parents focused on sharing how they support their child's development through a range of activities that develop aptitudes and skills (see Barron et al., 2009 for examples, and Chapter 3). In terms of sharing their plans for digital parenting, the priorities of toddlers' parents are diverse, with some strategies that include, or consciously exclude, providing access to technology.

For example, dad Scott Bernard wants sons William (Toddler) and Connor (Preschooler) to engage with multiple technologies and digital experiences. This is the opposite approach from that taken by the Jamesons, where Francoise and Craig hope sons Evan (Toddler) and Floyd (Preschooler) will build 'a foundation where they can actually think and play without [technology]', taking their children to sensory play classes to help achieve this aim. The Browns are another family that embrace a wide range of non-digital experiences. In addition to attending playgroup, gym-based TumbleTots and swimming lessons, son Simon is encouraged to 'pick up anything, whether it's like a real drill or anything like [that]. We'll supervise him, but we'd rather not, like, say "No". The rationale behind this approach, they say, is 'Don't kill the scientist'.

It is unsurprising that parents adopt different approaches to creating possibilities for their child's future, given the wide range of conflicting messages in this area (e.g. AAP, 2011, 2016; WHO, 2019, see Chapter 3). Messaging includes readily available advice, from the AAP's (2016) public health-based injunction not to 'feel pressured to introduce technology early; interfaces are so intuitive that children will figure them out quickly once they start using them' to more recent educational research findings such as Hurwitz and Schmitt's (2020) analysis indicating that 'digital skill in early childhood was a marginally significant positive predictor' of academic performance in middle childhood. This latter finding is strengthened by Juhaňák et al's (2019) research across twenty-one European OECD countries concluding 'that children who start using a computer at a later age (after the age of seven) demonstrate significantly lower ICT competence and ICT autonomy at the age of fifteen' (2019, p. 1). As Lauricella et al. argue (2015), parent and child factors play a complex role in this area.

Parents in this research tell us that a skill which may start as an engaging digital media activity on an irregular basis can transition to become a child's habit or expectation. This perspective informs the technology-resistant Jameson family's focus on promoting son Evan's capacity to 'disconnect'. Rita Chen believes videogames to be addictive and does not allow Lavinia to play them. Louisa Langridge has equivalent concerns about Jasper's use of the iPad, noting that persuading Jasper to relinquish it can risk a 'huge drama'. She shares her view about how Jasper's desire for digital media play seems to feed itself. Both the Langridge and Brown families have a strategy of not offering digital media to their children, hoping that an 'out of sight, out of mind' approach will minimize device-dependence whilst supporting the development of other skills and interests. While these perspectives might appear to indicate parental resistance to technology, the nuance described by Plowman et al. (2010) around 'complexities in families' attitudes to and uses of, technology' (p. 63) is evident in the vignettes.

Television sets are less easy to hide away than portable digital media. Parents Isabelle and Malcolm in the Davis family have strict rules around TV use before and after the school day (sister Phoebe, five, contributes to the Preschool cohort while Jacob, ten, is a primary school student) and apply the rule to toddler Emma. Other rules that some parents say they find useful include Klara and Jerry Brown's prohibition on pre-bedtime iPad use. Their concern is that when Simon is tired and grumpy, he doesn't want to turn the iPad off once he starts watching it. There's a similar situation in the Andrews-White family, where mum Kate prohibits interactive digital media in the evening after dinner and bath time, before Scott (two and a half) and older brothers Liam (almost five, Preschool) and Ben (eight) go to bed. Such rules are in line with the AAP's (2016) advice recommending 'no screens during meals and for one hour before bedtime'. Kate says she knows 'other parents who have the technology box and all the technology goes in there and they've very, very strict about it' but sees herself as relaxed, by contrast. Asked about other technology rules operating in her home, Kate turns the question on its head to talk about her children's implied rule for her: 'They get very upset if we've had a busy afternoon and they haven't had a chance to have their screen time.'

The toddler participants provide ample evidence of the attractiveness of information communicated via digital media. Although several families mention *Reading Eggs*, positively in the Davis case; less so for the Andrews-Whites, the cultural value of some digital media-based programs is highlighted by Rita Chen when she notes that *Peppa Pig* helps educate Lavinia about everyday Australian customs, such as Christmas, as well as providing social capital that Lavinia will be able to share in the future with her peers at school (Stevenson et al., 2021).

The Davis family is one of several – another is the Tosetti family – to note that digital media doesn't teach children patience but is more likely to frustrate them when their expectations aren't swiftly met. This contrasts strongly with the family of Sergei Mansi who, at twenty-three months, was on the brink of transitioning from the infant into the toddler cohort. In that case, mum Nadia notes the value of education around the notion of technology needing 'to charge': 'If he [breast] feeds a lot during the day, ... I will tell him the milk needs to charge.' (This example of technological metaphor and learning is discussed further in Chapter 11.) Dad Rohan adds, 'If the [digital] connection goes, he'll say "Oh, it's a poor connection".' These parents feel that digital media has helped

Sergei learn patience, but that Sergei also uses digital media to teach them life lessons of their own: 'If you explain things to him, [and] you don't just kind of take [digital media] things away, then he's generally okay', says Rohan, 'but if it's quite an abrupt sort of ending to whatever he's doing then he can't accept it'.

This vignette (see Chapter 7, Infants) implies that Sergei and his parents are exploring the value of co-negotiation which, as Savic et al. (2016, n.p. citing boyd, 2014) argue, offers potential benefit when the 'spontaneous and natural processes of family negotiations ... can help parents and children to collaboratively create "*a networked world in which they all want to live*" (boyd)'. A similar approach underpins the AAP's (n.d.) policy recommendations around 'A Family Media Plan' and it is to the evolving policy settings for the toddler age group's digital media use that this chapter now turns.

Toddlers' media use: Policy considerations

In policy terms, for children at the toddler stage, screen time remains the primary topic around which professional guidance revolves. As noted above, the AAP (2016) calls for no screen time at all for children until about eighteen to twenty-four months except for videochatting and says children aged two to five should be limited to an hour or less of screen time per day. AAP (n.d.) also encourages parents and children to negotiate and agree boundaries and limits to their technology use and advocates the development of the aforementioned 'Family Media Plan' as children get older.

However, as the ethnographic vignettes in this chapter illustrate and as discussed in Chapter 3, toddlers already inhabit a digital environment and are surrounded by numerous digital devices in typical home settings so that the notion of screen time itself becomes rather artificial and an ineffective measure of the pervasiveness of digital technologies in the lives of children. As the research shows, play activities stand out in the busy lives of toddlers. Parents are keen to ensure a balance between physical and technology-based play and, while none of the parents in the study cohort sought to exclude digital technology, they are mindful of its appeal to children and, in a variety of ways, direct and in many cases restrict its use.

Despite the ease with which the youngest children learn to use and navigate their way around different digital devices, we are reminded constantly that most digital technologies are not designed with children in mind, let alone designed for their use. Of key policy concern, therefore, is the provisioning of a reliable knowledge base for parents of children at this all-important stage. Authoritative guidance is often lacking with sometimes confusing and contradictory information about the most suitable technologies, the availability of content for children and the best ways for parents to support their children's digital skills. Age-based classification labels only go so far and don't provide the kind of detailed information and guidance that parents need and ask for.

Policymakers at governmental level, therefore, have an important role to play in setting standards, as well as guiding and aligning nationally relevant policies towards children and the digital environment. Thus, raising awareness across all sectors of key elements of safety by design, privacy by design (Livingstone & Pothong, 2022) and building in considerations of children's best interests in the evolving digital environment is central to the leadership role of government and state agencies.

Educationalists likewise can support children's and parents' experiences by introducing education activities using digital technologies that support learning, creativity, skills and play activities, thereby giving parents greater confidence as to how to manage the home digital environment. Parenting organizations can also play a key role here in providing more detailed guidance about the digital environment. Professional groups such as clinicians, paediatricians and child development specialists are similarly a crucial source of influence for parents. Here, developing guidance, learning strategies and programmes can be an important and beneficial intervention that is likely to reach many parents. Most importantly, however, it is within the private sector that a key responsibility lies in ensuring that digital products and services likely to be used by children are safe, developmentally appropriate and meet the needs of parents and toddlers alike. This requires a prioritization of and investment in, design with children in mind so that, rather than an afterthought, children's digital activities intentionally reflect the reality of the digital world they live in and offer the kind of positive nurturing opportunities that children deserve.

9

Preschoolers

In Australia, where compulsory schooling begins at the start of the calendar year when a child turns six, the preschooler cohort is situated in the final years before compulsory schooling, with four-year-olds attending elective kindergarten or preschool. In the UK, however, compulsory schooling commences when a child turns five and enters the first year of schooling; the primary school reception class. Before reception, a UK four-year-old may attend an elective kindergarten or preschool. For the purposes of this chapter, four- and five-year-olds are all called preschoolers. In both countries, given that four-year-olds are moving towards mandatory education, parents are often concerned that their preschool child will have the skills that meet teachers' expectations, enabling the child to start on a level pegging with peers.

This chapter is less concerned with an educational construction of preschoolers' abilities, focusing instead upon their developing sense of identity and sociality, both of which are mobilized in formal education settings. It responds to a point made by Christopher et al. (2022), referencing earlier work by Pelo (2008), that early childhood education 'continues to have a growing emphasis internationally on school readiness to social and emotional learning and development' (2022, p. 1). Building on this thought and having talked with preschoolers and their parents, the question we ask is: 'What evidence is there that preschoolers develop social and emotional skills in digital engagement?'

A slightly higher number of participant children fall within the preschool cohort compared with the infant and toddler groups: eleven children are aged four and five, rather than the nine children in each of the younger groups. Along with a greater number of eligible child participants, more of the preschoolers than any other cohort have siblings in another group. Two preschooler contributors, Libby Kramer and Michael Lim-Park, have siblings who feature in the Infants chapter. Four preschoolers, Liam Andrews-White, Connor Bernard, Phoebe Davis and Floyd Jameson, have siblings in the Toddler group. Five families contributed solely to the preschooler group, leading to the introduction of these families for the first time in this book: Imelda Spinner, Ellen Brent, Leela Palmer, Ben Lawe-Tammell and Freya Petersen. Six of the preschooler cohort live in Australia; five in the UK. Table 9.1 (below) shows the children contributing to this chapter, in their approximate age order.

The preschooler cohort includes the smallest proportion of first-born children. Indeed, eight of the eleven participants have at least one older sibling who has already blazed a digital trail, helping parents set and refine their approach to digital parenting. Children in this age group are less prone than younger ones to tantrums, although most have had more practice in arguing and better language skills to argue with. Toilet training is generally complete although children aged four and five are not immune to accidents. Preschool participants usually have better technical skills than their younger siblings and are increasingly likely to have family members call upon them for help, as we see in mum Isabelle Davis's aside to Emma, aged two (see Toddlers chapter) referencing Emma's older siblings Phoebe (five, this chapter) and older brother Jacob (ten).

Children aged four and five are often mature enough and have the understanding required, to provide informed consent with regard to

Table 9.1 Preschooler participants

Family	Name	Birth Order	Group	Age	M/F	AU/UK
Kramer	Libby	1	Preschool	4 yrs 1 mth	F	UK
Spinner	Imelda	3	Preschool	4 yrs	F	UK
Lim-Park	Michael	1	Preschool	4 yrs	M	AU
Brent	Ellen	3	Preschool	4 yrs 6 mths	F	UK
Palmer	Leela	2	Preschool	4 yrs 6 mths	F	UK
Andrews-White	Liam	2	Preschool	4 yr 11 mths	M	AU
Lawe-Tammell	Ben	3	Preschool	5 yrs	M	AU
Bernard	Connor	4	Preschool	5 yrs	M	AU
Davis	Phoebe	2	Preschool	5 yrs	F	AU
Petersen	Freya	2	Preschool	5 yrs	F	AU
Jameson	Floyd	1	Reception	5 yrs 4 mths	M	UK

contributing to research. Some of the interviewers' research techniques and collaborative, consultative protocols are consequently surfaced via preschool interview transcripts and a selection is shared here. Throughout this project and across all our work with children, parents provide written consent before a child is invited to take part. As children begin to understand the concept of helping with research, they are invited to give their agreement to doing so. Given that few preschoolers read or write, this invitation and the child's acceptance are performed verbally, as part of the audio (or sometimes video) recording. In the exchange that follows from the Davis family transcript, Kylie checks that Phoebe is willing to be photographed as well as audio-recorded. As the principal Australian interviewer-researcher, Kylie introduces her colleague Kelly to Phoebe. Kelly's role in the research is to focus on the activities of the child, while Kylie is immersed in interviewing one, both, or all parents and children.

> Kylie (to Phoebe): Now, you know how I said this is my friend Kelly here?
> Phoebe: Yeah
> Kylie: ... She helps me talk to you by, as well as recording things so I remember what you say, Kelly's going to take some photos of what you do, so we can remember what you do. Is that okay with you?
> Phoebe: Yeah

In addition to photos taken by the interview team, families are offered the opportunity to contribute videos of their child's everyday digital activities. This involves leaving a video camera with the family, since the family's own recording device may be the technology used by the child for digital play. Sometimes, families can provide examples of autonomously produced videos of their child engaging in digital contexts; this was the case with the Petersen family. Mum Claire had shown Kylie a snippet of Freya (five) in a pretend-play vlogger role, spruiking her make-believe Etsy store, performing a piece to camera while older sister Elsa (nine) operated the camera. With that extract in mind, Kylie explains the rationale and procedure of leaving a project video camera with the family in the hope that they might video the children, noting:

> Even videos of your videos would be really useful to show some of the activities that [your children do] ... [Rather than] getting Freya to engage with the technology, we're actually capturing it, or you're actually capturing it – thank you – in real time, as it happens, in real circumstances. So, it will be quite useful to see the girls watching vloggers and things like that. But we also know how incredibly busy and complex people's lives are so, if you don't get a chance to ... that's okay, you know, really. We leave it [the camera] with you for a month.

What often happens is I ring up four weeks later and … someone says 'Oh, hang on, I've forgotten about that!' So, then we leave it for another two weeks, so it's – we don't want it to be onerous but capturing that sort of real-life experience that they have with technology, like the girls were doing then is, would be, fantastic for us to see.

(Kylie, to Claire and Jeff, Freya's parents)

In fact, as well as contributing research-specific recordings, Freya and her family were happy to share Freya's vlogging video for research purposes, provided it was not copied or otherwise recorded and provided all identities remained confidential. That video became the basis of a stand-alone case study (Stevenson, Green et al., 2019).

In addition to being recognized for their capacity to consent to research, preschooler participants appreciate being thanked for their contribution. Acknowledging that interviews disrupt household routines and add stress to daily life, parents and children are both offered tangible tokens of gratitude after interviews finish. Under ethics protocols, such honoraria should not be so great an incentive as to induce a reluctant interviewee to take part, but they should be sufficiently significant to offer compensation for the inconvenience experienced. Instead of giving cash to adults or children, however, ethics protocols require that store 'gift vouchers' are used to allow the family some choice in their reward. As well as store tokens to adults and children (to give to their parents), Kylie also offers specific token of thanks to the child. Here, at the end of her interview, Phoebe Davis is keen to return to her routine:

> Phoebe: I might play upstairs with Emma [2, Toddlers chapter]
> Kylie: Yes, so, I'm going to stop talking to you and let you go and play with Emma. Would you like to come back here [first] and I'm going to give you a sticker for helping me?

Phoebe goes to Kylie and seems delighted with her sticker.

Kylie: Alright? So, we'll turn that off now [indicating the audio recorder], so thank you very much Phoebe for answering [my questions].

On another occasion, when Kylie finishes interviewing the two children under six in the Barnard family, she finds herself explaining the honoraria vouchers to the children before starting to interview their mum, Sarah. William (three) and Connor (five) had both been involved in interviews while older brother Xavier (thirteen), well beyond the research age group, also took an active interest, chipping in his own perspectives on occasion:

Kylie, to William and Connor: So, what I need to do now, is, I need to talk to your mum.

Kylie, to William: Now, I have something to give you and your brother to say thank you for listening to me, but mum is the boss of these, okay?

The boys see the vouchers and nod.

Kylie: Alright. So, here's one for William [handing a voucher to him], thank you so much; and one for Connor, but mum's the boss of these. So, thank you very much.

William and Connor give the vouchers to Sarah.

Sarah: Thank you, Kylie!

Kylie, turning to Xavier: And I didn't know you were going to be here, Xavier. So, I'm sorry, I haven't got anything for you.

Whole of family engagement in projects that focus on a specific age-group, as with the *Toddler and Tablets* research, prompted the research team to address ethical issues around inclusion and exclusion, resulting in a chapter that acknowledges the implications and complexity of restricting research to certain categories of children when their siblings are keen to take part (Stevenson, Jaunzems, Holloway, Green & Stevenson, 2019).

Having contextualized some of the interview practices and procedures, this chapter now turns to the vignettes relating to preschool children and their families before moving to an over-arching discussion of the research focus around evidence relating to preschoolers' use of digital media in developing their social and emotional skills.

Libby Kramer, four years, one month, commuter town, north of London

Mum Stella (thirty-one) learns her parenting of preschooler Libby and sibling Owen (Infant, nineteen months) through observation and discussion: 'I have lots of friends who have children so, yeah, [I learn through] mainly chatting'. She responds to her children's interests, noting that Libby currently 'wants to learn to read.' As a result, Stella has downloaded trial materials from *Reading Eggs*: 'It's not necessarily about teaching her to read 'cause obviously she'll learn that when she goes to school anyway … it's just, 'cause she really wanted to do it and she was asking us questions and we weren't sure how to do it properly.'

Unlike some parents, Stella sees Libby as having started her digital play in a hesitant way. Libby was about two when she first used a tablet and would 'play a little bit but … she wasn't used to the scrolling and she'd easily turn it off and start doing something else'. It was a shock to Stella to go to a parents' evening at Libby's nursery and learn that technology was a curriculum-based competency: 'She wasn't scoring highly or she, you know and I was, like: "Oh no! this is dreadful! We've got to do something about this" – so I started letting her use my tech a little bit more.'

At 'about three – oh well, coming up four', Libby discovered a program for taking and decorating selfies: 'she goes: "I've just taken a picture", says Stella, adding: 'and I was like, "I don't want you to take pictures!"' Libby's selfies, however, are part of the *CBeebies* app and designed for children. Users can move from the selfie to making digital stickers, 'So she'll take pictures of herself … and make stickers and stick it everywhere, like, on the app.' Libby also loves using Stella's smartphone to contact her grandma who lives in a different city: 'If my mum doesn't answer FaceTime', says Stella, 'Libby will ask to call her and then say "Nanna, will you FaceTime?"'

When Leslie returned to the Kramer's home to make a follow-up video, prompting the 'reindeer' exchange between Libby and younger brother Owen (nineteen months) discussed in the Infants chapter, Libby showed Leslie a game she likes where a player chooses between two curly straws. One straw puts a coloured liquid in a cup (the 'right' response), the other spills it on the table 'and the monster wipes it away', explains Libby, 'because he gets cross if gets on the floor. It's funny. It makes me laugh!' Leslie notes that Libby sometimes seems to deliberately choose the 'wrong' straw to see the monster's hand appear and wipe the coloured liquid off the table.

Imelda Spinner, four years, gentrified area, south London

Dad Daniel (forty-two) and mum Karla (forty-one) believe that Imelda is a lucky child because, as Karla explains, her two older sisters Belle (seven) and Alice (nine) 'will quite happily sit and do a puzzle with her or play a game'. At the same time, when Leslie returned for a second visit and Imelda wanted her sisters with her, it was Imelda's sisters who did most of the talking. In fact, as well as talking, Belle took the iPad from Imelda to demonstrate something to Leslie. The transcribed video records the interchange between the competing siblings:

Imelda: Belle! [takes the tablet back].
Belle: (To Imelda) I'm just doing one more thing …

Belle takes the tablet off Imelda to do something on screen and Imelda immediately pulls it back.

Imelda: Belle!

Imelda can activate a dormant screen and navigate through apps and icons, but she has gaps in her knowledge such as how to turn the iPad on if the power is off. Karla says, 'I'd only have to show her and then she'd know', but Imelda's many family helpers might mean she doesn't need to learn some skills. Later, when showing Leslie how she plays Subway Surfer, Imelda says: 'Belle helps me to change the character because I don't know how to.' Interestingly, Imelda had stated that she likes the game 'because you can change the character' despite not being able to do this independently.

Karla thinks Imelda had been using the iPad since she was about fifteen months of age, motivated by seeing her sisters use it. But Karla also says the children forget about digital media if devices are put away for a day or two: 'They can literally go a couple of weeks without touching the devices pretty much and then go two weeks where they don't lift their heads out of them.' This episodic engagement is reassuring to Daniel who, working in advertising, believes that dopamine systems are activated in digital media use and can lead to 'smartphone addiction [which] is something that I, you know, I'm sort of very aware of'. He adds that, while the girls' friends may have their own digital devices, in the Spinner family, 'we're a long way off'.

The parents use the iPad 'for emergencies' such as when Imelda goes with her parents to watch her sisters' back-to-back hour-long ballet classes, or when the family goes out for a meal and Imelda wants to leave just as the starter arrives. Karla emphasizes that it's not the case that Imelda would 'sit down in the restaurant and that [digital media] would be the first thing, it's like, your emergency [back up]'.

Michael Lim-Park, four years, multi-generation household, northern Perth suburb

Living in a multi-generational home with Korean-speaking mum Mi Na (forty), grandmother Yu Na (sixty-five) and Mandarin-speaking dad Andrew (forty-two), preschooler Michael (four) and Emily (Infant, twenty-three months) enjoy a rich multicultural and multi-lingual environment with all three adults involved in regular caregiving. Michael did not use words until he was twenty-seven months, which was when Emily was born and Mi Na took him to a speech therapist. Mi Na says, 'It was a big shock to me when I [… was told] not to speak any other language but English because we live in Australia.' Michael now attends a multicultural Montessori kindergarten class four full days per week and his parents (generally) follow the school's 'no digital media below ten years old' recommendation. Mi Na is both proud and regretful to note that nowadays 'he's speaking more and more English'. (See Stevenson, Green et al., 2021 for an alternative narrative around English as Another Language skill acquisition with respect to the Zhang/Chen family in the Toddlers chapter.)

Both parents have IT-related jobs, with Mi Na teaching digital game design. She notes that Michael, like her, is very visually oriented: 'We like playing pictures [matching cards], we like playing shapes, we like playing very much, you know, visual things.' Like many parents and even in face of the school's recommendations, Mi Na uses her phone on occasion to occupy Michael 'when I really have to attend to my daughter or I'm doing something for a period of time'. Michael knows her iPhone PIN number but he also knows that he must ask to use Mi Na's phone and can only watch Kids YouTube. Michael also accesses dad Andrew's phone and they play an educational puzzle app together designed to help children learn the Chinese language: 'The word will come out once the puzzle is completed', says Mi Na. At four, Michael uses voice recognition to create internet search terms, rather than typing words. Mi Na remembers the activity starting very soon after Michael began to speak: 'I didn't even know there was such a function!'

Mi Na's main concern about digital media prior to Michael enrolling in the Montessori school was around the impact of superhero role models. She says Michael's 'first teacher at school told me that Michael screamed really loud and tried the punching action against his friends. That was when he was exposed to iPad quite heavily and he had a choice to watch, like, Spiderman and those characters'. Michael's teacher suggested the family stopped allowing Michael's access to Superman content: 'I even changed his lunchbox', says Mi Na 'and, after a while, one or two weeks, [we] noticed a difference, yeah'.

Ellen Brent, four years, six months, south London

Living in a small, semi-detached house with parents Elisabeth (forty-three) and Ted (forty-four) and brothers James (nine) and Andrew (eleven), Ellen has impairment issues related to speech. When Ellen was diagnosed at sixteen months with a genetic syndrome that complicated her development milestones, including her language ability, mum Elisabeth found a children's programme, *Mr Tumble*, which teaches Makaton signing. The entire family learned to sign from watching *Mr Tumble*, not just Ellen. Now at an inclusive preschool that welcomes special needs children, Ellen interacts with the staff who all use Makaton. Elisabeth likes the high student-teacher ratio and that Ellen is socializing and 'not permanently being told "No, I just need to do this with your brother".'

Before Ellen turned three, she was given near-exclusive access to her mother's iPad. Elisabeth downloaded an augmented and assisted communication app for Ellen's use because she 'wanted her to have as many ways of being able to communicate as possible'. Ellen is highly motivated to learn to speak and found her own strategy for doing so, using a non-English-speaking-background children's language teaching programme called *Steve*, much to Elisabeth's surprise: 'I have no idea where [she found it]'. *Steve* allows viewers extensive repetition of everyday words in a comedy setting.

Ellen has a compartmentalized approach to her life. She wanted to name colours verbally, as well as sign them and found an online teaching tool to practise with: 'now she can say all the colours', says Elisabeth smiling and 'it's all "up, down, under, in".' Ellen likes a TV programme, *Our Family*, but, although there's only one television, she doesn't want to watch *Our Family* on the iPad. 'I do sometimes say "Why",' says Elisabeth, 'and she just says "No, TV – Family – TV. iPad, *Steve*".' Ellen doesn't like people to help her unless she asks first, but she does have a local authority-provided tablet with an offline-assisted communication program which sounds out letters to help her speak words. Elisabeth explains the benefit for Ellen: 'She's now at the stage where she pointed to my t-shirt this morning and went: "Sh, i, n, y!"'

Ellen enjoys cooking, especially with eggs: 'We make an omelette and she's in charge of the eggs.' In a follow-up video interview, Ellen shows interviewer Leslie a *CBeebies* app which involves a cake-making game where the child clicks ingredients, including eggs, and decorates the result. Leslie's transcript takes up the story:

[Ellen turns to him and] makes a kissing sound while expanding her fingers and thumbs and moving them away from her mouth (the gesture that means 'that is magnificent')
Leslie: (Laughs) Tasty, eh!

Leela Palmer, four years, six months, flat in a block on the outskirts of inner London

Leela (four and a half) lives with her single mum Linda (thirty-three) and big sister Marissa (fifteen) in an ethnically mixed high density London housing estate. Leela first started in day care at two years old. Linda was delighted because 'they've got a big outdoor area, they've got a big sandpit, they've got a climbing frame or the slides. They've got bikes, a trampoline …'. When Leela is at home, Linda prioritizes messy play and does painting, gluing and scrapbooking with her.

Leela has accessed her mum's iPad since she was 'around two and a half', initially to sing along with nursery rhymes. She likes YouTube videos now. Linda has a relaxed parenting style around digital media. When Leslie tells Linda there's a Kids YouTube she says, 'Oh, is there? … I didn't know you could do that. Oh, I'll have to look into that.'

Quite recently, Linda heard Leela talking to herself and she explained to Leslie how she asked Leela what she was doing: 'She's like: "I'm talking to my friend Siri"':

Linda (to Leela): But you know it's not a person now, don't you? It's the iPad
Leela: No, it's a person [… they listen to Siri]
Linda (to Leela): Is that your friend that talks to you?
Leela: Yeah
Linda: Yeah
Leela: He has an iPad
Linda: Does he?

Leela implies that she thinks Siri uses his iPad to communicate with her. Linda subsequently concludes 'she thinks it's a person then' and seems unfazed.

Linda describes how, at one point in the past, Leela was watching a video involving a character who was stealing. Linda heard it in the background: 'So then I went "No, you can't watch this" … and now she asks me if she can watch a video or if she can't.' Linda explains how, when Leela wants to watch something new, 'like P J Masks', Leela will type it into the search bar:

Linda: And it comes up and then I see what it is.
Leslie: So, what is it? I've never seen it.
Linda: I haven't actually watched it.

Some of Leela's digital activities are inspired by her teenage sister. 'The first time she started *Snapchat*' says Linda, was with Marissa 'and they just started taking selfies together and then eventually I downloaded it just to do the pictures.' In a follow-up interview, Leela shows Leslie 'all different ones' that illustrate the digital effects that augment selfies. She snaps a sample image of herself with purple lipstick and purple eye make-up. Leela (excitedly): 'It's got a ring on my nose.' The transcript notes 'Leela touches her own nose where the ring on the screen would be', as if she's checking there's no ring there. (There isn't.)

Liam Andrews-White, four years, eleven months, southwest of Perth

Liam, 'nearly five' lives at home with mum Kate (forty), older brother Ben (eight) and Scott (two and a half: Toddlers chapter). Dad Richard (forty-eight) is fly-in, fly-out and Kate sometimes finds herself parenting solo. It's a tech-rich household, even though the children prefer hard copy books. Kate says that apart from occasionally asking for help with navigating her phone, Liam has the skills to do 'whatever he wants to do' in digital contexts. Liam's preschool teacher has recently asked parents to provide individual headsets for each child for use with the class iPads and Richard and Kate are planning to give Liam his own tablet as a fifth birthday present.

Kate compares Liam's early digital experiences to Ben's, noting that Ben was born before touchscreens, 'whereas Liam has grown up flicking through [virtual] flash cards, seeing animals and all that'. Liam is described as having serial 'obsessions' and is currently crazy about Skylanders: 'it's all he's interested in. So, I find it a bit frightening', says Kate, 'and I really should put some rules [in place]'. But Kate recognizes that Skylanders is a point of contact for Liam with his peers and his imaginative connection to them fuels their offline play. 'Liam and his little group of mates will take [toy] Skylanders with them to each other's houses' says Kate, 'and then they'll go outside and they'll either play with the figures or they'll play as the characters.' She notes a difference in play styles between Liam and older brother Ben, where Liam plays shooter games with friends and Ben 'didn't play those games because he didn't have the exposure'. On the other hand, while Liam isn't frightened by his interactive digital activities,

Kate notes that he 'gets frightened of ABC3' (now ABC Me, Australian older children's TV programming).

Kate's concern is that kids like Liam 'have by-passed computer and laptops and gone straight to touchscreens', possibly missing out on coding skills and 'learning how to create their own things ... they don't have that full internet experience that you get on a computer'. She highlights one strict, digitally focused rule in their house: 'After about 6.00 p.m. we say, "no more!"' Kate says the rule is generally well-accepted, except for maybe a couple of nights a week: Liam and Ben can 'get very upset if we've had a busy afternoon and they haven't had a chance to have their screen time!'

Ben Lawe-Tammell, five years, riverside suburb, southern Perth

Ben is the youngest child and only boy in a family with mum Rosalie (fifty), dad Richard (forty-seven) and sisters Amelia (twelve) and Samantha (sixteen), who live together in an affluent suburb within the Perth metropolitan area. As one of the older children in the study, using technology 'all his life [... from] maybe six months [old]' according to mum Rosalie, Ben's digital play might be constructed as having become more 'gendered' as he's got older. Telling Kylie how he plays in game-worlds where 'you have to kill baddies', Ben shows her his *Minecraft* avatar in flight:

> Kylie: Is that you with a sword in your hand?
> Ben: Yeah.
> Kylie: What did you just do to that chicken?
> Ben: I whack it, like, I go to that chicken – Whack!

Among the benefits Rosalie sees in Ben's technology use is that Ben is usually 'Mr Active and he can get a bit fired up and it does help him relax and have some quiet time'.

Taking Kylie on a tour of the family's technology, Ben fetches Rosalie's iPhone ('Mum's password is 2002') and says if the phone's not available, he plays on the iPad and if that's not available, he plays on the computer. Just as Ben's concept of password privacy is developing, so is his understanding of 'real, real, real money'. This heightened awareness arose when Ben briefly had fingerprint access to his dad Richard's phone, allowing him to also access Richard's online credit. Fortunately, Rosalie saw the first in-game purchase register and Ben's fingerprint access was swiftly removed.

Richard often works away from home and Rosalie, an online business owner, says: 'I'm the mum who goes, "Not me, don't ask me" … there's too many responsibilities as a mum to be responsible for electronics as well.' She thinks Ben's learned his digital skills from his sisters, but Ben interjects: 'No, no, no, myself!' There are two device rules operating in the Lawe-Tammell home: 'no tech before school' because, says Rosalie, 'I cannot get him to eat his breakfast and put his clothes on and brush his teeth [if he's in a videogame]', and 'download free content only, using the Wi-Fi'. In extremis, says Rosalie, 'I'll just snatch it [tech] away. I don't tend to negotiate. Well, I do a little bit!'

Rosalie doesn't check the age-appropriateness of what Ben does online but is confident that his sisters do. Essentially and in alignment with the philosophy of the school Ben attends, which is an independent alternative-education model community school, both Rosalie and Richard trust their children to be moving successfully in a direction of self-regulation: 'What goes on in the inside is kind of up to the kid.'

Connor Bernard, five years, Perth northern suburbs

Mum Sarah helps dad Scott (both early forties) run their family business from home while parenting their five children. Connor goes to preschool three days a week and he and William (three, Toddlers) attend childcare for half a day on the other two days. In his interview, a rueful Connor (five) told Kylie: 'My daddy took the Xbox away.' Connor's parents' business includes the supply and installation of solar panels and dad Scott is very aware of how much power is consumed by different technologies. As Sarah says, 'Connor can't play Skylanders now'.

Sarah sees young children's digital skills as 'amazing': 'you think: "Oh my God!"' Even so, she remembers a time when Connor was so frustrated with Skylanders that 'He's like "MUM!!!" and you can hear – and he's actually thrown the controller before in rage – so I'll go in there and I'll go, "What's wrong?" … I'll work it out and I'll show him and he'll go, "Oh!" And I'll go: *"Thanks, Mum!"* "Thanks Mum" and he'll move onto the next [stage].'

Connor uses his mum's phone to show Kylie his favourite shark game:

Kylie (about the shark): Is he looking for gold?
Connor: [He's] eating them [people].
Kylie: Oh! He's eating them! It's very West Australian!
Sarah: Disgusting!
Connor: Blood!!!

Sarah: I don't know who downloaded that one. I've got two games on my phone and they're both – one dude crashes on a bike and snaps his neck and then that one eats people!

With five children, this family has a 'free apps only' default setting. Connor is also passionate about YouTube videos of monster trucks. Sarah says: 'If he sees my phone or Scott's phone on the bench, if he's got a couple of minutes he'll sit there and log into YouTube.' While Connor's parents pass their old Samsung devices down to younger family members and the three older children each have second-hand phones, Xavier (thirteen) has the only phone with a service plan and data. Sarah is generally happy with how her children all accommodate each other in their digital activities. She only intervenes 'when we hear someone say, "Give me back my horse!" Or "You took my house!"' Her starting point is a warning: '"If you can't play nicely", you know, but then if they continue, as in: "Oh my god! Why did you kill me?"', Sarah's response is definitive: '[I'm] like; "That's it! TURN IT OFF!"'

Phoebe Davis, five years, semi-rural Perth outskirts

Phoebe is older sister to Emma Davis (two, Toddlers) and is in preschool full time. Monday through Wednesday, when both her parents work, she and older brother Jacob (ten) also attend before and after school care, typically arriving by 7.10 am in the morning and being picked up between 5.30 and 6.00 pm that evening. This reflects the family's location in the Perth hills district, a comparatively long commute from Perth city where Phoebe's parents work. When mum Isabelle (forty-one) is at home on Thursday and Friday, the children are with her before and after school hours.

Isabelle navigates a complex dynamic around Phoebe's 'device envy'. Brother Jacob was given an iPad for his fifth or sixth birthday by his paternal grandparents, Isabelle can't recall the exact birthday, but 'I was staggered' says Isabelle, 'amazed that I didn't know, or permission wasn't sought, to say "Should we buy him his own device?"' She adds, as if seeking affirmation, 'I would have thought that would be something you ask a parent?' Even though Phoebe can get ready access to her mum's device, as she shows Kylie a game that she and Jacob both play, she says:

Phoebe: Jacob has a – iPad but when I will get a – iPad we could both do it together.

Kylie: On your own iPad?

Phoebe: (agreeing) ... and see who wins ... I play on Mummy's iPad and Jacob plays on his own iPad. He has a white stripe and then a blue stripe for the cover ... and it's his own one.

Although outside the research age group, older brother Jacob (ten) sat with Phoebe and sometimes interjected, dominating the conversation. In addition to referencing how Jacob has an iPad and she doesn't, Phoebe explains to Kylie about the limitations of one of her favourite iPad animal games. In this game app, pressing a picture of an animal displays its name and the sound it makes. Sometimes, continued pressing offers a different species of the same kind of animal, as Phoebe explains: 'But if you press "frog" it changes to a different frog.' She goes on to say ' ... but you can't get all of them 'cause they haven't been buyed yet ... we only buyed these ones [indicating a set of animal images]'. Mum Isabelle notes that Phoebe, at five, has reached a key stage in her maturity where she is ready for rules around digital media. More than 'a convenience babysitter', Isabelle believes that for children over the age of five, the threat to remove device access is 'a really good punishment!'

Freya Petersen, five years, southern Perth suburbs

Preschool student Freya (five) lives with older sister Elsa (nine), mum Claire (forty-three), dad Jeff (forty-one) and grandma Barbara. Barbara lives in a granny flat in the garden. The two primary rules operating in the Petersen household are: 'don't post anything online without permission' and 'mum must approve downloads'. Claire has several online businesses and uses her technology savviness to 'deliberately try and keep the tech a bit boring', limiting its appeal. Even so, Freya's favourite activity in the previous twelve months was watching YouTube vloggers, especially Stampylonghead. Claire says that after Freya's alternating kindergarten days, the five-year-old is 'so exhausted! The next day she'd be not up for very much at all'. In this context, Claire sees Freya's digital media use as restorative relaxation.

Reflecting her vlogger fandom, Freya plays on her parents' outdated unconnected iPhone 4 pretending to be a vlogger, with Elsa (nine) as camera operator and producer recording the video on the phone's unconnected memory. The children don't have social media accounts, but their mum sometimes posts their work to a restricted circle of family and friends. Claire notes that she posts less as the girls get older 'because, I guess, their privacy'. Claire has 'safe searches switched on' and thinks her family is a little more vigilant than most around digital media. She limits the girls' screen activities to about two hours a day, split before and after school, and uses a kitchen timer with a 'five- or ten-minute warning. [Even so ...] Freya used to throw massive tantrums' when her time was up. Claire adds: 'and I know they're tech tantrums.'

Although Claire says her family doesn't use 'learning apps', she notes that they do have one about learning French language. 'Yeah', says Freya, practising her French, '[le] sconse ... A skunk'. Claire likes that Freya enjoys science-show vlogging by Stampy and art and craft 'makes' suggested by another vlogger. Claire searches for the name ... 'CookieSwirlC', volunteers Freya. Claire encourages her children to be creative and 'do a drawing or paint a picture or make something', but, referring back to CookieSwirlC, Jeff says: 'The idea of watching a twenty-something playing with dolls, as opposed to playing with your own dolls, I don't get that', adding, 'it's about consumerism, you know?'

As with many parents of younger aged children, Claire says: 'There's a guilt attached to [it] – for me, I feel guilty about the amount of time my kids play on devices. And I ... feel they're missing out on their childhood [when] staring at a screen.' She sees an opportunity for parents to do more digital co-playing with children and notes it's something that grandma Barbara does with the girls. Claire, as a self-starter businesswoman, says: 'I think I've let them watch too much during the week because it's been – it's helpful to me at times.' (Stevenson, Green et al., 2019, addresses the Petersen family case study, along with one of Freya's vlogging videos, referring to Elsa as Emma.)

Floyd Jameson, five years, four months. inner city London

The Jameson family has concerns around children's technology use. When mum, Francoise (forty-one), told Leslie that Floyd and Evan (three, Toddler) use an iPad at home, dad Craig (thirty-eight) implied this wasn't the case, except when travelling 'in the car or on the train so they don't get cranky'. Leslie prompted: 'So you've got movies preloaded on there then?' Francoise replies: 'Yes'; however, Craig replies: 'But they don't use an iPad 'cause they're not allowed to.' This suggests a complicated family-specific sense of what it is for a child to 'use' an iPad.

Throughout their early years, Francoise has consciously introduced her sons to diverse experiences. These include classes that expose the boys to 'different textures and sounds to wake up their senses' and newborn swimming where 'you actually get them under water, just put them under water, it's quite amazing'. Francoise worries that while Floyd (five) 'loves the water, I probably have not been as good with that with Evan', who is three.

Francoise talks about how her boys play with 'so much imagination. They are so resourceful, effectively they just get on with … playing dinosaur versus tiger, whatever'. She contrasts this with the perceived impact of television viewing: 'It's like being a zombie. You try to talk to Floyd, you can't get his attention, he's mesmerized.' She notes TV has value, however, since 'they learn a lot' but sees importance in selecting 'intelligent programmes'. She also believes that shared viewing experiences offer children a point of contact with each other, talking about shows they enjoy, noting: 'You don't want them to get left out!'

Craig sees his children as 'too young to have a rational discussion … Floyd is really building it up but he can't articulate it'. Craig believes interactive media will be useful when the boys are 'maybe ten and above … and want to know about something. Fine, Google [it]', adding 'the only thing they'd probably be capable of doing [now] would be playing games'. But Francoise protests: 'I don't want them to watch video games.' Although the parents take pride in the fact that 'our children love books', Craig notes that he often reads books on Kindle ''cause I don't want to take two massive books [on holiday …]'. He muses: 'Do they perceive that as always being on technology?'

Craig sees one clear advantage in media on demand, however, having used it to explain to his children how volcanoes erupt. 'In a normal kids' book, it's just a grey mountain with a little bit of orange running down the side'. (Discussion of the Jameson family is included in Green et al. (2019), with Evan referred to as Owen.)

Floyd Jameson and his family complete the discussion of individual case studies distilled from the ethnographic and interview data. This chapter moves now to discuss the possibility that digital engagement may support development of preschoolers' social and emotional skills, integrating relevant observations with literature. It finishes with consideration of policy settings around digital media for preschool-aged children and their caregivers.

What evidence is there that preschoolers develop social and emotional skills in digital engagement?

Parents of preschoolers have a range of reasons for using digital media to distract their children and such reasons often have an emotional component.

For example, Karla Spinner talks about how she uses an iPad to help daughter Imelda manage the (boring) hours in which she sits through her two older sisters' ballet lessons and when she waits for food to arrive in a restaurant. Karla emphasizes that digital media access is never her first port of call for Imelda but instead provides an emergency backup, implying that the strategy makes her feel uncomfortable. Claire Petersen also expresses unease, describing herself as feeling 'guilty' about her daughters' device use. She's grateful to grandmother Barbara, however, who co-plays digital games with Freya and Elsa. Claire thinks that's a way in which parents could meet children half-way, sharing their digital engagement. Indeed, Toh and Lim (2021) endorse this perspective noting that 'active adult involvement in children's play can increase the social level of play and impart a beneficial impact on children's cognitive growth' (2021, p. 8).

Mi Na Lim-Park uses digital media to occupy Michael (four) when Mi Na needs to attend to daughter Emily, twenty-three months. Emily draws on walls and climbs on and over furniture, requiring Mi Na to take urgent action. Linda Palmer, a single parent with young daughter Leela (four and a half), became aware during their interview that Leela (still) constructs Siri as an actual person. Having explored that perspective, Linda was unfazed and somewhat amused by the situation, explaining to Leslie: 'I'm like "Who are you talking to?" She's like "My friend Siri".' From Linda's point of view, it's fine if the iPad operates both as a distraction for Leela and as a technological imaginary friend she can talk to and confide in. Given the established tradition of 'imaginary friends' in some children's play, it is possible that the Siri example in this case provides an equivalent sense of socio-emotional connection offered in other contexts by an imaginary friend.

Mi Na Lim-Park gladly shares how trilingual Michael 'knows how to search on YouTube Kids using voice recognition … I didn't even know there was such a function!' That statement and other positive comments made by parents illustrate the ego-boosting value for children of their digital skills and active agency in online contexts. As Mikelić Preradović et al. (2016) argue: 'Regarding the benefits of DT [digital technology] for young children … Firstly, digital technology can help children to visualize difficult concepts. Secondly, new interactive technologies facilitate the creation of an environment in which children can learn through action, providing them with the opportunity to create and explore.' (2016, p. 130).

Rosalie Lawe, mum to Ben Lawe-Tammell (five), believes his older sisters Amelia (twelve) and Samantha (sixteen) take responsibility for checking the age-appropriateness of what he does online, presumably in a socio-emotional exchange with their younger brother. Rosalie mentions that she and husband Richard are both 'very, very, very relaxed but confident parents'. At the same time, Rosalie doesn't 'negotiate' around tech: sometimes she will 'just snatch it away'. In contrast to this approach, other families appear to value discussion around technology and media as a site for negotiating with their young children. Such skills can implicate a developing understanding of 'needs and necessities', an area in which children and parents may have different perspectives (Cortés-Morales & Main, 2022). Sometimes, the social skill of negotiating may be more implicit than explicit: Leslie noted how infant Owen Kramer, nineteen months, distracts preschool sister Libby (four) from demonstrating her digital media skills and is rewarded with access to her reindeer toy, which she had previously denied him. Other parents aim to manage their children's use of connected media by applying time limits, sometimes as well as negotiating, as in the Andrews-White family. The Petersens activate a kitchen timer and give their children five- or ten-minutes' warning of disconnection. Even so, Claire Petersen notes that, until recently, daughter Freya would throw 'tech tantrums' (Hiniker, Suh, Cao & Kientz, 2016).

Isabelle Davis takes for granted that she can use an iPad to distract daughter Phoebe (five), but also sees it as a means of managing her child's behaviour. Isabelle uses access to digital media as a reward and denial of access as a punishment. Eichen et al. (2021), in a study of 150 Austrian parents with children aged between eighteen months and six years old, note that 'more than half of the parents agree that they use digital media as a reward or for motivational purpose (52.7 per cent)' (p. 2173). Such strategies are unlikely to be without emotional consequences: even though Isabelle is keen to explain that the strategy only works for her and her family once a child is old enough, at about five, implying that the use of rewards to motivate desired behaviours is an index of socio-emotional maturity.

Parents' constructions of children's capacity to reason and their right to have their opinions respected impact children's development opportunities. This may explain one aspect of the AAP (n.d..) recommendation that parents and children collaborate on a Family Media Plan. None of the participant families said they had such a plan, but most implied that their preschool child's views were acknowledged in their management of children's media access. The exception was in a family where children's digital media use is significantly discouraged. Craig Jameson's view is that Floyd (five) is 'too young to have a rational discussion. I think maybe once they're maybe ten and above [they can]'.

Craig's approach to recognizing the validity of children's wishes can be contrasted with Stella Kramer's. Stella sees school as the appropriate place to learn literacy skills but downloaded the *Reading Eggs* app for her preschool daughter, Libby (four), because Libby 'keeps saying how much she wants to learn to read'. In the Andrews-White household, mum Kate acknowledges that Liam (almost five) and older brother Ben (eight) get upset if a busy afternoon means they 'haven't had a chance to have their screen time'. The implication here is that Liam and Ben feel they have a right to a daily opportunity for digital play. At five, Phoebe Davis conceives the world as being a fair place. This inspires Phoebe's conviction that she will get an iPad eventually, since her brother Jacob has had one for some years.

Although children in this age group experience a wide range of rules around digital media, enforced with varying degrees of family-differentiated consistency, such rules would generally involve discussion and explanation, mobilizing social and emotional engagement.

Several parents of preschoolers believe that digital media access plays an important role in creating common socio-emotional ground for children's play. This benefit of digital technologies, 'sharing an activity with siblings, friends and sometimes with other family members', has been identified by Chaudron (2015, p. 61) as a major motivation for children's digital engagement. In that research, Chaudron studied children aged up to eight across seven European countries. In Australia, Kate Andrews-White talks about how son Liam uses his passion for Skylanders to connect with his friends in physical as well as online spaces. Connor Bernard also has a passion for Skylanders but his hopes for social connection via that passion have been stymied. As he told Kylie, his dad took the Xbox away and thus he can't play Skylanders anymore. Connor serves as a counter-example to mum Karla Spinner's perception that if devices are put 'up on a shelf after a day or two, they [the children] forget pretty much about them'. Even Floyd Jameson's family, given that their children aren't allowed to play on iPads, recognize digital media's role in helping children create shared cultural capital (Bourdieu, 1979). As mum Francoise notes, echoing Rita Chen's perspective in the Infants chapter, she wouldn't want her sons to feel excluded just because they're not allowed to use digital media.

Comparatively few parents identify digital media engagement as a legitimate way for children to have fun and/or relax while undertaking the socio-emotional labour of identity exploration and self-care (Jelic, 2014). Yet this is a common motivation for many of the children we spoke to wanting to use connected media. Libby Kramer talks excitedly to Leslie about how she creates stickers on her *CBeebies* selfies. Leela Palmer, who uses Snapchat for her selfies, shows Leslie how she decorates her image with a ring through her nose. Both examples offer evidence of arm's length identity play. Rosalie Lawe describes her son Ben as 'Mr Active', saying that digital media helps him 'relax and have some quiet time', exploring his less active persona. Similarly, Claire Petersen talks about Freya's early stages of preschool, alternating her childcare centre and home three days a week. The routine left Freya exhausted, notes Claire adding: 'Sometimes all she wanted to do was watch Stampy.'

Ellen Brent, who has special needs, offers a further example of parent-supported digital media use for identity development. She is allowed almost total access to mum Elisabeth's iPad as a means of helping her communicate, to the chagrin of brothers James (nine) and Andrew (eleven). Further, mum Elisabeth eagerly notes how Ellen's active and successful searching for programmes, such as *Steve*, have supported her development of communication skills. In contrast with Ellen's proactive search strategies, Stella Kramer was horrified when daughter Libby's first preschool report indicated that her 'online skills were below her peers'. Stella says she hadn't realized that digital media are part of the preschool curriculum and notes that, upon Libby first accessing connected media, 'she wasn't used to scrolling and she'd easily turn it off and start doing something else'. This anecdote provides a counter-example to views around children's 'natural' facility with devices and the AAP (2016) perception that 'interfaces are so intuitive that children will figure them out quickly'. Taken together, these examples offer a range of family-specific socio-emotional motivations for supporting children's digital media use.

Parents also have a range of concerns, however. Some parents, for example the Petersens and Mi Na Lim-Park, are worried about content. Claire Petersen uses safe search protection on connected media to restrict her daughters' access to inappropriate sites, while Mi Na notes that son Michael had behaviour issues when watching too much Spiderman, so his digital media access was reduced along with his exposure to superhero influences. The Jameson and the Spinner families both worry about the 'addictive' quality of digital media. Francoise Jameson says that even in the comparatively non-interactive setting of television viewing her preschool son Floyd can appear 'totally mesmerized'. Analogously, Daniel Spinner believes children risk digital media addiction through activating the brain's dopamine pathways. These parental concerns may indicate an intuitive grasp of hypotheses that link 'the avoidance of interpersonal relationships [via the …] search for compensation via online engagement' (D'Arienzo, Boursier & Griffiths, 2019, p. 1113).

While Kate Andrews-White is also concerned about whether her son Liam is obsessed with digital media, she has a supplementary worry that children growing up in a touchscreen environment are less well-placed to master skills such as coding. Thus, Kate's fears relate to the future as well as to the present.

Several families express implicit, or explicit, concern over ways in which digital media supports consumerism, possibly echoing Ron Ross's views about the negative impact on daughter Penny (three, Toddlers) of watching twerking videos. Jeff Petersen comments on a twenty-year-old internet influencer who videos herself playing with dolls. He argues that stars like Cookie Swirl C 'go to the shop and buy the toys that my children can't buy, get them home, unwrap them, play with them. So, it's all about consumerism'. Ben Lawe-Tammell, on the other hand, had a crash course in what he calls 'real, real, real money' after he made an in-app purchase as a result of having fingerprint access to his dad's digital phone. Phoebe Davis, at five, displays a basic understanding of commercial culture when she notes, regretfully, that a favoured app is restricted to a limited set of animals because these are the only ones her parents 'buyed'. Arguably, these parents' worries around commercialization also develop the child's awareness of social realities, as related discussions with young children about matters such as these help them 'question the cultural story being told and decide how to act on their new awareness' (Harste, 2003).

Another matter characterized by diversity in parents' views is the appropriate age at which a child might have a device 'of their own'. Although the Royal Children's Hospital in Melbourne discovered that 36 per cent of preschoolers, at about the same time as the *Toddlers and Tablets* research, had their own device (Rhodes, 2017), mum Isabelle Davis was horrified when Jacob (at about five or six, she couldn't recall exactly) was given an iPad by his grandparents. She was 'amazed that I didn't know, or permission wasn't sought'. The Spinner family would have agreed. Referring to her older daughters Belle (seven) and Alice (nine), mum Karla talks about how a 'lot of their friends' have their own devices, but that her family applies a different set of rules whereby 'we're a long way off'. This clearly contrasts with the Andrews-White family where Kate says that 'Liam is going to get one [a tablet] for his [fifth] birthday in a couple of weeks'. Claire and Jeff Petersen have found a middle path for daughters Freya (five) and Elsa (nine), who have access to a hand-me-down iPhone that's not connected to the internet. Claire's ambition is to 'keep the tech a bit boring' to reduce its attractiveness, while still allowing creative play, for example, her children's exploration and development of 'vlogging' personas.

Children's digital media access also allows preschoolers to learn about non-digital activities and phenomena. Thus, Ellen Brent and her family learned Makaton signing from watching *Mr Tumble*. Mum Elisabeth actively supports Ellen's digital media use, given her special needs around communication and in alignment with Keech et al.'s (2018) argument that preschoolers' parents see their role as providing 'supportive behaviours that inductively aligned with the conceptualizations of social support' (2018, p. 252). Even parents like the Jamesons, who say their children are 'not allowed to' use an iPad, acknowledge the existence of some 'intelligent [video] programs' and recognize the value of children seeing educational and scientific images online, for example, of 'lava or "what is a volcano" rather than just, you know, the rudimentary pictures in a baby's book' (Craig Jameson).

Given this diversity of parental approaches to digital media, it is important that policy settings respect differing family dynamics. Further, robust policy should respond to the many ways in which families engage with digital media to help their children prepare socially and emotionally for their years in 'big school'. It is to such policy considerations that this chapter now turns.

Preschoolers' media use: Policy considerations

This chapter illustrates that, as children approach school-going age, they are already immersed in the world of digital devices and content. Over the course of this developmentally crucial preschool period, children, typically aged four to five, acquire more refined motor skills, greater powers of communication and growing independence. Digital technology use will feature to some degree in all children's experiences at this time in their lives and the nature of that experience becomes an ever more prominent concern for parents. While the digital worlds of infants and toddlers often lie in the shadow of their parents' uses of digital technology, children in this age group exhibit growing autonomy and develop digital skills and preferences to the extent that they will have (or rather their parents will have created for them) their own profile on their favourite apps and services, thus underlining their growing identity as digital actors.

At this all-important stage as children prepare for compulsory schooling, parents' needs are also more defined in terms of beneficial activities and developmental experiences for their children. Parents become ever more conscious of the quality of the content with which their child may interact, the amount of time they spend with digital devices and the role this plays in their developing capacities. Regardless of whether the preschooler is a first child or has older siblings who have to some extent paved the way, as the accounts reveal, this is always a new experience given the fast pace of change in the digital landscape. As powerful multimodal devices, digital tools and technologies continue to evolve and offer ever more opportunities for children to play and explore – often to the surprise and wonderment of their parents.

As at previous stages of childhood, the need for professional guidance and trust in safety standards are a paramount policy issues for parents. Parents will have legitimate concerns about the potential impact of digital technologies on family life and their ability to manage their children's consumption and exposure. Given the intensification of children's use of certain apps and devices, for example, YouTube Kids and other video-sharing platforms or tablet devices, parents need accessible controls and features that empower them to make appropriate and informed choices about the content and technology their children use. Affordances of digital technology are often notoriously fixed and not necessarily tailored to parents' or children's needs. The requirements therefore for high-quality standards of design and age appropriateness become ever more pronounced as children's digital participation expands and becomes more autonomous. This is as true for the preschool child as it is for teenagers and, accordingly, a key policy priority is that the wider digital eco-system and in particular the content and technology industry take seriously questions of design and safety when children are likely to use their services.

Policy discourses to date have focused on protectionist measures, often retrofitted to existing technologies and services. Yet, as the various studies illustrated here show, that is hardly sufficient given the pervasive presence of the digital in households and family settings. A better-defined and targeted emphasis on the best interests of the child in all aspects of digital design is called for. Whether in terms of privacy and the traces of children's personal data, or the potential impact on their health and well-being, or the needs for appropriate digital literacy and skills, children's interests are now key policy concerns for the digital sector – manufacturers, connectivity providers, software and content providers – requiring increased attention at governmental and societal level. Such developments may be at an early phase but, as increasingly recognized by children's rights organizations, these are crucial if policy is to keep pace with twenty-first-century childhood.

10

The Bases for Diversity in Children's Digital Experiences

The above chapters on infants, toddlers and preschoolers have in part focused on some commonalities in parents and children's experience at these points in their lives, to be developed further in the conclusion. But they also reveal a vast range of factors that may lead children to have different experiences of these technologies beyond standard socio-demographics like gender, socioeconomic status, parental educational attainment, ethnicity and religious affiliation.[1] It is as important to understand the bases of such variation in experience, alongside the more common themes that have emerged across the chapters of this book.

Hence, this chapter more systematically follows up on some of this diversity, looking at factors that contribute to specificities in children's digital worlds. First, it focuses on differences in parents' technological orientation, their general parenting style and their specific aspirations that can have a bearing on children's digital experiences. Second, it explores further the role of siblings since they can play an important role in children's digital lives alongside the parents, grandparents and preschool carers discussed in other chapters. Finally, it moves into new territory in the family structures covered so far to consider how the interaction between divorced parents can influence children's exposure to the digital world.

Toddlers and Tablets findings

Characteristics of the parents: Technological orientations, approaches to parenting and aspirations

How much parents value digital technologies, how much they are enthusiastic about digital media – in other words their own technological orientation – can clearly have a bearing on what their children encounter.

In the chapter on Parenting and digital media, the Tosetti family (UK) were happy for two-year-old Leopoldo to engage with a range of activities on touchscreens whenever he wanted, although Mirabella thought this decision was made easier because their son was equally interested in other non-technological activities. As will be discussed in the next chapter, Parents' evaluation of children's learning through digital media, the Tosettis actively encouraged Leopoldo to engage with a wide range of ICTs. Both parents had trained in computer graphics and thought that what was available in the digital world now offered great opportunities for children and much more than had been possible in their own childhoods. Commenting on a nursery she had visited, Mirabella (UK) explains:

> They were really against technology, they have just one very old-fashioned computer and they allow them ten minutes a day and there were some parents were saying: 'Oh, it's just ten minutes? 'Cause more than that it would be really bad'. And I was thinking why? I don't understand why. Why all this fear of technology? (…) I never worried about, you know, 'Oh he's not going to read, he's not going to study if he has too much access to digital technology' …. I never worried about that.

In the case of the Bernard family (AU), it was husband's Scott's own personal passion for technology that meant that their five children, including three-year-old William, experienced some of his technological enthusiasm, although wife Sarah had some reservations. Sarah: 'Scott is all about technology, so he wants the kids to be exposed to it. I mean, we'll go camping and he'll bring a one-metre screen with a projector to the camping place. I'm like: "Really?"'

And later in the interview:

> Sarah (AU): 'Our fish tank switches off at 8:00 at night and, if it doesn't, he's got Wi-Fi attached to his phone, he can just press a button and the power socket switches it off. The pool pump runs on like Wi-Fi timers and stuff. And when we went camping, he bought a fridge which you could check to see the temperature on your phone … I'm the kind of person that's not old and scared of technology but he embraces it, he loves it, he just craves more and more and more.'

Parents' views on parenting in general and how they described their parenting style could also carry over into how they handled their children's digital activities. Returning to the Tosetti (UK) family, husband Lorenzo had experienced significant parental constraints when he himself was a child: Lorenzo: 'My parents were trying to protect me and they put me, we say in Italy [in] "a padded cell" … and in a way I felt frustrated. I had all the stereotypical symptoms. I was obese and suffered from, you know, anxiety like.' Mirabella expands on this: 'Yeah, (Lorenzo's) mum is very protective ... I know she's doing it with good intentions but, for example, when she was interacting with Leopoldo last time we were together, "Don't do this, don't do ... " "Come with me". "No, don't touch this, don't touch that" ... and Leopoldo was getting really frustrated 'cause he's used to this freedom.'

Partly in response to this authoritarian mode of parenting,[2] the Tosettis gave Leopoldo a good deal of freedom, in general letting him try things first and only intervening, gently, to give help if he was having problems achieving some goal. This was reflected in their lack of rules about touchscreen use. Mirabella: 'He's free to access them any time. I've never been ... I never thought it's good to be restrictive because I don't see the point, really.'

Meanwhile in the Lawe-Tammell family (AU), Rosalie explained how she really appreciated the ethos of the nursery that five-year-old Ben attended where 'they're free to play and have fun and learn the way they want to and wear what they want to'. Hence, Rosalie tried to carry this spirit over into home life, distancing herself from those parents that make rules about screen time: Rosalie: 'I know some people limit the number of hours you're allowed to be, you know, watching television or screen time or whatever. I'm not like that. No. No.'

The Brown family (UK) explained their general more embracing approach to parenting their two-year-old son Simon:

> Klara: We don't want to be over ... like authoritative ... you know we want to let him be a child and make a mess and you know to ...
> Jerry: 'Don't kill the scientist' is the phrase they use.
> Klara: He can get wet, he can get dirty if we wants to ... although he doesn't want to.
> Jerry: If he wants to pick up anything, whether it's like a real drill or anything like, we'll supervise him but we'd rather not say like: 'No!' (...) But the thing is like every time he sees something that interests him ... and we really like try and let him like interact with it as much as possible. And if it needs supervision, you know, we'll supervise but we ... I think we try and go out our way not to say like: '*No*'.

Finally, the aspirations of parents can make a difference to which particular aspects of the digital world their children experience. Here this is illustrated with the specific case of how the cultural and linguistic background of the parents can make such a difference, as some migrant parents encouraged their children to use apps featuring the parents' mother-tongue or used the technology to keep in touch with extended family in other countries. This can be first illustrated with the Mansi family (UK), consisting of Rohan, Nadia and twenty-three-month-old son Sergei. Rohan is a Canadian of Indian descent and speaks English. Nadia is from a Russian-speaking region of Ukrane and speaks to Sergei in Russian. The maternal grandmother, who spent up to six months every year in London with the family to help and be around her grandson, also spoke Russian to her grandchild. In addition, Nadia bought educational apps for the tablet to encourage Sergei to develop his Russian language further. Nadia: 'I found some educational cartoons in Russian because we feel English is not a problem, it's all around him. I speak Russian to him, it's not a problem as well but he may as well just have that reinforced.'

In the case of the Zhang/Chen family (AU), the emphasis was the opposite: to encourage their twenty-eight-month-old daughter Lavinia to learn English. Stanley Zhang and Rita Chen, both born in China, migrated to Australia and spoke Chinese at home. Rita's parents had moved to Australia from China after the birth of Lavinia and were now Australian permanent residents and lived a short drive away from the Zhang/Chen home. Rita's parents were Lavinia's primary caregivers during the working week, again speaking Chinese to their granddaughter. Lavinia talked to her other grandparents in China via videochat. Given all this exposure to Chinese, Rita had bought bi-lingual apps to help Lavinia's English. Rita (AU): 'This actually I brought back from China. I'm really selective on the toys 'cause it's hard to get her to learn English as well as Mandarin.'

Lavinia had an app for learning the names of animals in English and Mandarin, which Rita thought was helping Lavinia to be bi-lingual, although she was not totally sure. In addition, Lavinia watched episodes of *Peppa Pig* in both languages, sometimes viewing it in Mandarin and then watching the same episode in English. But mother Rita had another motivation for wanting her daughter to watch cartoons like *Peppa Pig*. In preparation for preschool, Rita wanted Lavinia to be aware of the programmes other children watched, to be aware of their culture, so that Lavinia could socialize with them when she started kindergarten:

> Rita (AU): Peppa Pig is very popular ... when she goes to kindy or pre-kindy and other kids talk about it, I hope she knows about it too. I don't want her to feel lonely and then there's no socialising with other kids.

Siblings

This section explores how the presence of older siblings can influence young children's experiences as they inspire, support or compete for the use of technological resources. In fact, there are a limited number of studies[3] of siblings' influence on the digital media use of younger children. Siblings are regularly mentioned in passing, for example, as when 'parents and siblings', or 'extended family and siblings' may have some influence on young children. Sometimes there is the hint that outcomes may not always be positive because of sibling rivalry. And since older siblings often do things on behalf of young children, the latter may not have as much chance to learn through experimentation (Plowman et al., 2008). One contribution of direct relevance to this chapter is Houen et al. (2021), a detailed ethnomethodological study of siblings seeking, offering and reacting to help when using digital media, since it provided a language to categorize the interactions (for example, 'solicited' and 'unsolicited' assistance and 'managing' that offer of help). Apart from younger siblings wanting to engage in what their older siblings are doing and learning by copying, many parents in both the UK and Australia noted how older siblings could often support younger ones in various ways and, on occasion, vice versa (Houen et al., 2021). One factor here can be the age of the older sibling and the age gap between the siblings. In the Palmer family (UK), preschooler Leela's older sister Marissa was fifteen and acted almost like an alternative parent, as was clear in the videos that Marissa took for the project. Since she could not read and write, Leela solicited assistance by asking her older sister to type in things for her, provide passwords and read instructions. Meanwhile, Marissa set up software for Leela, made suggestions about what she might consider when trying to proceed in the program, explained why some actions did not work, introduced concepts (e.g. 'delete') and generally encouraged Leela to be independent. As with some of the parents, Marissa prompted Leela to verbalize what she was doing by asking her questions (e.g. 'Do you want to tell me about it?' 'What are you going to show me?'), which required Leela to make evaluations and to express feelings and preferences. For example, Marissa asked 'Was that fun?' after Leela had been popping balloons on screen and asked her to name her favourite emojis when they were looking at a screen full of these icons. In other words, partly by virtue of Marissa's age, this was wide-ranging and sophisticated sibling support.

Meanwhile, in the Kramer family (UK), the videos taken by their mother showed how Libby (preschooler) invited Owen (infant) to join her in the game she was playing, suggesting he copy her actions to hide some characters ('You do some!'). When Owen was less successful, Libby tried to move his finger to the right place and, when that failed, she gave a verbal indication ('These, Owen!'). However, Libby was also willing to let Owen experiment on his own to see if he could work out what to do next. While this was all clearly not as sophisticated support as that shown by Marissa, it illustrates how even very young 'older' siblings can be helpful.

Siblings did not always show such support, however, as demonstrated in the Spinner family (UK), with sisters Imelda (four), Belle (seven) and Alice (nine). Belle regularly both played with Imelda and showed her how to do things on the tablet, but the oldest sister Alice admitted she personally only rarely helped her youngest sister. Yet, in the interview, Alice showed a detailed awareness of Imelda's digital capabilities and weaknesses, suggesting that Alice had been paying attention to Imelda's use of the tablet. This raises questions about how the dynamics of sibling relations may vary with the number of children. Admittedly Belle and Imelda were closer to each other in age but, if there had been no Belle to help out, would Alice have engaged with Imelda more?

This particular example also illustrates Plowman et al.'s (2008) point that older sibling support can reduce the younger sibling's chance to experiment. For example, it became clear that when Belle had been younger, she personally had learnt a good deal about the tablet through trial and error. In fact, when given the chance, Imelda showed that she too could work out how to do or find things on the tablet for herself. During the research, to the surprise of the whole family including Belle, Imelda located a gymnastics video on YouTube that she had not seen before. Siblings' 'helping out' could sometimes veer into 'taking over', however, and the Spinner family offers an instance of this. Although Imelda and Belle clearly had a close relationship, on occasion Belle took possession of the tablet Imelda was using in order to 'demonstrate' something. This happened twice during the family interview when Belle wanted to show Leslie her skills on the device, frustrating Imelda. Imelda managed the situation by eventually re-capturing the tablet from Belle and shouting at her older sister.

Finally, sometimes siblings' unsolicited 'help' may simply not be wanted as was clear in the videos of the Ross family (UK) with Penny (three) and son Frankie (six). While Penny was playing a game that involved matching items, Frankie tried to do some of these matches for her but she resisted ('My god, stop!') and even when he made verbal suggestions, they were rejected ('No thank you!'). But to show how things can change quickly, a few minutes later Frankie sincerely congratulated Penny when she achieved her goal and by the end of the video session the two siblings were singing together, with Penny copying Frankie's dancing to the music coming from the tablet.

Clearly siblings' influence upon digital media use is complex. This section demonstrates the potential nature of sibling support, which is sometimes quite sophisticated, while also noting how it can be problematic.

Parents' relations with each other: Children in divorced families

Relations between parents can be strained even within intact families and that can include issues such as different parental views about parenting or about technology. How such strains can have a bearing on young children's experience of touchscreens is illustrated here in the case of divorce.

In the UK, two divorced fathers, Brian and Neville, took part in the research, both with roughly equal access to the children as their ex-wives. Since they both belonged to an organization called 'Families need Fathers' (FNF), they could provide some examples from their discussions with other fathers as well as from their own experiences, although it seemed that many fathers had joined that particular organization because of problematic marriage break-ups and conflicts.

One issue is that of communicating with their children when the children are in the primary residential parent's home. A factor here can be the residential parent's wish to control that communication with the children, especially if a relationship with an ex-partner is not so positive. Brian had come across this in the FNF discussions: 'On the WhatsApp group, one particular guy had given his son an iPad or a phone or something so he can [keep in touch]. And then the mum just takes it away and that's it. And then the child doesn't use it or she's not teaching the kid how to use it and stuff like that' (Brian, UK).

Neville's divorce had involved conflict in the early days, as his ex-wife applied to have the children for more of the time, while Neville fought for equal access (involving solicitors). Later, when Neville gave his mother's old smartphone to his older seven-year-old child so that she and the three-year-old could stay in touch with the father, the mother initially did not want the child to have it. Neville (UK): 'She just wanted complete separation. She goes: "Neville, when the girls are with me, they're with me and they're not to talk to you."'[4] In fact, his ex-wife later relented and now often sends texts to the daughters when the children are with Neville. He is happy with this, believing that children should always have access to the other parent. Although, so far, he had not had any communication from his daughters when they were staying with his ex-wife, he thought this might be the daughters' choice, to keep the two worlds separate, also evident because they never talked about what it was like to be with their mother when they were with him.

Brian, who had always maintained cordial relations with his ex-wife Caroline, also saw giving his four-year-old daughter Mary telecommunications access as a precaution. Brian (UK): 'The reason why I brought her an iPad ... as a Christmas present just before I was moving out was because I didn't want to rely on Caroline for that communication. Not that ... I don't think she would ever at that point stop her talking to me, but I'd never wanted her to have that option.'

In this case, his daughter Mary FaceTimed Brian often when she was staying with her mother and even Caroline now FaceTimed him sometimes. Moreover, when Mary was staying with Brian, he sometimes reminded his daughter that she might consider Facetiming her mother. Clearly, in this case, neither the parents nor the child were worried about separating the two social worlds.

Another issue potentially relevant for the experience of touchscreens is where rules about children's use are different in the two homes (reflecting what the divorce literature more generally calls 'parallel parenting'; see, for example, Yarosh et al., 2009). In the case of Neville, although he and his ex-wife Jean had so far never discussed rules about technology, the parents simply recognized they might have different practices. Neville: 'All me and Jean have said is that the kids need to understand that there might be slightly different rules in each home and whatever Mummy says in her house and whatever Daddy says in his goes and that's it.'

Although not a technological example, Brian noted how things could go wrong when there were different rules. Once when Mary was at his home, she wanted to use sticking plasters repeatedly over the weekend when playing doctors, almost as another toy and Brian was quite willing to go along with this. When Brian brought Mary back to Caroline's home, their daughter immediately asked Caroline for a plaster, which Caroline refused to give her, arguing they were not to be 'wasted'. This led to Mary getting very upset and caused some drama resulting in Brian staying for several hours to discuss the issue with Caroline.

> Brian (UK): And then I got a text message saying: 'Please don't leave me to be the one to do all the discipline'. So, I said: 'Look, I think we need to agree that there are set rules as in 'be polite', 'wash your hands'. You know set rules. But if she comes to my house and she wants to play with a plaster, play doctors then she's going to play with plasters. I don't care. These are things that don't need to be fixated on.

Clearly, there is also the potential for such disagreements in relation to parents' different perspectives on their children's technology use, but it can take on an added dimension if there are underlying conflicts. Neville noted that in FNF, digital media use was not usually a major issue compared to other matters. But differences about appropriate parenting more generally could be a point of conflict, with either parent criticizing the approach of the other (as in differences of opinion about discipline that had been noted by Caroline). However, sometimes this interaction can reflect the general conflict between ex-parents as much as reflecting the fact that the parents have different practices. Brian (UK): 'There's a guy here who's just criticizing his ex-wife saying that all she does is stick [their child] in front of another cartoon on another tablet. So yeah, I mean it's just another reason for aggro if you want it.'

One last point arising is that, since family break-up can be very traumatic for the children, this could have a bearing on how strictly parents enforce rules, including rules about touchscreen use: Neville (UK) commented: 'I probably let my two use the devices more than I should but I'm in that transitional period at the moment when their mum only moved out sixteen weeks ago so I'm not going to rock the boat so to speak when they're in a transitional period when they're getting used to having two homes.'

In sum, these examples from divorced parents show multiple ways in which the strains or even conflicts arising from family break-ups can have consequences for children's experiences of digital media; be that in terms of contested access to the other parent, clashes over forms of parenting or relaxing some rules as a compensation for the trauma children may be experiencing from the separation process.

Conclusion

While there are limits to what a chapter can explore when looking at the factors leading to diverse experiences of touchscreen by young children, it can at least indicate some of the dimensions that could be considered. How technologies are valued by the parents (both for the children and for themselves), more general forms of parenting and mediation and parents' aspirations can all play a part in parental decisions relating to children's engagement with the digital world. Older siblings can have a complex influence on younger siblings' digital media use, where supporting that use can be multifaceted but also problematic. Lastly, the parents' own relationships with each other and any differences of approaches to parenting were dramatically demonstrated in the different ways in which divorce can have implications for young children's touchscreen experiences.

11

Parents' Evaluation of Children's Learning through Digital Media

In recent years there has been a shift in interest with the literature on early childhood education to evaluations of play, including digital play (Stephen & Edwards, 2018). However, in this study, when interviewed parents commented more on what learning processes were taking place. Hence, the main questions of this chapter focus on parents' perceptions of how touchscreens influence children's learning, their assessment of what different forms of learning are taking place and the role parents themselves play in fostering those different types of learning. Those parental perceptions are important because they have a bearing on parents' overall assessment of these digital media, while types of parental engagement in the learning process challenge the image of young children interacting with technologies in isolation.

Literature review: Parents' evaluation of children's learning

Parental perceptions of the importance of digital media for learning

Previous research has shown that while some parents are sceptical about whether digital media helped learning, others are enthusiastic about these technologies and keen to show what a difference they could make (e.g. Tőkés, 2016), while others may show an ambivalence (Kucirkova & Flewitt, 2022). Parental views about digital media's role in learning depend in part on a number of factors, for example, whether parents think that teaching, such as the teaching of reading, is really the role of the school rather than that of the parents, and when parents thought it was the right time for children to learn certain things (Stephen et al., 2013). Other research has stressed how parents tend to think of education benefits as more valuable than play and encourage the use of educational software (Verenikina et al., 2011). Meanwhile, in a study of tablet use, a survey looking at reasons for buying apps found that their role in supporting both creativity and learning was the major motivations for parents to acquire apps (Marsh et al., 2015).

Parental perception of what young children are learning through digital media

Studies have found that parents first and foremost tend to think of children's learning in terms of developing operational skills to use the technology (Plowman et al., 2010b). In the case of touchscreens, this might include opening and using apps, being able to operate the tablet independently and manage passwords (Marsh et al., 2015). Although that operational learning is sometimes the limit of parental horizons, researchers have explored broader senses in which children are learning through these interactions with technologies (Plowman et al., 2010b; 2010a) and, by implication, other ways in which parents may support that learning. For example, apart from developing operational skills to use the technology, children can learn about the world in general through technologies (Plowman et al., 2010a; McPake et al., 2012): learning to read, learning about numbers, shapes and colours, learning to count or learning to classify animals, or, more generally, to name things. They can do this through the cognitive operations such as matching and categorizing (Stephen, 2021).[1]

Through their experience of technology, young children can also enhance various dispositions to learn, which parents sometimes underestimate (Stephen et al., 2013). This can involve improving their ability to sustain attention, learning to follow instructions, developing problem-solving skills, exploring, building confidence, self-esteem and a sense of security, increasing perseverance, playing cooperatively and taking turns (Stephen & Plowman, 2008; Plowman et al., 2010, 2010b).

Finally, children can become acquainted with cultural values (Plowman, 2015) and cultural practices, for example, by talking to relatives on mobile phones, taking and printing digital photos, sharing memories by watching DVD recordings (McPake et al., 2012). Previous research argued that there were more opportunities for children to become aware of such cultural practices in the home than in preschool settings and yet parents were generally unaware of this level of learning 'in part because culture in which they lived was not visible to them – it was just the way things were' (Plowman et al., 2010b, p. 129).

While this section does not provide an exhaustive list of the types of learning supported by digital media, the discussion draws attention to the fact that such learning can cover very diverse elements. An example from Marsh et al. (2015), for instance, references potty training and the Tosetti (below) and Brent families both discuss using digital media in their potty training. Other authors also offer additional suggestions (e.g. Plowman et al., 2010b). Acknowledging this lack of completeness, however, the above categories at least provide a framework for examining parents' perceptions of how children may learn through their digital media use.

The role of parents in the learning process

It is important to appreciate some theoretical underpinnings in this literature on children, learning and digital media. One underlying framework from the field of child development for those interested in parental (and preschool staff) intervention is the work of Vygotsky (1978) and the importance he placed on social interaction supporting, or 'scaffolding', children's learning. This is in contrast to Piaget's view, which outlines how children learn by themselves in somewhat fixed stages (Plowman et al., 2010b; Roberts-Holmes, 2014; Wartella et al., 2016). Hence, Piaget's (1952) perspective emphasizes creating a rich (i.e. stimulating) environment in which children can learn by experimentation, usually in the form of (to various degrees directed or free) play. However, in the case of digital media it is argued that this latter approach does not work so well when young children encounter these technologies because they need a basic degree of support to operate them (Plowman & Steven, 2005). Stephen (2010) found that while a Piagetian worldview is well established in preschool settings, research has documented some examples of preschool staff interventions, or 'scaffolding': the 'guided interaction' described in Chapter 6, 'Digital media in preschool settings'.

In what ways do parents do the same? First, it is worth noting that while they may not explicitly intervene, parents unknowingly demonstrate uses of technology on a daily basis by simply letting children participate in activities and watch others. This allows children to learn even if the parents are not aware of it and has been called incidental learning (e.g. Plowman et al., 2008). Second, while parents themselves may not explicitly refer to these theoretical frameworks, the Piagetian and Vygotskian assumptions about child development are also reflected in different parents' views about parents' roles in children's learning. For example, some parents think that young children learn more through play without parental interventions and so do not help the children unless asked, preferring to let children learn by exploring (Stephen et al., 2013). Others limit their engagement to providing more technical assistance (Kucirkova and Flewitt, 2022). But some parents make many more interventions and this is most systematically illustrated by one in-depth study of four Scottish families (Stephen et al., 2013). These families were provided with various digital technologies – a games console (with some educational games), a reading system (with some puzzles) and technological pets – and the researchers drew on video material to show how parents' interventions in terms of scaffolding their children's experience are similar to the interventions of some staff in preschool. This includes monitoring, praising, encouraging, explaining, showing how things work and making suggestions about how to proceed (Stephen et al., 2013).

Toddlers and Tablets findings

Parents' evaluations of children's learning through digital media

Generally, most parents in the *Toddlers and Tablets* study thought that their children could learn things through digital media use, but some also had mixed views and a few were sceptical. The range and complexity of stances can be illustrated by looking in more detail at three families: the Spinners (UK), the Tosettis (UK) and the Petersens (AU).

Karla Spinner (UK) had bought various non-digital educational aids as well as ones to support physical development (for example, motor skills) but she had not prioritized equivalent digital learning supports. When the older girls were younger, Karla had decided not to buy educational games because she thought they were *gimmicky*. That said, the Spinners had subsequently acquired some educational software (for example, a game where children matched colours), including ones involving re-ordering items, ones like jigsaw puzzles and ones teaching numbers. Daniel was mainly annoyed by apps voiced over in the American language because he did not want the children growing up with *Americanisms*. As regards the alphabet and numbers, Karla had not tried to deliberately teach these but, instead, thought that the children would gradually become aware of such things.

Unlike many of the other families interviewed who interacted with their children when using such apps (as will be demonstrated later in this chapter), Karla specifically contrasted educational games that were being used in isolation by the child with higher quality parent-child interaction. In fact, on reflection, Karla noted that for the most part she and her husband did not interact with the children when they were using the touchscreens because the parents were usually too busy. Whenever they did find time to interact with the children, they would choose a non-digital activity such as drawing, rather than a technology-based one. Although she acknowledged that there might be apps to mimic such activities, Karla preferred the non-technology alternatives, like holding a pen.

In contrast, husband Daniel was more positive that actively engaging with touchscreen technologies was helping the children's cognitive development and that help was in addition to any entertainment value. But Karla worried specifically that the short-term and instant gratification of many such apps were detrimental to the development of children's attention span. Her point of reference from her own childhood was activities that took some time such as writing. Daniel, however, likened using digital apps to his childhood memories of more short-term activities like playing at drumming.

Daniel felt that current videos (on YouTube) were better than when he was younger, especially those produced by the BBC, which the girls watched more than the *Disney* or *Discovery* ones. He thought that these were quite educational and even Karla gave examples of where the girls mentioned something they had learnt from watching these programmes, for instance, their awareness of different types of illness. Daniel, although thinking more of his two older daughters, was also more positive about how the game *Minecraft* helped develop perseverance and imagination.

To put the Spinners into context, they were not unique in having reservations about educational apps and preferences for non-technological activities. Linda Palmer (UK) preferred books to software, even if she had acquired some of the latter for her daughter. Klara Brown (UK) had read criticisms of educational software, even if she had subsequently been impressed by some programs. Stella Kramer (UK) had bought software to support reading because her child Libby requested it, but the mother herself did not entirely believe in its effectiveness. Yet even the Spinners, especially Daniel, also said that there were some benefits and positive things about learning through technology.

The strongest contrast is with the Italian Tosetti family (UK), who made very positive comments about the internet. Mirabella had first introduced two-year-old Leopoldo to the iPad when he was six months old with a program called 'Nighty Night'. He could 'go' to different rooms in a house and when he switched off the light in that room the cartoon animals or people went to bed. The aim was to bring the app out at bedtime so that Leopoldo learnt it was time to go to sleep. It worked and she still uses the app sometimes. The next step was for Mirabella to get apps with English nursery rhymes, since the parents were from Italy and did not know the English versions. While Leopoldo mainly spoke Italian at home (in the little speech he yet had), he had learnt to sing the rhymes in English. There were also some games where the narrative was offered in a range of languages. Mirabella was happy for Leopoldo to be exposed to a variety of these (e.g. Norwegian). And, at the time of the interview, she was still trying to find apps for Leopoldo that related to whatever he was interested in at that time. Since Leopoldo was currently undergoing potty training, she had found a variety of apps – some with animations, some with real children – which showed Leopoldo what he was supposed to do. Since he was starting to actively engage in potty training, Leopoldo was also interested in the apps. In fact, Mirabella was amused by the fact that when sitting on his potty, he would hold the iPad in two hands in front of him, like reading a book.

Here the Tosettis, especially mother Mirabella who used to work as a graphic designer in the production of TV programmes for children, were clearly very enthusiastic about diverse forms of learning via the tablet, especially learning that was not linked to educational apps: learning the routines of going to bed, nursery rhymes (arguably an introduction to English culture), being made aware that there are different languages and potty training.

Finally, the Petersens (AU) were one of the families that had acquired educational apps but did not promote them and, in fact, the children did not use them. Mother Claire explained: 'You know, maybe if they had a mother who was geared towards education.' However, once again, educational apps were not the only touchscreen experiences the Petersen family associated with learning. Claire had been impressed by what five-year-old Freya had learnt from her decision to watch science vlogs on YouTube and how she and her older sister had even been inspired to create things after watching a vlog on crafting. Claire (AU): 'They've come off and they've been excited about making something. So that's great because often I haven't had the energy to think about what crafting activity they're going to do.' Later in the interview, father Jeff added, when reflecting on any benefits of touchscreens: 'Certainly I think as long as it's kind of something that encourages them still to be creative and building things and making things and doing that stuff and it's not just being passive.' In fact, one of the other outcomes of watching YouTube was that the daughters set up scenes with their dolls and videoed themselves playing at making their own vlogs.

Parental evaluations of what children learn through digital media

Learning about technology in general was important for some parents, which could mean just being immersed in a digital environment. Sherryl Cullen (AU), reflecting on the benefit of touchscreen devices, observed: 'I guess the good side is that it does give them more knowledge of things, technology-based, by being exposed to it ... probably Elle (16) didn't have [that] because the technology just it wasn't there ... whereas these kids ... and especially Finn (fourteen months), he doesn't know any different.' Like Stella Kramer (UK), discussed in the early chapter on Parenting and digital media, Rita Chen (AU) had a more specific reason for wanting her two-year-old daughter Lavinia to become familiar with tablets: next year Rita planned to send Lavinia to a kindergarten where they used tablets and she did not want her daughter to be disadvantaged.

As in the literature review, parents specifically mentioned various operational skills, sometimes being surprised by what their children had achieved given their age. For example, when asked about her daughter's skills, Linda Palmer (UK) referred to how Leela (preschooler) at three-years-old could delete files, put files in folders, navigate to and make choices in the Apps Store and use the backward and forward arrows. But Linda noted that Leela, eighteen months later, shifted to a different level, explaining that her daughter had worked out how to do some things in the games for herself: 'She's the one showing me how to do things.' In a similar vein, Sandra Ross was surprised and proud when three-year-old Penny worked out how to phone her father on the smartphone.

Compared to the claims made in the literature review, more of the *Toddlers and Tablets* parents volunteered different ways in which their children were learning about the world via the tablet: covering the standard list of counting, learning about shapes, colours and animals, to reading Bible stories and learning about the details of tooth cavities and airplane sickness from YouTube. Specifically, the Mansis (UK) noted that Sergei (nearly two) was making connections between what he had seen in an app or cartoon and what he saw in the outside world, such as the fact that a leaf resembled a rainbow. The Mansis were very positive about how this learning was sometimes reinforcing what Sergei had encountered from other sources. And given the multicultural nature of London and Perth, a number of family members came from other countries and, hence, language learning was mentioned by various families, whether that was learning English as an additional language (as with the Zhang/Chen family) or supporting first language acquisition (for example, reinforcing Sergei Mansi's Russian language abilities).

As regards dispositions, few parents initially volunteered these when asked what their children were learning but, later in the conversation, they spontaneously mentioned examples such as developing 'persistence' (Brown family, UK) or 'perseverance' (Ross family, UK). In a further example, Sergei Mansi's (UK) parents thought he had learnt to be patient through using the iPad: he had come to understand that he had to wait for things to load and did not get upset by that. He also learnt the words 'on charge' meant that something was not available, since the parents had sometimes told him the iPad was on charge when they did not want him to use it. In fact, having introduced him to the concept of non-availability through this digital experience, Nadia sometimes used it in other contexts: 'If he feeds a lot during the day … by feeds, I mean breastfeeds … I will tell him the milk needs to charge. And so, he knows that that's when he needs to wait.'

Lastly, a few parents mentioned forms of cultural learning. Rita Chen (AU) thought that *Peppa Pig* was educational not only in teaching about objects such as teapots (and how to use them) but because it also managed to convey the meaning of Christmas. Meanwhile the Tosettis (UK), who used the tablet to introduce Leopoldo to classical music, noted that he was, in addition, 'learning the grammar of audio-visual images' and appreciating cultural concepts, such as when they used an Elmo video to help explain what a 'birthday' meant.

The role of parents in supporting children's engagement with digital media

The role of parents in supporting learning can be illustrated through the videos of the Ross, Palmer and Kramer families (UK). For example, during one of Leslie's visits, mother Sandra Ross was teaching three-year-old Penny about the tablet. Sandra often commented on what Penny was doing, making suggestions about what to do next ('We need to do these ones'), what to press next ('That's it, press it again'), checking to see if Penny knew what came next ('Do you remember what mummy said you had to press?'), explaining why something did not work ('Because you haven't unlocked the pictures yet') and reminding Penny of the overall procedures in apps, for example, what Penny had to do next to achieve a goal (e.g. to earn a sticker). Sandra regularly gave Penny positive feedback whenever she was successful, even noting how quickly Penny had achieved a goal.

In the videos, Sandra pointed at an arrow icon and said 'press "Next", reminding Penny of the convention that the arrow is called 'next' and that pressing that key allows movement to the next screen. Later, Sandra showed Penny how to operate the volume control, how to navigate between pictures, the process of installing a new app and what she could expect to happen on screen. At one point, Penny had forgotten how to navigate to the page she wanted so Sandra reminded her. In addition, there was support relating to particular apps. As in other families, Sandra sometimes had to explain the nature of the task in the app, for example, showing Penny that she needed to trace the shape of a letter. Since Penny could not spell, Sandra offered guidance, like some other parents had, to explain what the written instruction said: 'Look, it says "play" and it says "pop the balloons".'

The Ross case study was particularly rich in showing what it meant to scaffold technology use, in terms of explaining how the technology operated, although all these elements could be found in the videos of other families. But additional forms of learning were also taking place. For example, Sandra explained at one point that Penny had pressed something to make the tablet update and described what Penny could then expect to happen and what she needed to do. Sandra: 'So, you've got to wait until this gets all the ways to the end' (points to a bar on the screen, more of which was gradually lighting up to indicate progress in the update). 'And this should say 100' (points to the percentages).

Over several more minutes, Sandra repeatedly asked Penny to describe how the update was progressing (for example, what percentage the update had reached) as another bar appeared in the charge icon, whilst also positively reinforcing Penny's patient waiting:

Sandra (UK): How does it look now then Penny?
Penny: It's down. Full to the top.
Sandra: It's filled right up to the top?
Penny: Yeah.
Sandra: And it still hasn't switched on?
Penny: Mm, mm.
Sandra: What do you think we have to do now?
Penny: We have to press it.
Sandra: I don't think we press anything. I think we have to wait a little bit still
   … even though it's all the way at the top.
(Penny looks at it for fifteen more seconds.)
Sandra: You're being very patient.
Penny: Yeah.
Sandra: Doing some good waiting.

It probably helped that, as the updating went through various phases, Sandra told Penny that the process was not yet finished. This expectation management arguably enabled Penny to remain patient and the constant questions and answers may also have assisted in passing the time. Ultimately, Penny waited quite a long while doing nothing, without making a fuss.

Finally, Sandra also went beyond talking about the operations of technology, when she was asking Penny to read the percentage points during the update (noted early), thus testing Penny's recognition of numbers. In one of the videos, a software app asked the user to pair up capital and small letters, but Sandra used the opportunity to see if Penny knew the associated sound as well. In another app, she asked Penny to read the scores and identify what colour the letters were, even though these were not among the tasks of the app. In other words, Sandra was constantly making use of what was happening in the app as a springboard to further scaffold development of Penny's cognitive and recognition skills. She frequently asked Penny to articulate what she understood to be happening and what she was seeing. This was more demanding than if Penny were to simply interact with the game on her own. Arguably, it was also more fun, because it was clear in other videos that Penny did sometimes get bored with games after a while when playing alone, but she appeared quite happy to interact with her mother and answer her questions.

During a visit to the Palmer family, Leslie asked to see the *Snapchat* app on the smartphone that allowed users to create images of their face combined with make-up or other special effects. Mother Linda opened the app on her phone (since preschooler Leela could not do that), saying to Leela: 'Let mummy get it up … 'cos it takes a while to come up.'

Leela sat quietly staring at the screen with Linda. After twenty seconds Leela commented: 'Wait.' Eventually the app opened and Leela could see her face on the screen and below this was a number of icons in buttons showing the different type of effects that could be superimposed on her own face.

> Linda (UK): (to Leslie): Stroll across and take a picture for the man. (NB Linda meant 'scroll'; the 'man' refers to Leslie)

Leela held the phone in her left open hand, with her right-hand fingers behind the bottom half of the phone using her right thumb to reach across the screen and make the icons scroll horizontally.

> Linda: (to Leslie) It's got all different faces and different things.

Leela held the smartphone up for her mother to operate it.

> Linda: No, you know how to do it. Hold it to your face so that you can see it.

Leela held her thumb on a smiling strawberry icon that made her face go very red on screen. Leela looked at it for a few seconds and then pressed something to take the picture. Linda encouraged Leela to take another. Leela put her thumb on a different face icon, but this time a keyboard came up covering the lower part of her facial image.

Linda: You're doing it too quick aren't you ... you need to wait for it to come.

Linda touched the upper part of the screen with her finger to make the keyboard disappear. Leela pressed something and the keyboard appeared again. Linda touched the screen to remove it once more. (It seems Leela must have been pressing something too early, without waiting long enough for Snapchat to react.)

Leela: (To Linda) What are you pressing?
Linda: Try a different one. (Leela touched an icon) There you go! I think it's gonna come. Right, hold it up to you and wait for it to come.

On screen the green stem of a cartoon strawberry appeared on Leela's forehead and some liquid appears to be pouring out of her mouth like a small, slow waterfall. Leela just looked at the picture for some seconds, smiling. She waited so long that the screen went blank, so Linda touched it to make the screen light up again with the special effects picture. Leela looked at it, laughing. After some more seconds, Leela took the picture. Leela then pressed another icon and her face on screen now had purple lipstick on her lips and purple eye make-up with a ring through her nose.

Leela: It's got a ring on my nose.

Leela touches her own nose where the ring on screen would be.

Linda: It's got a ring on your nose. But you haven't really got a ring, have you?
Leela: No.

Like Sandra Ross, Linda was initially encouraging her child to learn patience while the app loaded. Even Leela said 'wait' to herself. Later we see how Linda invited Leela to sort out the smartphone technology for herself rather than meeting Leela's request for her mother to do it for her – Linda wanted her daughter to do it independently ('You know how to do it'). Again, like Sandra Ross, Linda told Leela why some actions were not working ('You're doing it too quick, aren't you') and made alternative suggestions ('Try a different one'). But Linda also asked Leela to think about the more challenging question about how digital appearances differ from reality when talking about the snapshot image of Leela with a ring through her nose ('But you haven't really got a ring have you?'). Although Leela agreed, the fact that she was touching her nose where the ring appeared suggested she may not have been totally sure.

In the Kramer family (UK), four-year-old Libby was looking at an app on her tablet that was intended to teach her how to write words by hearing how they were pronounced. There was first a short story and then, to help the character progress in that narrative, Libby was asked by the program to spell the word 'wax'.

> Libby (UK): To mother Stella: 'Wax'. I don't know how it starts.
> Stella: W .....ax (stressing the 'w' sound).
> Libby: w. (presses the 'w' icon) What's next?
> Stella: What sound is next? W ... a ....x (stressing 'w', then 'a', then 'x').
> Libby: W ... a .... (presses the 'a' icon).
> Stella: And then ... w ... a ... x. What options have you got left?

Libby turned the screen around so her mother can see. Apart from W, A and X, several other letter options were offered.

> Stella: Can you make the sounds? (pause) W ... a ....x.

Libby paused, concentrating, her fingers hovering above different letters. She pressed one letter option – nothing happened, but there was no feedback from the app either. Libby tried a second. Nothing happened. She tried a third, which must have been X because she was congratulated by the program. The story continued and the next task was to spell the word 'fox'. Stella pronounced the different letters in 'fox' and Libby successfully found the F. Libby tried pressing a few things on screen. She blew out air from her mouth, as if indicating this was demanding. Libby then stared into space with her mouth open. She looked at the tablet and her fingers hovered about letter icons. She tried one. Nothing happened. She stared into space again. She pressed an icon. Nothing happened. She jabbed at the same key harder with her finger.

> Libby: I can't do it (she said in a very tearful voice).
> Stella: It's OK. When you say the word 'Fox ..... o ... x'.

Libby had another go and tried various keys. She must have been successful. The next word she had to find was 'mix'.

> Libby: I don't know it (looking at mum).
> Stella: Say the word. Mix.
> Libby: Mix.

Stella: Mix. M..i..x.
Libby: O?
Stella: No, if you put an 'o' in it, it would be m … o … x. M … i … x.
Libby: I don't know it. I don't know which one.
Stella: Listen to the sounds. M … i … x. Press the sounds on the app.
Libby: What's the app?
Stella: Well, on the game.

Libby's finger hovered above one icon.

Stella: Is that the one? No. What other ones are there?
Libby: W?
Stella: Er (the tone implied 'no').
Libby: F?
Stella: What word are you doing?
Libby: Er … mix.
Stella: Mix. So find the 'm' sound and then the 'I' sound and then the 'x'.

Libby presses a button, presumably 'm'.

Libby: What's next?
Stella: I.
Libby: I don't know which one it is.
Stella: Well listen to the sounds on the game. Press the buttons.

After thinking, Libby pressed a few buttons

Libby: Yes! (It looks as if she has been successful)

In this episode, Stella was always trying to give some guidance (for example, drawing attention to the sound of particular letters, encouraging Libby to say the word for herself and to listen to what it sounded like, asking what options were left). But at the start of the interaction relating to 'wax' and 'fox', there were more long silences when the mother said nothing, letting Libby try to sort it out for herself. One problem was that the app was giving no further feedback, providing no additional clues when Libby pressed the wrong buttons. Up to this stage, although the task seemed to be provoking serious reflection by Libby, it was also leading to some frustration. After this point, Stella started to engage more, to scaffold more and in different ways, now also telling Libby why a wrong answer was wrong (for example, what an 'o' in the word would sound like) and proposing to Libby that she should proceed by breaking the problem down into parts (that is, first find this sound, then find that sound). Arguably, if Libby had not had help and encouragement from her mother, she would only have had at best partial success when working with the tablet alone. Given Libby's reactions it seems likely that, without Stella's scaffolding, Libby would have given up.

Conclusion

One indication of the way in which parents value learning is their acquisition of educational apps. Many parents in both countries bought these, although the evaluation of the software ranged from appreciating the quality of some apps to being critical of them and not all parents promoted their use even when they were present in the home. But there were many other ways in which parents could appreciate different forms of learning through digital activities. This was best exemplified by the Tosetti family; however, the Petersen case demonstrated not only learning through YouTube, but also being inspired by it and how this influenced children's subsequent play.

Thinking about what children learn from playing with digital media, many parents prioritized the technologies children were likely to use in their (imagined) future lives. In some cases, parents' concern was to avoid their child being disadvantaged. Operational skills were important, and some parents were impressed by what their children could achieve, including how their child realized specific goals when using touchscreens. Following on from the types of learning identified in previous research, there were numerous examples of digital technologies helping children to learn about the world, in some cases reinforcing other sources. Building on concepts from previous studies, parents appreciated how the children were learning various dispositions, also illustrated by the Ross and Palmer families in the last section. There were a few examples where parents appreciated that the children were learning cultural concepts.

As regards parents' roles in that learning process, in the final three case studies of the Ross, Palmer and Kramer families, there are a variety of interventions to help scaffold technology use and in doing so support children's learning. Clearly there is a variety of ways in which parents can foster operational skills, such as showing children and explaining to them, reminding them how technology works, or what to do and expect in relation to particular apps. But these parents and indeed other parents do more than that. There are examples of parents motivating children by congratulating them when they are successful, encouraging them to manage the technology independently and actively helping to develop dispositions like patience. Moreover, parents sometimes go on to use children's engagement with these technologies as a starting point to ask further questions, to promote the child's other competencies, to get them to articulate their thinking or, in one example, to think about what is 'real' when encountering the digital world. In this sense, parents' interventions in relation to these technologies are equivalent to ones we might expect to see when children are engaged in non-digital activities – a point that is sometimes lost in discourses that stress the inauthentic nature of digital experience. These technologies and apps may provide, to varying degrees, a rich or poor medium in themselves, but arguably they are rich in the opportunities they offer for parents to take initiatives in relation to enriching their child's digital media experiences.

Parents, as evidenced throughout the ethnographic study, have mixed experiences of using educational apps and digital devices for learning, due in large measure to the uneven quality of provision in this field. App stores and online publishers host an enormous range of learning resources for this burgeoning market. Some participants in the study noted that there appeared to be a rise in the availability of professionally produced content and indeed according to some reports, this is a market that is set to grow by 26 per cent per annum in the period up to 2024.[2] However, key questions remain regarding quality control and educational appropriateness for parents as much as for educationalists. Participants in the research point to the 'gimmicky' nature of some apps or to the general lack of cultural or linguistic fit. This indicates a general lack of standards in this area and the need for much greater policy attention to appropriate accreditation, standards setting as well as testing and evaluation. While parenting organizations and online providers provide various ways to review educational content before trying it out, few professional standards exist in the all-important preschool stage when parents are keen to prepare children for the world of formal schooling. Trusted providers and brands with a tradition of producing high-quality content for children could take a lead in this area, expanding their own experience from the worlds of broadcasting or publishing into digital content, lending their own undoubted experience of educational development but also contributing to raising quality standards as the market and the digital environment continue to evolve.

12

Summarizing Our Research Findings

This book contains new research that captures the developing agency of the young child, as made visible in their personal, self-directed use of digital media. We have explored young children's digital engagement through ethnographic interviews and observation, play-based research with children and focus groups with parents and other significant caregivers. We have complemented this with a multifaceted review of relevant literature and an analysis of policy, advice and practice. The research also addresses how parents deal with the implications of their child's developing agency in a digital world. Caregivers' statements are an important means for making sense of how these key providers of opportunities and support for very young children approach their roles as mediators of and responders to children's growing interest and skills in relation to digital engagement. Some specific research questions have been addressed in the discussion sections of four previous chapters. Beginning with an overview question and narrowing the lens of enquiry to address specific questions, we asked:

- What does 'good' look like for young children's digital lives? (Chapter 3)
- What factors do parents consider when enabling digital media use in early childhood? (Chapter 7)
- How do parents perceive young children's use of digital media as creating or constraining possibilities for the future? (Chapter 8)
- Does early years' digital engagement support the development of social and emotional skills? (Chapter 9)

Rather than revisit the conclusions of those chapters here, we now weave together the separate strands to construct an overall picture of very young children's digital media use and the importance of families and educators in supporting their engagement with related media devices.

Parenting and digital media

Consideration of early years' digital media use involves reflecting upon the process of becoming a parent. Understanding how parenthood is a social construction (Lee et al., 2014), paralleling the social construction of childhood (James et al., 1997), involves appreciating the wider context of sometimes diverse discourses about how parents should act. Such injunctions are often embodied in parenting courses, advice books for parents and parent online forums and blogs. They are also, more traditionally, evident in the informal tips offered to new parents by their own parents, extended family and friends and shared within parents' social networks. The research interviews demonstrate how parents-to-be sometimes start the process of learning to parent before their first child is born, anticipating how their role will develop (Gager et al., 2002). Parents frequently supplement the tips and advice received from others by seeking out information from multiple sources while immersed in everyday parenting. By accepting some suggestions and approaches but rejecting others, parents navigate their own path through competing visions of 'how to parent', thus developing their own ethnotheories of the role (Harkness & Super, 1992).

Part of that personal process of learning-to-parent involves parents deciding what they should be concerned about. This takes place against the background of a history of anxious discourses about the detrimental effects on children of media and technologies (Critcher, 2008; Jaunzems et al., 2019; Tsaliki & Chronaki, 2020). Traditionally, many concerns relate to the content, such as representations of violence or sexuality, that children may encounter in the digital world, while other fears relate to children becoming dependent on technology, or meeting abusive strangers. These fears are similar for children under six and older children, although in the early years they are mitigated by parents of young children generally having more knowledge and control over what their children can do and when and how they access digital media. In contrast, parents of older children may feel themselves less familiar with the latest technology and less able to monitor their child's activities, especially when they are outside the home.

Most parents of early years' children focus on how they can support their child's development, although many are undoubtedly concerned about whether technology use might undermine that process, for example, by distracting their child from engagement in the 'real' world, or by undermining their capacity for imagination. Such concerns may be grounded in parents' memories of their own childhoods and their projections forward from that point (Livingstone et al., 2020). That said, some parents, like the Tosettis and the Bernards, have favourable evaluations of technology and hence fewer worries about it.

As parents formulate their ideas about parenting, to a greater or lesser degree they also forge and articulate their approach to digital mediation, usually aiming to help their child develop technological fluency (Barron et al., 2009) while avoiding what individual parents might construct as the pitfalls of media use (for example, the Jamesons). These parental ethnotheories, as Plowman (2015) discusses, become more complicated when parents find themselves mediating technologies that weren't part of their own childhoods. This complexity may be expressed in terms of the range of parenting genres each family adopts – resisting, balancing and embracing (Livingstone et al., 2020, p. 11; and see Chapter 3). Such terms indicate the strategies that parents aim to follow (as in, rules about children's use of digital media) understood in relation to parents' broader and often unstated techno-imaginaries for their child's future (perhaps a sci-fi world of hi tech jobs). Resisting, balancing and embracing are lenses through which to identify potential responses to indicators of concern (for example, their child becoming too attached to technological devices).

The parents interviewed in the *Toddlers and Tablets* project seem by and large to follow through on their personal visions and ideals as presented in their interviews. Or at least, they tend to tell coherent narratives about their parenting strategies and practices. Certainly their intentions appear authentic, as captured in the quotes cited in this book. But, confronted with unexpected contingencies, parents can change strategies, necessitating a rethinking (and re-narrating) of their approach. When Sergei Mansi (twenty-three months) was ill, when Lorenzo Tosetti (two) awoke with nightmares, when Simon Brown (two) ate less than his parents wished and when Ellen Brent (four) needed to take medication, their parents would use digital devices to distract or calm their children. One problem with offering guidance to parents about their use of digital media is that it fails to engage with such realities, focusing instead on ideal situations, principles and policies; and neglecting the compromises that parents feel they have to make when faced with particular and often challenging circumstances.

Similarly, much parental guidance appears to assume that parents are 100 per cent engaged in parenting duties, giving their full attention to 'the' child, that is, their 'one' child. But in the Brent home, where there are three siblings, mum Elisabeth says she will sometimes occupy Ellen (four) with the tablet so that she can engage with Ellen's brothers James (nine) and Andrew (eleven). In addition, parents have diverse roles and obligations and, while they are parents all the time, they do not always wear their parental hat or, at least, not with full attention. Parents face the everyday practicalities of managing a home, engaging in in- or out-of-home employment, study, self-care and care for others, such as going to the hairdresser or to a doctor, or visiting elderly relatives; or they may simply choose to spend 'adult time' with friends or a partner, possibly in a public space like a restaurant. Such activities may involve reciprocal adult attention and time off from full-on childcare when, once again, parents show themselves willing to use technological strategies to occupy their children.

As with occupying their children in public places when they are subject to competing demands, parents can also find it tricky to keep their children entertained on long journeys. Again, the cultural ideal, cited by several interviewees, is to give children crayons and paper to draw on. But while this may be considered a socially acceptable, even creative, activity, all the parents in this study admitted to occupying their child in various circumstances with a device. Some, like Sandra Ross, say: 'It does make sense sometimes to go, "You know what, you're going to be happy for five minutes; I'm going to be happy for five minutes. Yeah, why not?"' Others, like dad Jo Cheung-Yeo, see cultural variations in advice given to parents. But the dominant concern is that parents see their children's use of digital media in public places as leaving them vulnerable to critical, even hostile or shaming evaluation by outsiders, with parents such as Nadia Mansi admitting to feeling guilty about going down this path.

Other important adults: Grandparents and preschool staff

The *Toddlers and Tablets* project considers two other sets of key actors in very young children's lives: grandparents and early childhood care and education staff. These interviews and group discussions supplement the primary focus, which is on parents and children. As Chapter 5 (Grandparents) and Chapter 6 (Digital media in preschool settings) demonstrate, there are distinct research literatures regarding both grandparenthood and preschool practitioners. These literatures also include examples of and commentaries upon, the supplementary carer's constructions of parents' use of digital media and how their interaction with parents is also inflected by parents' views of grandparents' (Breheny et al., 2013) and preschool educators' use of digital media with their children (Plowman et al., 2010b). The aim of including these perspectives was to be holistic in valuing the contributions of all significant adults to the child's varied digital experiences, including times when parents are not present and grandparents, or alternatively childcare and preschool staff, are 'in loco parentis'. Each group comprises important adults with whom parents and children interact, including with regard to digital matters.

Grandparents' perceptions of digital media, their concerns and agendas prove to be sometimes (surprisingly) similar to parents' but also, on occasion, at odds. Hence, grandparents' contributions to children's digital development may be appreciated by parents but may equally be a source of tension. Sometimes parents in the same family may differ in their response to a particular grandparental initiative such as when Jacob Davis (at about age five or six) received an iPad from his paternal grandparents without his mother's knowledge or agreement. Other areas with potential to impact intergenerational relations include grandparents' advice to parents, how grandparents interact with their grandchildren and the support they offer to grandchildren in co-playing with a digital device (as in the Petersen family). The lived examples discussed in this book reveal that, in the wider social construction of grandparenting, the grandparental role is changing and uncertain, requiring considerable negotiation, for example, over how much they should 'interfere'. Generally, the exemplars from the *Toddlers and Tablets* research and from the literature highlight how grandparents need to be included in research if we are to gain a thorough understanding of the shaping of children's digital experiences.

Other key adults impacting this shaping become important when children take part in early childhood care and education settings, for example, in early learning centres, kindergartens, nurseries and other forms of preschool care and learning. The preschool staff participants reveal themselves as having their own agendas, chiefly around supporting child development, drawing on both their formal training and informal interactions with their colleagues at work. Preschool educators' perspectives are influenced by the demands of the early years' digital technology curricula in Australia and the UK, though individual educators also have their own concerns about the digital world. As we see with parents and grandparents, these staff co-construct a social world where there is a variety of digital media-related discourse. In the nurseries and kindergartens taking part in the project, staff engagement in young children's digital lives varied significantly, reflecting the resources of different institutions, the orientation of the different centres (as is the case with four-year-old Michael Lim-Park's Montessori school), specific policy environments and the resourcefulness of the staff themselves. An established theme in the preschool literature is the limited understanding that adults in both home and preschool settings have of what happens in the other location. They are likely to have even less appreciation of the child's specifically digital experiences in each of those other settings (Plowman et al., 2010b).

From birth to preschool

Integrating the information from the family-based parent and child ethnographic chapters, a developmental lens positions participant children on a continuum starting from birth with the infants' group, moving through toddlerhood to preschoolers. In relation to digital media, this birth to preschool age is a historically under-explored age cohort who were first enfranchised as active digital agents with the advent of touchscreen devices (Holloway et al., 2013). Our adoption of this birth-to-six trajectory has allowed visibility and appreciation of the commencement of a young person's lifetime engagement with interactive digital media as conditioned, enabled and bounded by parents' and caregivers' experiences and expectations. As the book has shown, from children's very earliest months onwards, there is ample evidence of caregivers learning to parent digitally as they perform their role, surprised and challenged in many instances by what they describe as their very young child's 'intuitive' engagement with digital media. Ready examples of this include Scott (two and a half) in the Andrews-White family who gained access as soon as he could reach for a device. In these early stages, the primary challenges parents identify as limiting children's productive media engagement relate to their child's still-developing motor skills, which are often shown to frustrate an infant's settled intention for digital interaction. Some parents provide clear evidence of their child's understanding of using associated workarounds within digital contexts when frustrated by physical barriers. For example, we saw how parent Isabelle Davis made her iPhone available to Phoebe (five) who can use apps but first must ask older sibling Jacob (ten) to facilitate access by opening the app and setting up her games.

One of the aphorisms of childhood is that the first stage is 'walking', the second stage 'talking'. If walking marks the metaphorical bridge from the end of (what this book terms) the infant period, it is the development of the verbal, talking child which is the hallmark of the toddler. As children develop their talking, they also experience significant growth in their conceptual understanding of the world around them. Thus, infants might initially be confused by Skype and Facetime, which deliver apparent access to someone they know well but then may frustrate the child's wish to interact fully with that person. In the case of the Campbell family, infant Julia (one) could get so distressed by seeing dad Adam on-screen but then losing him again when the call ended, that her parents considered video-calling each other only at times that don't involve Julia. Similarly, parents recalled memories of when their children were younger and would look around the back of a physical media device as if hoping to see the person they were talking to physically located there. This was the case in Mirabella and Lorenzo Tosetti's tale of Leopoldo (two) looking behind the iPad during a Skype call hoping to find his Italy-based grandparents in person, in addition to seeing them on screen.

Once children are toddlers, most feel more confident about their everyday physical movements and are better positioned to engage actively in the world around them. While this is true for both physical and mediated contexts, technology offers intoxicating examples of a child's growing capacity to act in the world. Imitative play remains important; recall, for example, toddler Emma Davis (two) playing with an unconnected games controller as brother Jacob (ten) plays a game and the broken laptop in the Peter Pan Nursery which the preschoolers pretend-play with. Indeed, much of childhood knowing is achieved through doing (Schank et al., 1999).

We also saw examples of children's impatience at being fobbed off with 'fake' technology, for often children's enjoyment of technology is related to the way digital interaction leads to an outcome, an impact on the world, almost independently of the child wanting to achieve any specific outcome. Thus, infant Emily Lim-Park (twenty-three months) uses the remote control not because she wants to watch a television programme but because she wants to activate a dark screen with content. As her mother notes, having turned the television on, Emily usually walks away. Toddlers in the research displayed differing reactions to the inevitable frustrations of wrangling technology to make it do as they intend. This was exemplified in a story told by parent Sarah of preschooler Connor Bernard's (five) earlier toddler years when parent Sarah responded to his anguished cry after he'd thrown the games controller in a frustrated rage. Interaction isn't always seamless, however, and children's desires for digital engagement can sometimes be frustrated by the quality of the available infrastructure. Parents were divided as to whether children learned 'patience' or 'impatience' from their experiences with connected media. Thus, Penny Ross (three) and Leela Palmer (four) were said to have learned they needed to wait for some technology to load and activate. In contrast, Emily Lim-Park (twenty-three months) and Leopoldo Tosetti (two) were described as being frustrated by technology's time lag. Similarly, parents talk about the ways in which children feel frustrated or surprised when their activities trigger the capitalist architecture underpinning much of the contemporary internet. This was the case, for example, when Scott Andrews-White (two and a half) had to manage pop-up advertisements and when Ben Law-Tammell (five) inadvertently activated in-game purchases after being enticed to click a link embedded within the free content of a game.

It is at this stage, as children first begin semi-autonomous digital activity, that parents may begin worrying about the algorithms that are designed for adults, but which attract and engage children's attention, possibly transporting their child through interconnecting links to inappropriate content. Parent Isabelle Davis shared this fear in relation to her daughter Emma (two), worrying what the toddler might find if she were to search the term 'Barbie'. According to his mum Mi Na, by the time Michael Lim-Park was four he had already mastered voice-activated internet search. Our research demonstrates that young children of Emma's and Michael's ages aren't necessarily protected from the full range of digital content by their limited keyboard skills or their poor grasp of spelling.

Once they develop the capacity to verbalize thoughts and action, as toddler William Bernard (three and a half) demonstrates, children begin to articulate an individual contribution to this research. In place of parents noting their child's likes, dislikes and activities, toddlers are increasingly able and willing to talk in their own words about what they like and enjoy about their digital activities and the things they don't like, as the exchange between Jasper Langridge (around three and a half) and interviewer Kylie exemplifies: 'Sometimes I get lots of telly … and I get grumpy.' Some of our vignettes demonstrate how a gentle researcher-offered challenge can motivate a child to talk about and execute digital media actions. This is evident in William Bernard's indignant declaration that the animal that Kylie suggests is a lion is actually a tiger, with William's verbal declarations supplemented by an expansion of the image of the animal discussed. On occasions such as this one, a child can marshal a range of skills and competencies that demonstrate independence of thought and action and a strength of purpose. This pathway is increasingly evident in children as they traverse the toddler years and move towards preschool.

The preschoolers, as the oldest age group in the book, personify 'negotiating' as a capstone competency, with confident talking as the hallmark of the older toddler and with walking defining older infants. Preschoolers often focus on activities that help the child develop and express their sense of self, a desire which Bertenthal and Fischer (1978) argue starts in late infancy, when children begin to recognize themselves in their reflection.

For preschoolers, the nuance of digital interactivity enhanced by artificial intelligence and linguistic processing can be sufficiently responsive for Leela Palmer (four) to construct Apple's digital assistant Siri as a real person. Leela's Siri has a male voice and her digital engagements with Siri are so persuasive that Leela thinks of him as her friend and believes that he, like her, has iPad access. Such 'imaginary companions' are well-established in the literature about children in this age group, with many parents – as is the case with Leela's mum, Linda Palmer – seeing their child as gaining some value from the imagined friendship (Majors & Baines, 2017).

Friendship-formation is also a motivation for some parents' support of their child's digital media use. As Rita Chen says of daughter Lavinia's (two years, four months) love of *Peppa Pig*, 'I don't want, you know, [that] she feel, you know, lonely and then there's no socializing with the other kids'. Rita sees a value of digital media use in helping Lavinia share cultural capital with other children. Such cultural connections become increasingly clear in the preschool years as children are becoming more aware of themselves as individuals who can make independent choices. This is discussed further in the next section since the cusp of preschool and school marks the point at which children's mainly domestic-informed exploration of the digital must adjust to the impact of peer culture and the curriculum-driven school-based agenda.

Only one child in the preschooler cohort, Floyd Jameson (five), was formally enrolled within the compulsory education system, having entered the Reception class at his Primary school in the year he turned five, as mandated by the UK schooling system. The interpolation of a school-based learning framework to direct a child's digital activity removes one aspect of child-driven choice from their patterns of digital engagement. In a sense, it creates dual sets of experiences in the digital world, with important congruencies and differences. As Kent and Facer note (2004), of nine- to eighteen-year-olds, there is 'a reconceptualization of learning on a continuum of formal and informal practices, with the specific location (of home or school) not in itself finally determining, instead rather providing a context for, which of these practices are adopted and approved' (p. 454).

The end-stage of the birth-to-six development journey is the graduation from preschool into school and the child's induction into a planned and managed educational framework. This is where our research stops, for there is already extensive research around the school/home nexus for school children (Kent et al., 2004). This greater body of research relating to school children's digital skills and engagement reflects public investment in curriculum and educational infrastructure and the need to recognize digital skill-based outcomes and competencies. Such research extends back for a generation since, historically, the comprehension and motor skills of school-aged children enabled their use of keyboard and mouse to access the internet. In contrast, the digital enfranchisement of infants, toddlers and preschoolers is comparatively recent.

Learning about more than technology

On the cusp of their formal engagement with the education system, preschoolers are actively learning about the socio-cultural world around them and actuating themselves as individuals and as proto-consumers and citizens. Much of this development is achieved through individual choice and personal self-expression. The preschooler age group naturally contributes more to the family-based ethnographic vignettes than the younger participants. Contributing with both what they do and what they say preschoolers provide evidence of nuanced understandings of their digital media use. For example, Libby Kramer's (four) actions indicate a child who values the opportunity to display her digital abilities and she uses other resources, for example, her toy reindeer, as a currency for distracting sibling Owen (nineteen months), to prevent him from disrupting her exchanges with Leslie.

As well as directly engaging with Leslie and Kylie during the research process, preschoolers are also more likely than younger children to talk about engaging with others during digital play. Often, they engage with siblings, as with Leela (four) and Marissa (fifteen) Palmer's co-use of Snapchat. Preschoolers also use digital play to engage with same-age friends. Kate Andrews-White, for example, talks about how son Liam (almost five) and his friends share their love for Skylanders across three contexts: playing Skylanders digitally, playing with their Skylander action toys and in make-believe games that see the boys pretending to be characters from the Skylanders' world.

While such play may appear gendered, it represents an outcome of interacting social and cultural forces which does not preclude alternative outcomes. Indeed, early research such as that conducted by Katz (1981) indicates that preschoolers' increasing awareness of themselves as individuals separate from others is associated with an increase in gender awareness. Katz notes 'that much of the basic perceptual and cognitive processes' for gender awareness have developed 'by the time the child is ready to enter the school' (1981, p. 40). In comparing children's developing awareness of racial and gender characteristics, Katz also notes that gender awareness is established earlier, speculating that this may reflect gendered parenting roles (1981, pp. 38–9), perhaps more salient in the 1980s than they are today. Indeed, the preschooler age group reveals significant self-differentiation and the development and expression of personal interests and enthusiasms.

Insofar as there is evidence for gendered interests, such as Liam Andrews-White's (four) Skylanders play, other examples include Ben Lawe-Tammell's (five) discussion of virtual 'rough and tumble' play: 'I whack it, like, I go to that chicken – Whack!' This contrasts with some of the girls' self-presentation-based imaginative play such as Leela Palmer's (four) Snapchat stickers and Freya Petersen's (five) use of filters in her make-believe persona as an Etsy-using entrepreneur. Possibly influenced by older sister Elsa (nine), Freya is one of the few children referencing others' uses of the internet and the activities of influencers and thought leaders such as vloggers Stampylonghead and Cookie Swirl C. All the same, dad Jeff rues the consumerist overtones of much of this context and expresses puzzlement at his daughters' preference in watching an adult vlogger who videos herself playing with dolls, rather than his children playing with dolls themselves. This resonates with some parents' comments about other older children, such as when mum Sarah Bernard discusses how Sean (eleven), older brother of William (three) and Connor (five), likes to watch videos of people playing *Minecraft* but doesn't play the game himself.

Diversity in children's digital experience

The discussion of infants', toddlers' and preschoolers' media use, supplemented with the latter part of this chapter, draws attention to some common experiences at different ages. But these also indicate alternative sources of diversity in children's digital lives. While it is more common to consider diversity through terms such as gender, class and ethnicity, the chapter on this topic aims to highlight other dimensions for consideration, especially in terms of possible impacts on digital engagement.

Sometimes diversity arises through parents' characteristics, such as their own orientation to technology. This is demonstrated, for example, in dad Scott Bernard's enthusiastic embrace of technology that he hopes to convey to his children. Alternatively, diversity can arise from broader parenting genres relating to the family's approach to technology, such as the Tosettis's willingness to let their son experiment with whatever he encounters in his environment, including the digital. Meanwhile, the role of parental aspirations is illustrated when digital resources play an important role in helping bridge cultures for bi-cultural families, particularly where parents have moved to a new country. Mum Rita Chen uses children's digital media to introduce Lavinia (twenty-eight months) to the festivals of the broader Anglo/Australian society. At the same time, Lavinia uses her digital skills to help maintain her family heritage, especially in accessing media in her mother tongue, Mandarin.

Birth order and sibling age both make a difference to young children's digital experiences in myriad ways: sometimes supporting, sometimes in conflict, sometimes negotiating (see Olafsson et al. (2017) for a discussion of this in older age groups). There is also a range of possible implications of strained relations between parents as demonstrated by the impactful and not uncommon cases of divorced families. While most families volunteering for this research were dual- or sole-parented rather than alternating-parented, tensions can be heightened when a child spends time in two homes where parents might have different approaches to digital mediation. This is exemplified in the perspectives of two sole-parent fathers contributing to the project who explained how a relationship breakup may involve residual conflict with the other parent that can influence access to and messages about, devices that allow communication between the absent parent and child.

Parents' evaluation of children's learning through digital media

A common thread running through parents' commentaries across these under-six age groups indicates shared awareness that digital media skills and content allow children access to specific communities of interest and cultural capital. As well as keeping them entertained and allowing parents to prioritize non-child centred activities, digital media engagement offers preschoolers an introduction to social interaction, cultural information, taste formation, educational content and skill development. In turn, these uses of digital media support possible trajectories towards imagined occupations. Indeed, one of the motivating frameworks for toddler Simon Brown's (2) parents' choice to empower Simon's exploration of his environment is 'don't kill the scientist'. In these digital imaginaries, as Livingstone and Blum-Ross (2020) make clear, parents see opportunities to support their child's crafting of an enhanced, self-determined, digitally engaged future. Yet skills and opportunities are directly determined by available resources of money, education and technology; any presumption that digital media can level an unequal playing field is illusory.

Most parents, irrespective of whether their child is a passionate and engaged user of interactive devices or not, seem to have a perception of advantages and disadvantages accruing to particular patterns of digital media use. Some parents of young children appear concerned that the mesmerizing impact of digital media might unbalance an otherwise multifaceted, well-rounded childhood.

This was the case with Sergei Mansi (twenty-three months) and Floyd Jameson (five years, 4 months).

Other families referenced concerns around commercialized culture and an induction to consumerism (for example, the Petersens), the capacity for children to unwittingly spend large sums of money online (for example, the Lawe-Tammell), or exposure to inappropriate content (for example, the Davis family). Those children tended to be in the upper age group in our study and often had older siblings at school. This was the case with Freya Petersen (five, with older sibling Elsa, nine); Ben Lawe-Tammell (five, with siblings Amelia twelve and Samantha sixteen) and with Phoebe Davis (five, with brother Jacob, ten).

By the time children are preschoolers, many parents have instituted rules they hope will help minimize risks while maximizing opportunities. Very few parents acknowledge, with Kate Andrews-White as an exception here, that children can also have expectations (and, by implication, rights) to have their own say in their family's rule repertoire. In the Andrews-White case, the children have an expectation of enjoying daily screen time – almost as a quid quo pro for accepting that parents might place limits on how much of that screen time they are allowed.

Although parents might promulgate and adopt rules, they rarely articulate a vision for their children's progressive engagement with technology throughout their childhood and adolescence. Apart from expressing general hopes (for example, the Petersen family) or fears (for example, the Jameson family), few of the families placed the rules and guidance they offer their children in the context of a perceived developmental agenda, where the family's preferred digital engagement strategy prepares its younger members for a specific way of relating to technology and digital media at a particular age and stage. For example, although Lavinia's (two) family (the Zhang/Chens) imagined an educational trajectory from preschool to primary school, no family provided an example of a longer-term digital media use strategy where 'we do this now to achieve such-and-such an outcome by the time my child reaches high school' (Green et al., 2019). These observations imply the absence of a progressive parental digital media strategy as part of parents' chosen ethnotheories (Plowman 2015).

The challenges confronting parents' planning for children's digital futures

While first-time parents sometimes had a plan as to when their child would use technology, as indicated by the Govender family, once children began to reach for a smartphone or seek out a tablet, parents became increasingly likely to provide access in an episodic manner. This was especially the case when the child was tired, needing a break or, as Craig Jameson admits, the parent was 'hung over'. As Green et al. (2019) note, even where parents had strong opinions about, for example, an age for toilet training a child, or their child's progress within the education system, as with the Zhang/Chen family, those parents did not articulate, to us as researchers, specific plans around their child's progressive engagement with digital media. Where parents said they had had a plan for digital media, prior to the birth of their first child, those plans seem generally to be forgotten when the second or subsequent child comes along, as noted in the Bernard and Cullen families.

One of the possible exceptions to the general rule of the parents' episodic mediation strategies relates to the age at which a child might get a personal digital device and, given that access, whether the device should be internet-enabled or capable only of playing content that parents had downloaded and made available off-line. Examples of this parental decision-making in the *Toddlers and Tablets* research include the Andrews-White family (providing a tablet for Liam's fifth birthday), the Spinner family (who are 'a long way off' giving older children Belle (seven) and Alice (nine) their own devices) and the Petersens, whose daughters Freya (five) and Elsa (nine) share a hand-me-down iPhone that can record video and play games but which is not connected to the internet. Significantly, all three of these families – the Andrews-Whites, the Spinners and the Petersens – include children in upper primary: the age at which parents might begin to think about these issues.

In one family, the awareness that a personal media device is a key parental decision appeared to be visible in the breach, rather than the planning. Isabelle Davis keenly felt the inappropriateness of her parents-in-laws' past decision to provide ten-year-old son Jacob with his own device when he was about five or six – Isabelle can't remember Jacob's exact age at that point. Yet, the fact of Jacob's access to a personal device was a vivid element in sister Phoebe's (five) interview, where she describes Jacob's device 'with a stripe' in considerable detail and imagines a future when she will be able to play games with him, with each child using their own tablet. Jacob's parents, when he was five or six, had possibly not discussed when he would have his own device and we were not told whether his grandparents had asked dad Malcolm for his thoughts about gifting a tablet.

While discussion of this kind might helpfully be formulated in advance and then shared with the broader group of people who take an active interest in the child's development, many parents in this age group would think their children are just too young. Indeed, a lack of clarity might simply reflect that this is often a matter of intense debate that parents will address in due course, but not quite yet. There may be a 'timetable' of different problems that preoccupy parents at different stages of their parenting journey, including in relation to digital media. For most families in this research, under six is too early to decide about this issue.

As it is, children in the under-six age group engage in negotiating, discussion and decision-making to borrow adults' and shared media devices. Two participant children were keen to share their perspectives on a relative loss or absence of media access, as when Connor Bernard (five) shared with Kylie that 'my daddy took the Xbox away'. Phoebe Davis has constructed a future situation 'when I will get a – iPad' as is the case with brother Jacob. These clear articulations of loss and longing indicate children's desire to articulate wants and needs clearly when digital media access is at stake.

Other parameters may also be addressed in discussions around young children's episodic use of digital media, including when digital media is generally kept out of sight to keep it 'out of mind' (as with the Langridge and Brown families). In households with siblings and shared access, the topics involved may include whose turn it is, who has the better reason for access and the important matter of when a device will be relinquished, including likely discussions about a time frame for personal use. Such dynamics were evident in the exchanges between Imelda Spinner (five) and older sister Belle (seven) that took place during Leslie's research with the Spinner family. Incidental verbalizing and the associated reasoning and persuasion all help promote young children's communicative skills while deepening their understandings of self and others.

Although parents sometimes acknowledge that they weren't entirely happy with their own digital habits (as with Francoise Jameson), they did not generally discuss how their personal experiences with digital media might influence their particular parenting ethnotheories or what they might hope to do differently to reduce the chance of their child developing similarly problematic digital behaviours. Even where parents were clear they wanted their child to have a particular approach to digital media, for example, mum Angie's hope for the very young Eliza Govender (four months) that Eliza would not be part of a 'selfie generation', or Jenna who doesn't want her daughter Julia Campbell (eleven months) to feel constantly connected to a device in the future, parents tended to focus on the here and now; for example, where Ben Lawe-Tammell (five) can't use digital media in the morning before going to preschool because he won't get dressed if he does, or where Liam (four) and Scott (two and a half) Andrews-White can't engage with interactive media after bath time because it stops them sleeping. Rather than suggesting an absence of pre-thought, however, parents' priorities indicate the just-in-time aspects of child-rearing, as if they feel 'we're busy enough with raising a young child: the future teenager will have their turn in due course'.

The range of families' approaches to children's digital media use and the different parenting genres in evidence in this research as sketched out in Table 1.2 underline the uniquely complex and demanding task confronting contemporary parents. Every parent we interviewed indicated the importance they placed upon supporting their child's digital media use. Our hope is that the wide and detailed range of stories and insights these parents have shared within this book might help counter some of the panic around children's activities online that regularly circulates in the public sphere (Jaunzems et al., 2019), complicating what is already a complex matter.

A clear role is also indicated here for policymakers who to date have given too little attention to digital technologies for children under six. As noted in earlier chapters, authoritative guidance is often lacking with sometimes confusing and contradictory information about the most suitable technologies, the availability of content for children and the best ways for parents to support their children's digital skills. Policymakers play key roles in setting standards, as well as shaping and developing policies that can influence those industries that provide digital technologies, services and content. As we have argued, raising awareness of the importance of designing for children, integrating safety by design, privacy by design and building in considerations of children's best interests in the evolving digital environment is central to this policy function and vital for planning for children's digital futures.

Parents' support of their young children's development

At this early stage in their child's life, parents appear to focus more on the physical environment than the digital one, allowing the child to explore their everyday world, encouraging them, interacting with them and demonstrating that they appreciate the child's achievements. The place of digital media in this process varies. Some parents, like Karla Spinner, treat the digital as gimmicky, while others embrace the digital world. One example of this is dad Lorenzo Tosetti, who argues that the internet and digital media provide son Leopoldo with a much more stimulating environment than he himself enjoyed as a child. Many parents, like Claire Petersen, express reservations about young children's digital media use while, at the same time, showing themselves impressed by what their child can do technologically and what children learn from their activities online.

For most parents, the clearest merit they see in digital device use is the role it plays in supporting children's learning. Building on and further exemplifying the work of previous researchers (e.g. Plowman et al., 2008; Plowman et al., 2010a), our interviews illustrated how learning with and through digital engagement is a multifaceted activity. It covers learning operational skills (how to use devices), learning about the world (numbers, shapes, counting, animals), developing dispositions (persistence, attention, exploring, problem solving) and encountering the socio-cultural world (birthdays, Christmas, music appreciation).

Threaded through these chapters on infants, toddlers and preschoolers are observations on other influences which impact on parents' understandings of and attitudes towards digital technology use. As the research shows, parents draw on diverse sources of guidance to help inform their digital parenting. Professional groups including clinicians, health professionals and educators stand out as important influences when parents come to consider issues such as how much digital use is appropriate, the developmental impact of different kinds of activities or balancing physical activity with digital engagement. Specific policy guidance for the age groups addressed in this book is often lacking, with professional discourses that frequently fall back on generalized admonitions about 'too much screen time' creating confusion and further dilemmas for parents who seek help in dealing with the practicalities of managing young children's busy lives. The research demonstrates that children are often surrounded by numerous digital devices in their homes, indicating that professional guidance appears out of touch with the reality of the place of digital technologies in the lives of children.

Finally and to balance stereotypes of children engaged with technologies in isolation, the project's video materials demonstrate how, at times, parents use digital devices to prompt their children's learning. While this certainly may involve assisting children to use hardware and software, it covers much more, including: helping the child to understand the world; aiding in the development of positive dispositions; and, harnessing the child's technology use as a springboard for raising other issues, just as a parent might do if reading a book aloud to their child (Barron et al., 2009). Throughout this research, parents offer numerous examples of how they engage in social and creative use of technology to help their child's learning processes and support a better understanding of the world around them.

Planning for children's digital futures

Parents' preparations for parenthood were as different as the approaches to parenting they said they had adopted. Some parents chose to embrace highly structured family routines (for example, the Lim-Park and Zhang/Chen families). Some had expected to parent in one way and found themselves adopting a very different style of parenting (the Mansi and Cullen families). Yet others took a 'whatever works' approach (the Andrews-White family and, to some extent, Sandra Ross). Not surprisingly, the children's digital experiences and patterns of technology use varied significantly, partly reflecting parents' approaches to digital mediation and partly reflecting children's individual characteristics (as in the Lim-Park and Langridge families). Penny Ross's (three) digital skills, for example, were compared negatively by mum Sandra to the 'scary good' digital competencies that sibling Frankie (six) had demonstrated at Penny's age. Along with the Lim-Park, Langridge and Ross families, many others indicated that parents' approaches to digital parenting varied over time, circumstance and with the specific needs of the child concerned, with Ellen Brent providing possibly the clearest example of this dynamic in action.

This book adds to the evidence base regarding the ways that parents of children from birth to six years old help their child design a desired trajectory through skill acquisition and device use that responds to the family context and to what the family imagines to be that child's emerging digital future. Although the participant families are overly middle class, well-educated and from the global North, there is ample evidence of a wide range of differing approaches to these issues reflecting particularities of family culture and circumstance. Tomorrow's technology will always differ from today's, but there are many ways in which parents actively help prepare their child for a lifetime of digital media use. One particular initiative that may help protect children against over-dependence on device use and support their capacity for disengagement might be a family decision not to have interactive media in bedrooms overnight (Green & Haddon, 2015, Nikken et al., 2018). If adopted, however, this kind of strategy is best introduced in the under-six age group, with parents modelling the practice (Livingstone et al., 2015).

Every parent in this research wants the best-possible outcome from their child's digital engagement, over time and in relation to an unfolding series of technologies. Even so, the digital is only one consideration among many and parents often have higher priorities for their children such as consideration for other people, playing in the open air, learning from and being stimulated by their environment, or regular enjoyment of physical activity.

The stories that parents and children shared with us indicate that each family interacts with digital media in their own way and often unpredictably decided in the moment, while also constructing rules and mutual expectations to maximize benefit. Each set of idiosyncratic rules and expectations reflects the family that chooses and adopts them, yet this does not mean that they are necessarily instinctive or intuitive, free of deliberation and choice: far from it. Yet the kind of information that can support such deliberation and help parents tailor their families' digital culture to meet their own hopes and aspirations has generally been lacking. The all-important information about active digital parenting in the domestic routines of children prior to their starting formal schooling has, in the main, been absent. This book aims to speak to that gap. We are immensely grateful to the families who generously shared their lives, perspective and histories of digital interactivity with us. Our case studies and family vignettes offer pointers to the diversity, creativity and exuberance that parents bring to digital parenting and to their children's experiences in digital media engagement. Along the way, this book has revealed multiple challenges faced by parents as they grapple with bringing up young children in a complex and changing digital world. It has also revealed many limitations on the resources they can access as they seek to resolve these challenges. However, by celebrating the range of approaches that families bring to this task and recognizing the contribution made by parents, grandparents and early years' educators to the positive outcomes of digital media use in early childhood, this book offers a fundamentally optimistic view of young children's digital futures.

Appendix

Families contributing to this research
(in pseudonymous alphabetical order)

This appendix offers vignettes of participant families organized in alphabetical order. Please see the Chapter 1 (birth to six years) for information about age-of-child order and please consult the index (by family name and by first name) to see their key contributions to chapters. Some families have two children in the target age group (birth to five years) and, in that situation, children from the same family are referenced in different chapters. Thus, the twenty-two research families contribute data relating to twenty-nine children across the three age groups: infants, toddlers and preschool. The contributing families and participating children in the reference age group are as follows:

1. Andrews-White (AU) children: Scott, male, two years, six months (toddler); Liam, male, four years, eleven months (preschool)

Parents Kate (forty) and Richard (forty-eight) have three children. Eldest, Ben (eight), is at primary school. Richard works away from home (fly-in, fly-out) while Kate is a part-time student and has home duties. They live in a southern suburb of the greater Perth Metropolitan area. The family has a range of digital technologies: two laptops, two iPads, a desktop computer, a tablet, three smartphones (Kate has two, sharing with the boys), an Xbox, a DVD player and four televisions. Kate trouble-shoots the iPads and smartphone; Richard is the laptop expert. The children are comfortable with FaceTiming Richard when he's away and Skyping their Brisbane-based aunt.

Ben was three and a half when he started playing with the iPad, but Liam first used it at one. Scott gained access as soon as he started reaching for it. Liam rarely asks for help but if he does, it's related to the phone and he asks Ben or Kate. Scott uses the iPad independently, but Kate has disabled Siri, which could not understand Scott's words causing frustration. Kate also prevents app deletion because Scott was accidentally deleting her apps. Parental controls and

Table A1 Family members participating in digital media use in early childhood – Birth to six

Family and country	Mum	Dad	Child 1	Child 2
Andrews-White (AU)	Kate	Richard	Scott (T)	Liam (P)
Bernard (AU)	Sarah	Scott	William (T)	Connor (P)
Brent (UK)	Elisabeth	Ted	Ellen (P)	
Brown (UK)	Klara	Jerry	Simon (T)	
Campbell (AU)	Jenna	Adam	Julia (I)	
Cheung-Yeo (AU)	Marie	Jo	Samuel (I)	
Cullen (AU)	Sherryl		Finn (I)	
Davis (AU)	Isabelle	Malcolm	Emma (T)	Phoebe (P)
Greenfield (UK)	Trish	Danny	Andrew (I)	
Govender (AU)	Angie	Yussef	Eliza (I)	
Jameson (UK)	Francoise	Craig	Evan (T)	Floyd (P)
Kramer (UK)	Stella	Michael	Owen (I)	Libby (P)
Langridge (AU)	Louisa	Dean	Cecilia (I)	Jasper (T)
Lawe-Tammell (AU)	Rosalie	Richard	Ben (P)	
Lim-Park (AU)	Mi Na	Andrew	Emily (I)	Michael (P)
Mansi (UK)	Nadia	Rohan	Sergei (I)	
Palmer (UK)	Linda		Leela (P)	
Petersen (AU)	Claire	Jeff	Freya (P)	
Ross (UK)	Sandra	Ron	Penny (P)	
Spinner (UK)	Karla	Daniel	Imelda (P)	
Tosetti (UK)	Mirabella	Lorenzo	Leopoldo (T)	
Zhang/Chen (AU)	Rita	Stanley	Lavinia (T)	

Key: (I) Infant; (T) Toddler; (P) Preschool.

Family vignettes are arranged in alphabetical order.

security settings have been enabled on the iPad and on YouTube. Kate worries about pornography, violence and 'shooter' games, potential bullying and griefing (of Ben, on *Minecraft*) and the possibility that gameplay stifles creativity. Kate notes, however, that playing games digitally inspires non-tech play offline.

Kate says the boys go online for about an hour a day after school (between 3.00 and 6.00 pm), but they do see screen-time at an 'entitlement'. Interactive screen time is extended on weekends and holidays but always ends at 6.00 pm because Ben has problems sleeping if he's online later. The family watches television in the evenings.

2. Bernard family (AU) children: William, male, three years, six months (toddler); Connor, male, five years (preschool)

The two youngest of the five Bernard children (Xavier thirteen; Sean, eleven; Chloe, nine; Connor, five; and William, three) contributed to the research. Parents Sarah and Scott (early forties) recently moved to a new-built house in Perth's outer northern suburbs, between the ocean and parkland. Together they run a family business selling solar panels. Sarah is home-based, while Scott does marketing, sales and site visits. Both come from large families themselves. Xavier is a hands-on big brother, helping with the two younger children. The family has a puppy and four canaries.

Xavier has a laptop, at his high school's request and Sean has just been given one because he's going to high school next year. Sean and Chloe currently attend the local state primary. Connor has kindergarten three days a week with William attending the same kindergarten for one day; they also attend childcare two half-days per week. With five children and a big mortgage, Scott and Sarah watch their spending. The three older children have hand-me-down phones while other devices are communal, with different tablets having different apps. William and Connor use whichever device is handy and charged, mainly to access YouTube and Netflix. They understand password requirements and ask if they need help.

Dad Scott is an 'early adopter' of technology, seeing children's digital media access as important preparation for their future lives. Sarah's concerned about safety online. She thinks children have access to too many devices, but she is 'amazed' at how Connor and William seem to intuitively know how digital media work. The parents believe their children self-monitor and withdraw from inappropriate content, but Scott has an alert on some apps that warns him if a child accesses adult content. Given the ages of the older children, parental controls limit viewing to below (not including) MA15+; excessively violent games are forbidden.

3. Brent family (UK) child: Ellen, female, four years, six months (preschool)

The Brents live in a semi-detached house in South London. Dad Ted (forty-four) has a post-graduate diploma and works in international development. Elisabeth (forty-three) has a degree and is a part-time finance officer for an NGO. They have three children: Andrew (eleven), James (nine) and Ellen (four).

Diagnosed with a chromosomal disorder 22Q Deletion Syndrome (also called DiGeorge Syndrome), Ellen struggles to talk. Four days a week she attends a special needs-friendly nursery. The staff can all sign and Ellen brings a tablet provided by her local authority to help her communicate. It's not a connected device, but pressing the key letters sounds out words. Despite the challenges she faces, Ellen is extremely motivated to speak and has used her own iPad (shared with her mother) to find help. She enjoys practising speech with 'Steve': an English-teaching program designed for children who are non-native speakers. Ellen likes Steve's comedic presentation and the opportunity to repeat words as often as she wishes.

Suffering from chronic digestive problems, a symptom of 22Q syndrome, Ellen needs to take foul-tasting medicine. Mum Elisabeth hides the medicine in pureed fruit and lets Ellen use the tablet as a distraction while she feeds her daughter. When Ellen needs to use the toilet, Elisabeth allows Ellen to take her iPad with her so she can relax, where she interacts with content of her choice (from YouTubeKids) to pass the time.

Ellen's two brothers have limits on their technology time but understand that Ellen requires different rules because she can't read and write whereas they can. Elisabeth anticipates that once Ellen learns to read and speak without help, her tablet hours will be restricted. The entire family (parents too) operate with technology rules such as 'no technology in bedrooms'.

4. Brown family (UK) child: Simon, male, two years (toddler)

The Brown family lives in eastern outer London, in a residential area with terraced Victorian housing. Jerry (thirty-eight) has a masters degree and is director of a family company. Klara (thirty-seven) is also masters-level educated in her native country, Slovakia, and has an accountancy qualification from the UK. She has lived in London for nine years and chooses not to undertake paid work while Simon (two) is young, noting that Slovakian maternity leave lasts for three years.

Klara is not worried about smartphone overuse since she only allows Simon limited access. She says he's very interested in everything around him. Jerry notes that, while they don't prevent Simon from accessing the smartphone when he wants to, they do encourage him to do more 'active' pursuits. Klara notes that Simon learned about numbers and letters from YouTube, well before she had planned to teach these to him. Once they realized Simon was keen to learn from YouTube, Jerry and Klara encouraged him to do so.

Simon has a genetic disorder that discourages him from eating. The smartphone distracts him, making it easier for his parents to feed him. Dinner time is consequently one of the main occasions that Simon has smartphone access.

Klara says she also uses her smartphone to occupy Simon when he might be bored: indeed, that's how Simon was originally introduced to the device, at six months old, on a flight to Slovakia. It's also clear that Klara actively helps Simon engage with software, overcome difficulties and understand tasks. The family occasionally uses Skype when Klara is with Simon in Slovakia, while Jerry stays in the UK. Simon recognized Jerry on the screen but, early on, lost interest in communicating this way.

5. Campbell family (AU) child: Julia, female, twelve months (infant)

Jenna and Adam are thirty-nine, raising only child Julia in inner-city Perth, near parkland and a lake. Julia's maternal grandma cares for her three days a week and lives five minutes' walk away. Her parents have flexible work arrangements, allowing them extra hands-on time. With nearby aunts and uncles and cousins aged five to fifteen, Julia is the baby in the family.

Adam and Jenna both have university business degrees, with Adam working in sales and Jenna in a health-related charity. Jenna has health issues and her pregnancy was a delightful surprise heralding an abrupt lifestyle change and re-evaluation. She sees herself as using TV and digital media to distract and entertain Julia, so she can work from home and attend to household chores. Jenna's mother chooses not to use technology on the days she cares for Julia.

An early adopter, Adam grew up using digital technology before his friends had it. However, he's concerned about privacy and on-call availability. Jenna is a more cautious tech user who worries about algorithms and social media and the psychological implications of constant connectivity. She hopes that regulation will eventually catch up with big tech.

The family has a variety of media including two TVs, smartphones, laptops, iPads, desktop, Nintendo Wii, a DVD player and a Kindle. Julia's favourite 'device' is the TV remote. She uses buttons to vary channel and volume and loves the cause and effect, while appearing not able to swipe touchscreens. Adam and Jenna don't so much limit Julia's screen time as prefer to share books, reading and active play with her. Easy-going, with an 'it takes a village' approach to child-rearing augmented by online and expert advice, the parents seek expert help for challenges like promoting good sleeping habits.

6. Cheung-Yeo family (AU) child: Samuel, male, twenty-one months (infant)

In a new family home in a southern Perth suburb, Marie, Samuel's mum, is from Vietnam while dad Jo was born in Singapore. They met in Australia while Jo was completing his PhD in IT and Marie was studying Law. Jo works full time for an internet service provider, while Marie works as a part-time lawyer. Most of their family live overseas and Jo and Marie aim to visit their families every year. Relatives come to Perth more rarely but, when they do, may stay with Marie and Jo for extended periods of time.

At twenty-one months, Samuel is quiet, yet active. When Samuel turned one, Jo resumed full-time work and Samuel started attending childcare two days per week. The centre has a strong music-based curriculum, reflecting a shared passion of his parents. Alongside musical instruments, the children practise meditation and yoga as part of their daily routine. The curriculum doesn't feature (~avoids) digital technologies, but educators use tablets to play music and take photos of the children, compiling daily visual diaries for parents. Samuel used to be a reluctant attender but now looks forward to childcare.

Jo is the more protective, conservative parent while Marie likes to experiment, introducing Samuel to new activities. She encourages Samuel's art-based play and involves him in cooking: they also enjoy being outdoors. Samuel's parents have a desktop computer, four laptops, three tablets and four smartphones. Jo and Marie have agreed between them on times and places where Samuel can access their devices and, while restricted in these ways, no tech is forbidden. Jo notes there seem to be culturally specific differences in advice for parents: for example, keep 'screen until later [age]' in Australia versus a 'way to occupy them when having meals, at the mall, when they're crying' in Singapore.

7. Cullen family (AU) child: Finn, male, fourteen months (infant)

Sherryl Cullen has four children, Elle (sixteen), Adam (twelve), Alexa (nine) and baby Finn (fourteen months). Sherryl is a sole parent: her first marriage ended some years ago and her second partner, Finn's father left while Sherryl was pregnant and they are not in touch. The three older children see their father every fortnight or so in line with his fly-in fly-out lifestyle. Elle and Adam attend the local high school and both have a genetic condition that requires regular monitoring. Alexa is a primary student.

The family currently lives in a large home in the north-eastern outskirts of the Perth metropolitan area, supported by Sherryl's parents, who live with them and help care for the children. This frees up time for Sherryl's university teaching degree studies which she started while pregnant with Finn. Sherryl sometimes uses the creche at the university and she and Finn also attend a mother and baby music class.

Sherryl feels her father has less of a parent role with her and her sister, but instead concentrates on being a grandparent. A stay-at-home mum in her first relationship, Sherryl, says she parented her three older children intuitively. Without Finn's father around to bounce ideas off, however, she feels less confident raising Finn. Further, her own mother sometimes makes suggestions that Sherryl finds unhelpful, especially in relation to Sherryl's 'attachment' parenting style.

Finn is a happy child and enjoys the company of the three adults and his older siblings. There is ample digital media in the house with the adults and the two older children each having smartphones (five in all) and with a shared desktop in the house, plus three personal laptops (for Sherryl, Sherryl's father and oldest child Elle). Elle is an academic achiever and her laptop is supplied by her school's gifted and talented program.

8. Davis family (AU) children: Emma, female, two years (toddler); Phoebe, female, five years (preschool)

Dad Malcolm (forty-two), mum Isabelle (forty-one) have three children: Jacob (ten), Phoebe and Emma. Living in the semi-rural hills area on the outskirts of Perth, they have chickens, two cats and a dog. Malcolm's family lives a long distance away on the eastern side of Australia, but Isabelle has a large family living locally. Malcolm's parents aren't comfortable with digital technology, so, in order for the children to talk to their paternal grandparents via Skype, Malcolm's brother needs to be with them. Otherwise, the family uses text. Malcolm and Isabelle work in the city: Isabelle Monday to Wednesday, Malcolm full-time, but with some flexibility in hours.

Phoebe (in preschool in the early childhood centre) and Jacob (in grade 5) attend a local primary school which is co-located with a 'before and after school care' centre. Emma's childcare is nearby and the children all go to school or childcare on the three days when Isabelle is working. There's a strict 'no TV or devices' rule before school and 'no TV after school' except Fridays.

Phoebe's class uses a Smartboard but doesn't provide access to individual devices. However, the Davis family share four iPads and Phoebe and Jacob use these for reading and maths homework, as well as entertainment. Isabelle is amazed at the children's digital skills, saying she's never taught them how to use digital devices. Emma can navigate YouTube and recognizes the photo icon on Isabelle's iPhone. Phoebe can use apps but prefers that Jacob opens and sets up her games, generally tiring of them quickly. Jacob is forbidden to play violent games, or *Minecraft*, which Malcolm sees as a waste of time.

9. Greenfield family (UK) child: Andrew, male, twenty-one months (infant)

Trish (thirty-five), Danny (forty-one) and only child Andrew live in a South London flat in a middle-class socioeconomic area. The closest shops are twenty minutes' walk; there's a park ten minutes away. Both parents work full time and Andrew attends a nursery every day. His parents feel this encourages a structured, social experience, but he needs to 'let off steam' at home. They've done a parenthood training course and are members of the online group, *mumsnet*, but feel there's no one way to raise a child because all children are different.

Danny is a master's degree-qualified careers advisor for university students; Trish is an arts graduate who designs digital projects and specializes in web interfaces. They are hands-on parents, with Trish more frequently engaging Andrew in conversation and play while Danny attends to the 'to do' list, such as changing Andrew at one point in the interview and running a bath for him. Trish doesn't allow Andrew to use portable media, tablets or smartphones and she expressed surprise that Danny is more liberal. Trish's preference is to engage tactile play at this stage of Andrew's development, feeling that Andrew can learn digital technology skills at school, or earlier if it's part of childcare. Andrew gets Trish to play his favourite YouTube videos on the family TV and can also persuade her to co-watch with him on her phone. Danny says he uses Andrew's YouTube viewing as a break, but Trish sees YouTube as a discussion starter. She's concerned that Andrew may become 'obsessed', even though he often wants to sample new content for a short time, rather than watch it through.

Trish uses FaceTime to connect Andrew with her father and Andrew recognizes him on screen. She finds Andrew is less grumpy and calmer if she shows him family photos on her phone.

10. Govender family (AU) child: Eliza, female, four months (infant)

The Govenders live in a northern Perth suburb close to amenities, a public transport node and a beach. Mum Angie (forty-one) is on maternity leave having given birth recently to first child, Eliza. Angie is a communications instructor for a university and does some teaching online. The family dog is a three-year-old Schnauzer, Ziggy.

Dad Yussef (forty) works as an Occupational Safety and Health manager in the resource industry and has a long commute to a manufacturing and processing hub beyond the metro area. He wasn't part of the interview, but Angie sends WhatsApp images to Yussef during the day to involve him in Eliza's routines.

Angie has many concerns about popular platforms such as Facebook, Instagram and Snapchat but uses Facebook to engage with family and friends, while limiting the photos she shares online of Eliza. Angie is Perth born and bred, with some family in Melbourne, but Yussef's family is international, spread between Australia and Zambia, where he was raised. Both sets of grandparents have divorced and remarried and Eliza has a global family network, including seven grandparents and a number of half- and step-aunts and uncles. Angie and Yussef keep in touch with absent family using Skype and FaceTime.

Eliza was born prematurely and spent her first few days in a Neonatal Intensive Care Unit at the local teaching hospital. In consultation with specialist midwives and her GP, Angie uses apps to help monitor Eliza's progress and development. Given her infancy, Eliza does not interact with digital media or television and her parents try to engage her in tactile play while foreseeing a point when they will introduce her to digital media.

11. Jameson family (UK) children: Evan, male, three years, six months (toddler); Floyd, male, five years, four months (preschool)

Mum Francoise (forty-one) and dad Craig (thirty-eight) are both dual nationals with Francoise originally from France and Craig from Australia. Craig runs his own business as a procurement consultant while Francoise works with a financial services regulator. Francoise has family living close by their inner-city home in London's Hackney borough, while Craig's close family are in Australia. These parents initially indicated they couldn't contribute to the research since they don't really 'allow their children to use smartphones and tablets'. This seemed interesting, but it became clear that it was an overstatement, with both children accessing digital media in a range of circumstances. Evan attends preschool while Floyd recently started Primary Reception class (from age five, in the UK).

Francoise describes herself as 'addicted' to her phone, preferring checking her iPhone for new emails than 'reading a magazine or book', while Craig says his technology addiction is to gaming. The family own several laptops, iPads, smartphones, Kindles, along with one games console, one DVD player and one smart TV. The children also have access to 'electronic toys', such as Leap Frog, which Francoise hopes will help the boys learn French.

Craig and Francoise have an ambivalent relationship with digital media, initially perceiving themselves as not allowing their children to use smartphones and tablets; however, they also reflect on how they've allowed the children to flick through photos on their phones. They observed with concern that their children now 'know intuitively how to flick' and how this has led the children to become intrigued and 'tempted' by technology. In addition, Craig and Francoise can both identify times when they have lent the boys an iPad to play with, including long car journeys, on the train and when Craig is 'hung over in the mornings'.

12. Kramer family (UK) children: Owen, male, nineteen months (infant); Libby, female, four years, one month (preschool)

Mum Stella (thirty-one), dad Michael (twenty-eight), Libby and Owen live in a terrace house on the edge of a commuter town located twenty miles from London. Stella completed A levels and works as a part-time receptionist in a local primary school; Michael is a diploma-qualified management accountant. The children attend nursery for a day and a half, a toddlers' group twice a week and a Bible study group. Stella was the main interviewee and had a friend in to play with the children, but they still interrupted, wanting her attention.

The family has a range of media including a computer, a Kindle Fire tablet, another tablet, a smartphone, another phone, a games console (mainly for Netflix), TV and a DVD player. The parents seem comparatively relaxed about their children's technology use, with Libby using apps before she was two, particularly on longer car journeys, although Stella prefers taking toys and colouring books to cafes. Allowed to play with a connected smartphone and tablet, Libby likes *CBeebies* games and *Storytime* but can get lost between apps. Owen is interested and copies Libby's activities, but can't yet use digital media. Stella is concerned that Libby has fewer ICT skills than her nursery peers and now encourages more computer-based activity at home.

Stella bases her parenting on experience of caring for younger siblings, talking with friends and work in a nursery. She tends to select friends with similar approaches to parenthood, ending a friendship with a family she felt was lax, although she recognizes the validity of differences in approach. Stella thinks nursery is a richer learning environment than home and tries to structure similar learning rich afternoon activities when she is caring for her children.

13. Langridge family (AU) children: Cecilia, female, nineteen months (infant); Jasper, male, three years, five months (toddler)

The Langridge family comprises mum Louisa (forty-one, from Belgium), dad Dean (fifty-one, from Ireland but with family in Perth), Cecilia, Jasper and Rufus the dog. They live in a 100-year-old cottage in the outer Perth metropolitan region of the Perth's hills. Though with European family connections, they last holidayed in Europe after Jasper's birth but haven't travelled overseas since.

Dean is a drive-in, drive-out mining supervisor working several hours' journey from Perth on a roster rotation that regularly changes his workdays. When he's home, Dean minds the children while Louisa is at work and Dean's parents also offer irregular care. Louisa, a part-time lecturer and freelance marketer, otherwise uses university childcare. She's grateful that childcare offers craft and messy play, since she prefers walking local trails with her children, or playing in the garden. Passionate about multiculturalism, Louisa is pleased the children's childcare community is a diverse one. She values the internet for its access to multilingual resources while still wanting Jasper and Cecilia to play in nature.

Jasper is a reserved child and struggles with toilet training, while Cecilia has a determined, independent personality. Jasper enjoys the family's trampoline and loves his parents reading to him. He accesses Louisa's smartphone and iPad but needs help to open apps and gets easily frustrated. Cecilia mimics Jasper's tech use and has accidentally phoned people and locked Louisa's phone. Louisa says she's addicted to tech herself, but she's pleased that Jasper can be distracted away from devices. Sometimes using media as an audio-only source, Louisa ensures that the children aren't always watching a screen. She admits to using technology as a childminder, to get on with her household tasks, while Dean is away. Indeed, Jasper and Cecilia have listened to a baby music app since they were weeks old.

14. Lawe-Tammell family (AU) child: Ben, male, five years (preschool)

The Lawe-Tammell family lives in a four-bed apartment in a stylish converted warehouse with ample outdoor space in an affluent but alternative southern suburb of Perth. There are three children—Samantha (sixteen), Amelia (twelve) and Ben (five); and parents Rosalie Lawe (fifty) and Richard Tammell (forty-seven). Samantha and Amelia care for two rescue cats and a dog and the family also has four chickens and is thinking about getting a duck.

Mum Rosalie did not complete high school and is now an entrepreneur with shares in two stores and an online retail business, while dad Richard is general manager of a boutique hotel chain and often travels for work. The older children attend a private girls' school while Ben is a preschool pupil three-days per week at the local community-based school previously attended by his sisters. On other weekdays Ben is in full-time childcare and has been since he was ten months old.

Everyone apart from Ben has a smartphone and Samantha has an iPad which she shares willingly. There's also a Mac for family use. Rosalie oversees the children's technology access and loves her iPhone, but pretends she can't turn on a TV. Although she is generally laissez-faire, the older children have signed 'user agreements' as part of a school initiative around cyber-safety. All the children are encouraged to self-regulate their digital activities.

Both Richard and Rosalie have laptops, but Rosalie leaves her laptop at work. Ben has free access to digital media and is a confident user. He plays *Minecraft*, including in multiplayer mode on a hosted server, with other children from school and childcare. He has a well-developed concept of 'goodies v baddies' and his games include fantasy violence such as killing dragons and blowing up trucks. His kindergarten class has a Mac, which Ben says is used for games, while the childcare centre makes use of a smartboard.

15. Lim-Park family (AU) children: Emily, female, twenty-three months (infant); Michael, male, four years (preschool)

Emily and Michael Lim-Park live in a multi-generational household with mum, Mi Na (forty), dad Andrew (forty-two) and matriarch grandmother Yu Na (sixty-five), who migrated to Australia to help out when Michael was a few weeks old. Residents of a leafy housing estate in a suburb twenty minutes north of Perth city Andrew's Mandarin-speaking extended family members live nearby. Because they were comparatively late to parenthood, most of the Lim-Parks' friends' children are in their teens.

Meeting as overseas post-graduate students in Australia Andrew (from Singapore) and Mi Na (from Korea) both work in IT-related areas. Andrew is employed by a sizeable multinational organization; Mi Na teaches digital game design to post-secondary students. Emily and Michael are mother-tongue Korean speakers with both Mi Na and Yu Na using Korean with them. Andrew tends to speak English at home, since it's the parents' common language, but the family also spends time with his nearby family, who speak Mandarin. Yu Na is Emily's principal carer when Mi Na is at work and Andrew does most of the preschool drop-off and pick-up for Michael (supported by Yu Na).

Michael attends a nearby Montessori school that recommends children should be ten before using digital media. Both parents now discourage their children's interactions with digital devices, but this wasn't the case originally. Mi Na removed access when Michael was three and Emily not yet one, upon advice from the school. She sometimes allows limited 'passive' viewing of YouTube Kids during snack time and, for Michael, when she is busy with Emily. Additionally, the family co-uses a Korean chat app Kakao Talk to connect with their Korean-based family. Teen cousins living locally are adept digital media users, but they know they shouldn't use it around Michael and Emily.

16. Mansi family (UK) child: Sergei, male, twenty-three months (infant)

The Mansi family lives in a spacious flat in a block of apartments in Camden, just outside central London in a wealthy middle-class area. Rohan (thirty-four), originally from Canada, works part time as an academic and part time as a yoga instructor. He has a PhD. Nadia (thirty-eight) is from Ukraine and has lived in the UK for seventeen years. She has an MPhil and currently stays at home with Sergei (twenty-three months). The maternal grandmother spends up to six months every year in London with the family to help and be around her grandson. The paternal grandmother is of Indian descent and visits often, too – both were in the home at the time of the interview.

Rohan and Nadia had been wary of letting Sergei access media before he was eighteen months, since Rohan had read that technology was not so good for brain development because it involved too passive an interaction. But when Sergei was six months old, Nadia had been alone and needed to distract him in his high chair, so gave him a tablet for some minutes while she prepared his meal. She had felt 'ashamed' about using the tablet as a babysitter and felt that there was some stigma attached to this.

In principle, Rohan said he would take the device away if Sergei played too long on it, but in practice Sergei was usually only on the iPad or smartphone for short periods, given that he has a short attention span due to his age. Sometimes Sergei just enjoyed looking at any app where that was something happening, like the British Airways app showing flights times. But he also had preferences – currently for trains and diggers. Sergei was also happy to watch real-world scenarios, like trains coming and going. He could also name the tube lines he wanted to watch.

17. Palmer family (UK) child: Leela, female, four years, six months (preschool)

Sole parent Linda (thirty-three) lives in a flat in a high-density, ethnically diverse, inner London housing estate. She has two daughters, Marissa (fifteen) studying for her General Certificate of Secondary Education qualifications (GCSEs) and Leela. Linda left school with GCSEs and work-oriented National Vocational Qualifications (NVQs). Currently outside the paid workforce, Linda hopes to find a job when Leela goes to school. At present, Leela attends the same preschool as Penny Ross (a toddler in this book) three days a week, along with cousin Charlemagne (Linda's sister's daughter). Linda sees raising Leela as very different from her experience of young motherhood with Marissa, when there were fewer resources and supports.

Services are patchy in the housing estate, including telecoms services. Linda leaves her flat and goes outside the building to get a reliable signal. The local shopping centre and tube station are a fifteen-minute walk, but there's a park nearby and some corner stores. When the interview started, Leela was playing with her toys but she asked to go on the tablet and accessed that while sitting on Linda's lap.

Leela first used a tablet when she was two and a half, mainly for accessing nursery rhymes but in the past year she is also accessing Linda's smartphone. There is some drama around Leela's tablet use, since Linda thinks Leela would be constantly on the tablet, given the chance. Leela has a strong sense of connection to the device and says she believes Siri is real. At the same time, Linda is pleased at the level of digital media skills that Leela has developed and surprised at the way YouTube videos have increased Leela's general knowledge. Linda worries that she may sometimes use the tablet to occupy Leela, for example, on journeys. Leela turns to mum, Linda, and sister, Marissa, in that order, if she needs support online or in-app.

18. Petersen family (AU) child: Freya, female, five years (preschool)

The Petersen family consists of dad Jeff (forty-one), mum Claire (forty-three), daughters Elsa (nine) and Freya (five) and Claire's mother Barbara, who lives in a granny flat in the garden. The main dwelling is an older three-bedroom cottage in an inner southern suburb of Perth. There are several pets: two small dogs, a cat and a goldfish.

Jeff works part time at an educational facility while Claire works three days per week as a medical illustrator and also runs several online businesses, through eBay and Etsy shops. They share childcare with grandmother Barbara, juggling schedules to cover the girls' activities. Jeff's parents live overseas and the families keep in touch with FaceTime and Skype.

The Petersens have only lived in their current home for the past twelve months. The girls attend a primary school in the next suburb, with Elsa in grade four and Freya in pre-primary (preschool). There are closer schools, but Jeff and Claire did not want to disrupt Elsa's friendship networks when they moved house, so they did not move the girls to a new school.

A centrally located desktop computer is used by all family members and Jeff and Claire both have iPhones. The girls share a hand-me-down iPhone 4 that is not connected to the network and is mainly used for music, games and for the girls to use to make recording videos. The parents have concerns around the girls accessing inappropriate content and take care to monitor their children's digital activities, but don't use any software for this. They actively encourage 'real-world play' and, as an artist, Claire makes sure to have art and craft supplies on hand.

Claire is the more tech-savvy of the parents and maintains the family iTunes account, acting as the gateway parent for new apps and games. She uses a fingerprint scan on her phone, whereas the girls both know their father's password.

19. Ross family (UK) child: Penny, female, three years, three months (toddler)

The Ross family lives in a Victorian terraced house in a residential area on the outskirts of inner London (not far from the Palmers). Mum Sandra (thirty) works part time in a hotel and left school at sixteen with basic qualifications. Dad Ron (thirty-one) is a bus driver and left school without academic qualifications. Son Frankie (six) is full time at school, while daughter Penny (three) attends a nearby nursery (childcare) on the weekday afternoons for three hours each day.

Sandra said that screen time was not an issue since Penny had many activities and digital media use was only one of them. In fact, if Penny didn't see the tablet, she didn't think about it. Ron clarified that he and Sandra had 'different rules' and she concedes that there is 'Daddy time' when Sandra is at work and Ron is in charge allowing Penny to do whatever digital activities she wants. Penny often tries to copy older brother Frankie on his videogames and Ron says: 'She's kind of all over him to watch what he's doing.' Given that Penny finds some digital content (such as an animal being hurt) very upsetting, Sandra checks the content Penny might see and has replaced the adult YouTube feed with Kids YouTube plus 'really strict filters'. One of Penny's favourite outings is to Sea Life Centre, which Sandra says they visit 'about ten times a year, if not more'. The family has a Virtual Reality (VR) headset with Penny watching 'Under the Sea' VR content during the interview.

When Penny got stuck in her tablet use brother Frankie would take the tablet and say he would sort it out – but he rarely showed her how to overcome the problem and was likely instead to solve it himself but then carry on using the tablet rather than giving it back to her.

20. Spinner family (UK) child: Imelda, female, four years (preschool)

The youngest of three children, Imelda lives with mum Karla (forty-one), dad Daniel (forty-two) and big sisters Alice (nine) and Belle (seven) in a terraced house in a recently gentrified, now middle-class, South London suburb. There's specialist shopping, an overground rail station and a park a few minutes away. The children mostly play in the dining room, but different activities are assigned to different areas of the house. There's no desktop in the home, but the adults have a laptop each and the older girls share one. Each parent has an iPad and a smartphone and the girls share Daniel's old iPad and a no-longer-connected smartphone. There are two TVs, a DVD and a Kindle but no games consoles. Imelda has used the iPad since she was fifteen months old and can hold it and swipe the screen. Generally, however, parents take other toys to cafes or outings and only use digital media in 'an emergency'.

Daniel is a graduate working in advertising while Karla, with a social science degree including child development units, chose to be a stay-at-home mum for nine years before taking a part-time IT role supporting her brother's business. Karla sees benefits in childcare but once she decided not to return to work, she relied on playgroups and children's activity classes, like ballet, for added socialization.

At the same time, Karla feels guilty she hasn't played more with the children over the years, preferring to read books to them. Imelda attends preschool three and a half days per week, spending time with her mother otherwise. Karla and Daniel see themselves as flexible parents with some friends stricter than them, others more liberal. They ban tech for the hour before children's bedtimes, while the children's laptop has a set time limit and will also shut down at 8.00 pm.

21. Tosetti family (UK) child: Leopoldo, male, two years (toddler)

The Tosetti parents are Italian-born who have lived in the UK for about sixteen years. They live in a compact one-bed flat in a middle-class, cosmopolitan area of north-west London. Mirabella (forty-one) has a communications degree: Lorenzo did not go to University. Both trained to be graphics designers. Mirabella gave up that work when she had Leopoldo (two), but Lorenzo (forty-one) continues his work in animation and special effects.

Mirabella mentioned things that Leopoldo learns through using technology: the 'time for bed' routine, counting, colours, animals' names, classical music. As graphic designers, Leopoldo's parents teach him the grammar of audio-visual images and use videos to explain complicated concepts, such as an Elmo video to help him understand what 'birthday' means. They say that Leopoldo doesn't much enjoy children's programs, preferring amateur YouTube videos of washing in a washing machine, people opening packages, vacuuming and children his own age doing things.

The Tosettis are positive about the way Leopoldo interacts with technology. Lorenzo likes how Leopoldo tries hard to work out how to do things on the iPad and how actively engaged he is. For dad Lorenzo, as a child growing up in what he saw as an over-protective family, he felt he was kept in a 'bubble'. Even now, when Lorenzo's mother visits, she tells grandson Leopoldo what to do and what not to. This can frustrate Leopoldo because his parents allow him considerable freedom to do what he wants, provided it's not dangerous. Mirabella's recollection of her own childhood in a small town in Italy was that there was little to do and she was always bored. She contrasts this with Leopoldo's experiences, his rich engagement in nursery and all the possibilities presented by the digital world with access to so many images and ideas.

22. Zhang/Chen family (AU) child: Lavinia, female, two years, four months (toddler)

The Zhang/Chen family lives in a three-bedroom house in an eastern suburb of Perth. Stanley Zhang (thirty-six) works in IT for a mining company while Rita Chen (thirty-three) works in Finance for an Australian bank. They have one child, Lavinia (twenty-eight months). Stanley and Rita were both born in China but met in Australia. Both have degrees and are proficient in English, but they speak Mandarin at home and with Lavinia.

Soon after Lavinia was born, Rita's parents also moved to Australia and have permanent residency. Sun and Lily Chen are in their late fifties and speak little English. They are Lavinia's primary caregivers during the week. They live nearby and grandmother Lily commits herself to an active social calendar with

Lavinia, which includes library story-time, swimming and three-days per week at playgroup. At the same time, there is a firm commitment to routine and it's important to Lily that she is home by 2.00 pm every day for Lavinia's nap.

In terms of digital media in the Zhang/Chen home, Stanley has a laptop that he uses for browsing after work and both he and Rita have iPhones. They also have an iPad that is purely for Lavinia's use and loaded with apps that they have selected as appropriate for her. Lavinia also has the use of a LeapPad-style device that Rita bought in China which features a bilingual language app. The family television is usually used to stream web programs controlled via Rita's phone and the use of a dongle.

Rita considers herself moderately strict in terms of Lavinia's digital access. She and Stanley are against computer games but see the value of programs and apps with educational content. They believe that most schools use iPads and they want Lavinia to be able to use the technology before she starts school.

Glossary

Rather than offer a volume-specific Glossary, we recommend that readers consult a specialist Glossary, such as the *Glossary of terms relating to children's digital lives* produced by the Digital Futures Commission (Atabey et al., 2023), https://digitalfuturescommission.org.uk/wp-content/uploads/2023/03/DFC-Glossary-180323-ready.pdf

Notes

Chapter 4

1. For a review of children's internet use (specifically birth to eight-year-olds), see Holloway et al. (2013).
2. This was originally a term used to describe television (Tizard & Hughs, 1984).
3. For details about participant parents, see Table 1.2.
4. This case study is elaborated in Chapter 9, 'Preschoolers'.

Chapter 5

1. In fact, there is more than one typology of grandparenting styles, as reviewed in Thiele and Whelan, 2006, although some of the categories are similar across typologies.
2. In the light of some very positive representations of grandparenthood, studies have shown that one in five grandmothers was unhappy, unaffected or held mixed emotions about the role, while one in three grandparents expressed disappointment or difficulty with the role (Thiele & Whelan, 2006, p. 102).
3. This refers to Prensky's (2001) distinction between children who were 'digital natives' having grown up with new technologies and parents were 'digital immigrants' who had first encountered technologies as adults.
4. This refers to arguments that over time parents have become less authoritarian, often called 'the detraditionalization of the family' and associated with Giddens. For an elaboration see Williams and Williams (2005).
5. This is a UK TV programme where an 'expert' nanny visits families who feel they are having problems with their children and she takes charge of the children for a short while.
6. See Chapter 4, 'Parenting and digital media'.
7. This shows a different strategy from that noted in the Elias et al. (2019) study, where some grandparents enforced rules less when the children were at their house and means that we cannot assume grandparents are generally more permissive because of their age-stage (discussed in Elias et al., 2019).

Chapter 6

1. The term comes from Prensky (2001) and has been much criticized (e.g. Herring, 2008; Selwyn, 2009).
2. See the chapter on Parents' evaluation of children's learning.
3. These terms are cited here because they capture staff's representations of both themselves and children.
4. Gillen et al. (2018, p. 5) in a policy brief written by most of Europe's key researchers in this field note that 'digital literacy has not yet become an integral part of early year's education in most settings across Europe'.
5. Hence, other writers have tried to develop taxonomies of play that include digital elements (Marsh et al., 2016).
6. A free-to-air channel for children under seven provided by the BBC, the UK public broadcaster.
7. A questionable assumption discussed in Stephen and Edwards (2018).
8. *Tapestry* facilitates creation of a digital record of a child's early years educational journey.
9. This can be compared to the discussion of parents occupying children in the chapter on Parents.
10. See the discussion of such interactivity in the chapter on Parents evaluating children's learning.

Chapter 8

1. Lavinia is the focus of a published case study: Stevenson et al. (2021), and discussion of the Zhang/Chen family is also included in Green et al. (2019).

Chapter 10

1. The importance of different aspects of family context is also noted in a range of other studies and reviewed in Stephen and Edwards (2018).
2. See the literature review discussing parenting styles in the Parenting and digital media chapter.
3. European studies examining siblings and digital media include Farrugia and Haddon (2014), Ólafsson et al. (2017) and Chaudron et al. (2018). For a brief summary of the mixed positive and negative interactions between siblings in relation to ICTs, see Stephen (2021).
4. Also noted in Yarosh, Chew and Abowd (2009).

Chapter 11

1. While these may be worthwhile, they can be achieved by non-digital activities. More critically, Stephen makes the point that fewer digital activities promote 'exploration, problem-solving and creative expression' (p.59).
2. Technavio (2021). Global Education Apps Market | $ 46.88 Billion growth expected during 2020–4.

References

AAP (2011). Media use by children younger than 2 years: Policy statement from the American Association of Pediatrics Council on Communications and Media. *Pediatrics*, 128(5), 1040–5. https://doi.org/10.1542/peds.2011-1753

AAP (2016). Media and young minds: Policy statement from American Association of Pediatrics Council on Communications and Media. *Pediatrics*, 138(5), e20162591. https://doi.org/10.1542/peds.2016-2591

AAP (n.d.). *Family Media Plan*. [website] American Academy of Pediatrics. https://www.healthychildren.org/English/media/Pages/default.aspx

Atabey, A., Pothong, K., & Livingstone, S. (2023). *Glossary of terms relating to children's digital lives*. Digital Futures Commission, 5Rights Foundation. https://digitalfuturescommission.org.uk/wp-content/uploads/2023/03/DFC-Glossary-180323-ready.pdf

Aubrey, C., & Dahl, S. (2008). *A review of the evidence on the use of ICT in the early years foundation stage*, Becta report. http://dera.ioe.ac.uk/1631/2/becta_2008_eyfsreview_report.pdf

Aubrey, C., & Dahl, S. (2014). The confidence and competence in information and communication technologies of practitioners, parents and young children in the Early Years Foundation Stage. *Early Years*, 34(1), 94–108. https://doi.org/10.1080/09575146.2013.792789

Austin, E. (1993). Exploring the effects of active parental mediation of television content. *Journal of Broadcasting & Electronic Media*, 37(2), 147–58. https://doi.org/10.1080/08838159309364212

Bakardjieva, M. (2005). *Internet society: The Internet in everyday life*. Sage.

Ballagas, R., Kaye, J., Ames, M., Go, J., & Raffle, H. (2009). Family communication: Phone conversations with children. *IDC '09: Proceedings of the 8th International Conference on Interaction Design and Children* (pp. 321–4). Association for Computing Machinery. https://dl.acm.org/doi/proceedings/10.1145/1551788

Bangerter, L., & Waldron, V. (2014). Turning points in long distance grandparent–grandchild relationships. *Journal of Aging Studies*, 29, 88–97. https://doi.org/10.1016/j.jaging.2014.01.004

Barron, B., Martin, C., Takeuchi, L., & Fithian, R. (2009). Parents as learning partners in the development of technological fluency. *International Journal of Learning and Media*, 1(2), 55–77. https://doi.org/10.1162/ijlm.2009.0021

Bates, J., & Taylor, A. (2013). Grandfather involvement: Contact frequency, participation in activities and commitment. *The Journal of Men's Studies*, 21(3), 305–22. https://doi.org/10.3149/jms.2103.305

Baumrind, D. (1991). The influence of parenting style on adolescent competence and substance use. *The Journal of Early Adolescence*, 11(1), 56–95. https://doi.org/10.1177/0272431691111004

Bazalgette, C. (2022). *How toddlers learn the secret language of movies*. Palgrave Macmillan.

Beck, U., & Beck-Gernsheim, E. (2002). *Individualization: Institutionalized individualism and its social and political consequences*. Sage.

Bennett, S., Maton, K., & Kervin, L. (2008). The 'digital natives' debate: A critical review of the evidence. *British Journal of Educational Technology*, 39(5), 775–86. https://doi.org/10.1111/j.1467-8535.2007.00793.x

Berger, J. (2008 [1972]). *Ways of seeing*. Penguin Books.

Berger, P., & Luckmann, T. (1966). *The Social Construction of Reality: A Treatise on the social construction of knowledge*. Anchor Books.

Bergman, C., Dimitrova, N., Alaslani, K., Almohammadi, A., Alroqi, H., Aussems, S., Barokova, M., Davies, C., Gonzalez-Gomez, N., Gibson, S.P., Havron, N., Horowitz-Kraus, T., Kanero, J., Kartushina, N., Keller, C., Mayor, J., Mundry, R., Shinskey, J., & Mani, N. (2022). Young children's screen time during the first COVID-19 lockdown in 12 countries. *Scientific Reports*, 12. https://www.nature.com/articles/s41598-022-05840-5

Berlin, I. (1969). Two concepts of liberty. In *Four Essays on Liberty* (pp. 118–72). Oxford University Press.

Bertenthal, B. I., & Fischer, K. W. (1978). Development of self-recognition in the infant. *Developmental Psychology*, 14(1), 44–50. https://doi.org/10.1037/0012-1649.14.1.44

Beyens, I., & Beullens, K. (2017). Parent-child conflict about children's tablet use: The role of parental mediation. *New Media and Society*, 19(12), 2075–93. https://doi.org/10.1177/1461444816655099

Blum-Ross, A., & Livingstone, S. (2019). Connecting learning: Parents and young children in museum makerspaces. In A. Blum-Ross, K. Kumpulainen, & J. Marsh (Eds.), *Enhancing digital literacy and creativity: Makerspaces in the early years* (pp. 148–64). Routledge.

Bourdieu, P. (1979). Les trois états du capital culturel. *Actes de la recherche en sciences sociales*, 30(1), 3–6.

boyd, D. (2014). *It's complicated: The social lives of networked teens*. Yale University Press.

Breheny, M., Stephens, C., & Sprilsbury, L. (2013). Involvement without interference: How grandparents negotiate intergenerational expectations in relationships with grandchildren. *Journal of Family Studies*, 19(2), 174–84. https://doi.org/10.5172/jfs.2013.19.2.174

Bronfenbrenner, U. (1979). *The ecology of human development: Experiments by nature and design*. Harvard University Press.

Bronfenbrenner, U. (2005). Bioecological theory of human development (2001). In U. Bronfenbrenner (Ed.), *Making human beings human: Bioecological perspectives on human development* (pp. 3–15). Sage.

Bruner, J. S. (2006). *In search of pedagogy Volume I: The selected works of Jerome Bruner, 1957–1978*. Routledge.

Burr, V. (2015). *Social constructionism* (3rd ed). Routledge.

Butsch, R. (2000). *The making of American audiences: From stage to television 1750–1990*. Cambridge University Press. https://doi.org/10.1017/CBO9780511619717

Centers for Disease Control and Prevention. (n.d.). *Child development: Positive parenting tips: Toddlers (2–3)*. Retrieved 18 April 2022, from https://www.cdc.gov/ncbddd/childdevelopment/positiveparenting/toddlers2.html

Chaudron, S. (2015). *Young children (0–8) and digital technology: A qualitative exploratory study across seven countries*. Joint Research Centre. https://publications.jrc.ec.europa.eu/repository/handle/JRC93239

Chaudron, S., Di Gioia, R., & Gemo, M. (2018). *Young children (0–8) and digital technology, a qualitative study across Europe*. JRC Science for Policy Report. EUR 29070. https://doi.org/10.2760/294383

Chen, C., Chen, S., Wen, P., & Snow, E. (2020). Are screen devices soothing children or soothing parents? Investigating the relationships among children's exposure to different types of screen media, parental efficacy and home literacy practices. *Computers in Human Behavior*, 112, 1–14. https://doi.org/10.1016/j.chb.2020.106462

Christopher, V., Turner, M., & Green, N. C. (2022). Educator perceptions of early learning environments as places for privileging social justice in rural and remote communities. *Education Sciences*, 12(1), 40. https://doi.org/10.3390/educsci12010040

Clarke, L. (2011). Parental mediation theory for a digital age. *Communication Theory*, 21(4), 323–43. https://doi.org/10.1111/j.1468-2885.2011.01391.x

Clark, L. S. (2013). *The parent app: Understanding families in the digital age*. Oxford University Press.

Colvert, A. (2021). *The kaleidoscope of play in a digital world: A literature review*. Digital Futures Commission.

Corkin, M. (2021, November 11). *Studies suggest no causal link between young children's screen time and later symptoms of inattention and hyperactivity*. The Conversation. https://theconversation.com/studies-suggest-no-causal-link-between-young-childrens-screen-time-and-later-symptoms-of-inattention-and-hyperactivity-169943

Cortés-Morales, S., & Main, G. (2022). Needs or wants? Children and parents understanding and negotiating needs and necessities. *Childhood Vulnerability Journal*, 4(1), 13–36. https://doi.org/10.1007/s41255-021-00020-5

Council on Communications and Media. (2016). Media and young minds. *Pediatrics*, 138(5), e20162591. https://doi.org/10.1542/peds.2016-2591

Couse, L., & Chen, D. (2010). A tablet computer for young children? Exploring viability for early childhood education. *Journal of Research on Technology in Education*, 43(1), 75–96. https://doi.org/10.1080/15391523.2010.10782562

Critcher, C. (2008). Historical aspects of public debates about children and media. In K. Drotner & S. Livingstone (Eds.), *The international handbook of children, media and culture* (pp. 91–104). Sage.

Crotty, M. (2020 [1998]). *The foundations of social research: Meaning and perspective in the research process.* Routledge.

Crowley, A., Larkins, C., & Pinto, L. M. (2021). *Listen – Act – Change: Council of Europe Handbook on children's participation. For professional working for and with children.* Council of Europe. https://rm.coe.int/publication-handbook-on-children-s-participation-eng/1680a14539

Danby, S., Davidson, C., Theobald, M., Schrive, B., Cobb-Moore, C., Houen, S., Grant, S., Given, L., & Thorpe, K. (2013). Talking activity during young children's use of digital technologies at home. *Australian Journal of Communication*, 40(2), 83–99. https://eprints.qut.edu.au/65579/

D'Arienzo, M. C., Boursier, V., & Griffiths, M. D. (2019). Addiction to social media and attachment styles: A systematic literature review. *International Journal of Mental Health and Addiction*, 17(4), 1094–118. https://doi.org/10.1007/s11469-019-00082-5

DeLoache, J. S. (1987). Rapid change in the symbolic functioning of very young children. *Science*, 238(4833), 1556–7. https://doi.org/10.1126/science.2446392

Department for Education (UK). (2021). *Statutory Framework for the Early Years Foundation Stage*. Retrieved 22 November 2021 from https://www.gov.uk/government/publications/early-years-foundation-stage-framework-2

Desmond, R., Singer, J., Singer, D., Calam, R., & Colimore, K. (1985). Family mediation patterns and television viewing: Young children's use and grasp of the medium. *Human Communication Research*, 11(4), 461–80. https://doi.org/10.1111/j.1468-2958.1985.tb00056.x

DigiLitEY. (2018). *Using augmented and virtual reality in the early childhood curriculum*. Retrieved 27 February 2022 from http://digilitey.eu/wp-content/uploads/2018/06/DigiLitEY-Policy-VR.pdf

Dimitrova, N., Bergmann, C. Alaslani, K., Almohammadi, A., Alroqi, H., Aussems, S., Barokova, M., Davies, C., Gonzalez-Gomez, N., Gibson, S. P., Havron, N., Horowitz-Kraus, T., Kanero, J., Kartushina, N., Keller, C., Mayor, J., Mundry, R., Shinskey, J., & Mani, N. (2022). Young children's screen time during the first COVID-19 lockdown in 12 countries. *Scientific Reports*, 12, 2015. https://doi.org/10.1038/s41598-022-05840-5

Dong, C., Cao, S., & Li, H. (2020). Young children's online learning during Covid-19 pandemic: Chinese parents' beliefs and attitudes. *Children and Youth Services Review*, 118, 105440. https://doi.org/10.1016/j.childyouth.2020.105440

Doty, J., & Dworkin, J. (2014). Online social support for parents: A critical review. *Marriage & Family Review*, 50(2), 174–98. https://doi.org/10.1080/01494929.2013.834027

Dubey, H., Sharma, R. K., Krishnan, S., & Knickmeyer, R. (2022). SARS-CoV-2 (COVID-19) as a possible risk factor for neurodevelopmental disorders. *Frontiers in Neuroscience. 16*. https://doi.org/10.3389/fnins.2022.1021721

Dunfield, K., Kuhlmeier, V. A., Oconnell, L., & Kelley, E. (2011). Examining the diversity of prosocial behaviour: Helping, sharing and comforting in infancy. *Infancy*, 16, 227–47. https://doi.org/10.1111/j.1532-7078.23010.00041.x

Dunifon, R., Near, C., & Ziol-Guest, K. (2018). Back-up parents, playmates, friends: Grandparents' time with grandchildren. *Journal of Marriage and Family*, 80(3), 752–67. https://doi.org/10.1111/jomf.12472

Eastin, M., Greenberg, B., & Hofschire, L. (2006). Parenting the internet. *Journal of Communication*, 56(3), 486–504. https://doi.org/10.1111/j.1460-2466.2006.00297.x

Education (2023). *About early childhood education and care in Australia: What is early childhood education and care?* Government of Australia, Department of Education, https://www.education.gov.au/early-childhood/about-early-childhood-education-and-care-australia

education.gov.uk (2023). *Statutory framework for the early years foundation stage: Setting the standards for learning, development and care for children from birth to five*. UK Government: Department for Education, https://assets.publishing.service.gov.uk/government/uploads/system/uploads/attachment_data/file/1170108/EYFS_framework_from_September_2023.pdf

Edwards, S. (2016). New concepts of play and the problem of technology, digital media and popular-culture integration with play-based learning in early childhood education. *Technology, Pedagogy and Education*, 25(4), 513–32. https://doi.org/10.1080/1475939X.2015.1108929

Eichen, L., Hackl-Wimmer, S., Eglmaier, M. T. W., Lackner, H. K., Paechter, M., Rettenbacher, K., & Walter-Laager, C. (2021). Families' digital media use: Intentions, rules and activities. *British Journal of Educational Technology*, 52(6), 2162–77. https://doi.org/10.1111/bjet.13161

Elias, N., & Sulkin, I. (2017). YouTube viewers in diapers: An exploration of factors associated with amount of toddlers' online viewing. *Cyberpsychology: Journal of Psychological Edwards, Research on Cyberspace*, 11(3). https://dx.doi.org/10.5817/CP2017-3-2

Elias, N., Lemish, D., & Nimrod, G. (2021). Grandparental mediation of children's digital media use. In L. Green, D. Holloway, K. Stevenson, T. Leaver, & L. Haddon (Eds.), *The Routledge companion to digital media and children* (pp. 96–107). Routledge.

Elias, N., Nimrod, G., & Lemish, D. (2019). The ultimate treat? Young Israeli children's media use under their grandparents' care. *Journal of Children and Media*, 13(4), 472–83. https://doi.org/10.1080/17482798.2019.1627228

Eun, B. (2019). The zone of proximal development as an overarching concept: A framework for synthesizing Vygotsky's theories. *Educational Philosophy and Theory*, 51(1), 18–30. https://doi.org/10.1080/00131857.2017.1421941

Farrugia, L., & Haddon, L. (2014). Mediation by siblings and other relatives. In D. Smahel & M. F. Wright (Eds.), *Meaning of online problematic situations for children. Results of qualitative cross-cultural investigation in nine European countries*.

EU Kids Online, London School of Economics and Political Science. http://eprints.lse.ac.uk/56972/

Fenty, N., & McKendry Anderson, E. (2014). Examining educators' knowledge, beliefs, and practices about using technology with young children. *Journal of Early Childhood Teacher Education*, 35(2), 114–34. https://doi.org/10.1080/10901027.2014.905808

Findley, E., LaBrenz, C. A., Childress, S., Vásquez-Schut, G., & Bowman, K. (2022). 'I'm not perfect': Navigating screen time among parents of young children during COVID-19. *Child: Care, Health and Development*, 48(6), 1094–102, https://doi.org/10.1111/cch.13038

Flewitt, R. (2005). Conducting research with young children: Some ethical considerations. *Early Child Development and Care*, 175(6), 553–65. https://doi.org/10.1080/03004430500131338

Flewitt, R., Messer, D., & Kucirkova, N. (2015). New directions for early literacy in a digital age: The iPad. *Journal of Early Childhood Literacy*, 15(3), 289–310. https://doi.org/10.1177/1468798414533560

Ford, T. G., Kwon, K. A., & Tsotsoros, J. D. (2021). Early childhood distance learning in the US during the COVID pandemic: Challenges and opportunities. *Children and Youth Services Review*, 131(106297), 1–9. https://doi.org/10.1016/j.childyouth.2021.106297

Forghani, A., & Neustaedter, C. (2014). The routines and needs of grandparents and parents for grandparent-grandchild conversations over distance. In *CHI '14: Proceedings of the SIGCHI Conference on Human Factors in Computing Systems* (pp. 4177–86). Association for Computing Machinery. https://dl.acm.org/doi/proceedings/10.1145/2556288

Gager, C. T., McLanahan, S. S., Glei, D. A., Halfon, N., & McLearn, K. T. (2002). Preparing for parenthood: Who's ready, who's not. In N. Halfon, K. Taaffe McLearn, & M. A. Schuster (Eds.), *Child rearing in America: Challenges facing parents with young children* (pp. 50–80). Cambridge University Press.

Game, A. (1991). *Undoing the social: Towards a deconstructive sociology*. Open University Press.

Garvis, S., & Phillipson, S. (2019). Teachers' and families' perspectives in early childhood education and care: A reflection of 19 countries. In S. Phillipson & S. Garvis (Eds.), *Teachers' and families' perspectives in early childhood education and care*. Routledge.

Gee, E., Takeuchi, L., & Wartella, E. (2017). *Children and families in the digital age: Learning together in a media saturated culture*. Routledge.

Gillen, J., Marsh, J., Bus, J., Castro, T., Dardanou, M., Duncan, P., Enriquez-Gibson, J., Flewitt, R., Gray, C. Holloway, D., Jernes, M., Kontovourki, S., Kucirkova, N., Kumpulainen, K., March-Boehnck, G., Mascheroni, G., Nagy, K., O'Connor, J., O'Neill, B., Palaiologou, I., Poveda, D., Salomaa, S., Severina, E., & Tafa, E. (2018). *Digital Literacy and young children: Towards better understandings of the benefits* and challenges of digital technologies in homes and early years settings. A policy brief from COST Action IS1410/ EECERA Digital Childhoods SIG. https://e-space.mmu.ac.uk/624237/

Given, M., Winkler, D., Willson, R., Davidson, C., Danby, S., & Thorpe, K. (2014). Documenting young children's technology use: Observations in the home. *Proceedings of the American Society for Information Science and Technology*, 1(51), 1–9. https://asistdl.onlinelibrary.wiley.com/doi/full/10.1002/meet.2014.14505101028

Green, L., & Haddon, L. (2015). *Parents' reflections upon mediating older teens' gaming practices*. Media@LSE Working Paper Series, Paper 37. https://www.lse.ac.uk/media-and-communications/research/working-paper-series

Green, L., Haddon, L., Livingstone, S., Holloway, D., Jaunzems, K., Stevenson, K., & O'Neill, B. (2019). *Parents' failure to plan for their children's digital futures*. In B. Cammaerts, N. Anstead, & R. Stupart (Eds.). Media@LSE Working Paper Series. http://www.lse.ac.uk/media-and-communications/assets/documents/research/working-paper-series/WP61.pdf

Haddon, L. (2015). Children's critical evaluation of parental mediation. *Cyberpsychology: Journal of Psychosocial Research on Cyberspace*, 9(1). https://doi.org/10.5817/CP2015-1-2

Haddon, L. (2017). Domestication and the media. In P. Rössler (Ed.), *The international encyclopedia of media effects* (Vol. 1) (pp. 409–17). John Wiley and Sons. https://www.academia.edu/download/48486032/Domestication-and-media.pdf

Haddon, L., & Holloway, D. (2018). Parental evaluations of young children's touchscreen technologies. In G. Mascheroni, C. Ponte, & A. Jorge (Eds.), *Digital parenting: The challenges for families in the digital age* (pp. 113–23). Nordicom.

Haddon, L., & Livingstone, S. (2014). *The meaning of online problematic situations for children: The UK report*. EU Kids Online. http://eprints.lse.ac.uk/60514/

Haddon, L., & Vincent, J. (2015). *UK children's experience of smartphones and tablets: Perspectives from children, parents and teachers*. Net Children Go Mobile. http://eprints.lse.ac.uk/62125/

Harkness, S., & Super, C. M. (1992). Parental ethnotheories in action. In I. Sigel, A. V. McGillicuddy-DeLisi, & J. J. Goodnow (Eds.), *Parental belief systems: The psychological consequences for children* (2nd ed) (pp. 373–92). Psychology Press.

Harste, J. C. (2003). What do we mean by literacy now? *Voices from the Middle*, 10(3), 8–12.

Hatzigianni, M., & Kalaitzidis, I. (2018). Early childhood educators' attitudes and beliefs around the use of touchscreen technologies by children under three years of age. *British Journal of Educational Technology*, 49(5), 883–95. https://doi.org/10.1111/bjet.12649

Helsper, E. (2021). *The digital disconnect: The social causes and consequences of digital inequalities*. Sage.

Herring, S. (2008). Questioning the generational divide: Technological exoticism and adult constructions of online youth identity. In D. Buckingham (Ed.), *Youth, Identity and Digital Media* (pp. 71–92). MIT Press.

Hiniker, A., Suh, H., Cao, S., & Kientz, J. A. (2016, May). Screen time tantrums: How families manage screen media experiences for toddlers and preschoolers. In *Proceedings of the 2016 CHI conference on human factors in computing systems* (pp. 648–60). Association for Computing Machinery. https://doi.org/10.1145/2858036.2858278

Holloway, D. J., & Stevenson, K. J. (2017). Parent as field collaborator when interviewing the preverbal and early verbal child [blog post], *DigiLitEY: The Digital Literacy and Multimodal Practices of Young Children* [COST Action IS14100]. https://digilitey.wordpress.com/2017/01/24/parent-as-field-collaborator-when-interviewing-the-pre-verbal-and-early-verbal-child/

Holloway, D. J., Green, L., & Livingstone, S. (2013). *Zero to eight: young children and their internet use*. http://eprints.lse.ac.uk/52630/; (the most recent download numbers are here: http://eprints.lse.ac.uk/cgi/stats/report/eprint/52630)

Holloway, D., Green, L., & Love, C. (2014). 'It's all about the apps': Parental mediation of their preschoolers' digital lives. *Media International Australia, Incorporating Culture & Policy*, 153, 148–56. https://doi.org/10.1177/1329878x1415300117

Holloway, D., Willson, M., Murcia, K., Archer, C., & Stocco, F. (Eds.) (2021). *Young children's right in a digital world*. Springer International Publishing.

Horsfall, B., & Dempsey, D. (2015). Grandparents doing gender: Experiences of grandmothers and grandfathers caring for grandchildren in Australia. *Journal of Sociology*, 5(4), 1070–84. https://doi.org/10.1177/1440783313498945

Houen, S., Danby, S., & Miller, P. (2021). Siblings accomplishing tasks together: Solicited and unsolicited assistance when using digital technology. In L. Green, D. Holloway, K. Stevenson, T. Leaver, & L. Haddon (Eds.), *The Routledge companion to digital media and children* (pp. 130–43). Routledge.

Hughes, R. (1998). Considering the vignette technique and its application to a study of drug injecting and HIV risk and safer behaviour. *Sociology of Health and Illness*, 20(3), 381–400.

Hurwitz, L. B., & Schmitt, K. L. (2020). Can children benefit from early internet exposure? Short-and long-term links between internet use, digital skill and academic performance. *Computers & Education*, 146. https://doi.org/10.1016/j.compedu.2019.103750

Jack, C., & Higgins, S. (2019). What is educational technology and how is it being used to support teaching and learning in the early years? *International Journal of Early Years Education*, 27(3), 222–37. https://doi.org/10.1080/09669760.2018.1504754

James, A., & Prout, A. (Eds.) (1997). *Constructing and reconstructing childhood: Contemporary issues in the sociological study of children*. Falmer Press.

Jaunzems, K., Holloway, D. J., Green, L., & Stevenson, K. J. (2019). Very young children online: Media discourse and parental practice. In L. Green, D. J. Holloway, K. J. Stevenson, & K. Jaunzems (Eds.), *Digitising early childhood* (pp. 16–27). Cambridge Scholars Publishing.

Jelic, M. (2014). Developing a sense of identity in preschoolers. *Mediterranean Journal of Social Sciences*, 5(22), 225–34. https://doi.org/10.5901/mjss.2014.v5n22p225

Jeon, H. J., Diamond, L., McCartney, C., & Kwon, K. A. (2022). Early childhood special education teachers' job burnout and psychological stress. *Early Education and Development*, 33(8), 1364–82. https://doi.org/10.1080/10409289.2021.1965395

Juhaňák, L., Zounek, J., Záleská, K., Bárta, O., & Vlčková, K. (2019). The relationship between the age at first computer use and students' perceived competence and autonomy in ICT usage: A mediation analysis. *Computers & Education*, 141. https://doi.org/10.1016/j.compedu.2019.103614

Katz, P. A. (1981). *Development of children's racial awareness and intergroup attitudes*. https://files.eric.ed.gov/fulltext/ED207675.pdf

Kay, L., Brandsen, S., Jacques, C., Stocco, F., & Zaffaroni, L. G. (2023). Children's digital and non-digital play practices with cozmo, the toy robot. *M/C Journal*, 26(2). https://doi.org/10.5204/mcj.2943

Keech, J. J., Hatzis, D., Kavanagh, D. J., White, K. M., & Hamilton, K. (2018). Parents' role constructions for facilitating physical activity-related behaviours in their young children. *Australian Journal of Psychology* 70(3), 246–57. https://doi.org/10.1111/ajpy.12195

Kelly, C. (2015). 'Let's do some jumping together': Intergenerational participation in the use of remote technology to co-construct social relations over distance. *Journal of Early Childhood* Research, 13(1), 29–46. https://doi.org/10.1177/1476718X12468121

Kent, N., & Facer, K. (2004). Different worlds? A comparison of young people's home and school ICT use. *Journal of Computer Assisted Learning*, 20(6), 440–55. https://doi.org/10.1111/j.1365-2729.2004.0010.x

Kontovourki, S., Garoufallou, E., Ivarsson, L., Klein, M., Korkeamaki, R. L., Koutsomiha, D., Marci-Boehncke, G., Tafa, E., & Virkus, S. (2017). *Digital literacy in the early years: Practices in formal settings, teacher education and the role of informal learning spaces: A review of the literature*. COST ACTION IS1410. http://digilitey.eu/wp-content/uploads/2017/01/WG2-LR-March-2017-v2.pdf

Kuby, C. R., & Rowsell, J. (2017). Early literacy and the posthuman: Pedagogies and methodologies. *Journal of Early Childhood Literacy*, 17(3), 285–96. https://doi.org/10.1177/14687984177157

Kucirkova, N. (2014). iPads in early education: separating assumptions and evidence. *Frontiers in Psychology*, 5(715), 1–3. https://doi.org/10.3389/fpsyg.2014.00715

Kucirkova, N. (2017). An integrative framework for studying, designing and conceptualising interactivity in children's digital books. *British Educational Research Journal*, 6(43), 1168–85. https://doi.org/10.1002/berj.3317

Kucirkova, N., & Flewitt, R. (2022). Understanding parents' conflicting beliefs about children's digital book reading. *Journal of Early Childhood Literacy*, 22(2), 157–81. https://doi.org/10.1177/1468798420930361

Kuczynski, L., & De Moi, J. (2015). Dialectical models of socialization. In W. F. Overton, P. C. M. Molenaar, & R. M. Lerner (Eds.), *Handbook of child psychology and developmental science: Theory and method* (pp. 323–68). John Wiley & Sons. https://doi.org/10.1002/9781118963418.childpsy109

Lansdown, G. (2005). *The evolving capacities of the child*. UNICEF. https://www.unicef-irc.org/publications/pdf/evolving-eng.pdf

Lauricella, A., Wartella, E., & Rideout, V. (2015). Young children's screen time: The complex role of parent and child factors. *Journal of Applied Developmental Psychology*, 36, 11–17. https://doi.org/10.1016/j.appdev.2014.12.001

Lave, J., & Wenger, E. (1991). *Situated learning: Legitimate peripheral participation*. Cambridge University Press.

Leaver, T. (2017). Intimate surveillance: Normalizing parental monitoring and mediation of infants online. *Social media+ society*, 3(2). https://doi.org/10.1177/2056305117707192

Lee, E., Bristow, J., Faircloth, C., & Macvarish, J. (2014). *Parenting culture studies*. Palgrave Macmillan.

Levickis, P., Murray, L., Lee-Pang, L., Eadie, P., Page, J., Lee, W. Y., & Hill, G. (2022). Parents' perspectives of family engagement with early childhood education and care during the COVID-19 pandemic. *Early Childhood Education Journal*, 5 (Aug), 1–11. http://doi.org/10.1007/s10643-022-01376-5 [Online First].

Livingstone, S. (2002). *Young people and new media*. Sage.

Livingstone, S. (2014). The mediatization of childhood and education: Reflections on *The Class*. In L. Kramp, N. Carpentier, A. Hepp, I. Tomanic-Trivundza, H. Nieminen, R. Kunelius, T. Olsson, E. Sundin, and R. Kilborn (Eds.), *Media practice and everyday agency in Europe*. Bremen: Edition Lumière.

Livingstone, S. (2021). The rise and fall of screen time. In V. Strasburger (Ed.), *Masters of media: Controversies and solutions* (Vol. 1, pp. 89–104). Rowman & Littlefield.

Livingstone, S., & Blum-Ross, A. (2020). *Parenting for a digital future: How hopes and fears about technology shape children's lives*. Oxford University Press.

Livingstone, S., & Helsper, E. (2008). Parental mediation and children's internet use. *Journal of Broadcasting & Electronic Media*, 52(4), 581–99. https://doi.org/10.1080/08838150802437396

Livingstone, S., & Pothong, K. (2021). *Playful by design: A vision of free play in a digital world*. Digital Futures Commission. https://digitalfuturescommission.org.uk/wp-content/uploads/2021/11/A-Vision-of-Free-Play-in-a-Digital-World.pdf

Livingstone, S., & Pothong, K. (2022). Imaginative play in digital environments: Designing social and creative opportunities for identity formation. *Information, Communication & Society*, 25(4), 485–501. https://doi.org/10.1080/1369118X.2022.2046128

Livingstone, S., & Third, A. (2017). Children and young people's rights in the digital age: An emerging agenda. *New Media & Society*, 19(5), 657–70. https://doi.org/10.1177/1461444816686318

Livingstone, S., Stoilova, M., & Nandagiri, R. (2019). *Children's data and privacy online: Growing up in a digital age: an evidence review*. LSE Research Online, London School of Economics and Political Science. https://eprints.lse.ac.uk/101283/

Livingstone, S., Mascheroni, G., Dreier, M., Chaudron, S., & Lagae, K. (2015). *How parents of young children manage digital devices at home: The role of income, education and parental style*. EU Kids Online, https://eprints.lse.ac.uk/63378/

Livingstone, S., Ólafsson, K., Helsper, E. J., Lupiáñez-Villanueva, F., Veltri, G. A., & Folkvord, F. (2017). Maximising opportunities and minimising risks for children online: The role of digital skills in emerging strategies of parental mediation. *Journal of Communication*, 67(1), 82–105. http://eprints.lse.ac.uk/68612/

Livingstone, S., Blum-Ross, A., Pavlick, J., & Ólafsson, K. (2018). *In the digital home, how do parents support their children and who supports them?* Parenting for a Digital Future: Survey Report 1. LSE. http://www.lse.ac.uk/media-and-communications/assets/documents/research/preparing-for-a-digital-future/P4DF-Survey-Report-1-In-the-digital-home.pdf

López-de-Ayala-López, M., & Haddon, L. (2018). *The parental mediation strategies of parents with young children.* Media@LSE Working Paper 50. LSE. http://www.lse.ac.uk/media-and-communications/assets/documents/research/working-paper-series/WP50.pdf

LSE (2021). *EU Kids Online: Researching European children's online opportunities, risks and safety.* https://www.lse.ac.uk/media-and-communications/research/research-projects/eu-kids-online

Lull, J. (2000). *Media, communication, culture: A global approach.* Columbia University Press.

Lupton, D. (2017). 'It just gives me a bit of peace of mind': Australian women's use of digital media for pregnancy and early motherhood. *Societies*, 7(3), 25–37. https://doi.org/10.3390/soc7030025

MacKenzie, D., & Wajcman, J. (1999). *The social shaping of technology* (2nd ed.). Open University Press.

Majors, K., & Baines, E. (2017). Children's play with their imaginary companions: Parent experiences and perceptions of the characteristics of the imaginary companions and purposes served. *Educational and Child Psychology*, 34(3), 37–56. https://discovery.ucl.ac.uk/id/eprint/10022746/

Margolis, A. A. (2020). Zone of proximal development, scaffolding and teaching practice. *Cultural-Historical Psychology*, 16(3), 15–26, https://doi.org/10.17759/chp.2020160303

Marsh, J., Brooks, G., Hughes, J., Ritchie, L., Roberts, S., & Wright, K. (2005). *Digital beginnings: Young people's use of popular culture, media and new technologies.* University of Sheffield.

Marsh, J., Plowman, L., Yamada-Rice, D., Bishop, J., & Scott, F. (2016). Digital play: A new classification. *Early Years*, 36(3), 242–53. https://doi.org/10.1080/09575146.2016.1167675

Marsh, J., Plowman, L., Yamada-Rice, D., Bishop J., Lahmar, J., & Scott, F. (2018). Play and creativity in young children's use of apps. *British Journal of Educational Technology*, 49(5), 870–82. https://doi.org/10.1111/bjet.12622

Marsh, J., Plowman, L., Yamada-Rice, D., Bishop, J. C., Lahmar, J., Scott, F., Davenport, A., Davis, S., French, K., Piras, M., Thornhill, S., Robinson, P., & Winter, P. (2015). *Exploring play and creativity in pre-schoolers' use of apps: final project report.* http://www.techandplay.org/reports/TAP_Final_Report.pdf

Mascheroni, G., & Haddon, L. (2015). Children, risks and the mobile internet. In Y. Zheng (Ed.), *Encyclopedia of mobile phone behavior* (pp. 1409–18). IGI Global.

Mascheroni, G., & Siibak, A. (2021). *Datafied childhoods: Data practices and imaginaries in children's lives*. Peter Lang.

Mason, J., May, V., & Clarke, L. (2007). Ambivalences and the paradoxes of grandparenting. *The Sociological Review*, 55(4), 687–706. https://doi.org/10.1111/j.1467-954X.2007.00748.x

McClure, E., Chentsova-Dutton, Y., Barr, R., Holochwost, S., & Parrott, G. (2015). 'Facetime doesn't count': Video chat as an exception to media restrictions for infants and toddlers. *International Journal of Child-Computer Interaction*, 6, 1–6. https://doi.org/10.1016/j.ijcci.2016.02.002

McPake, J., Plowman, L., & Stephen, C. (2012). Pre-school children creating and communicating with digital technologies in the home. *British Journal of Educational Technology*, 44(3), 421–31. https://doi.org/10.1111/j.1467-8535.2012.01323.x

Mikelić Preradović, N., Lešin, G., & Šagud, M. (2016). Investigating parents' attitudes towards digital technology use in early childhood: A case study from Croatia. *Informatics in Education*, 15(1), 127–46. https://doi.org/10.15388/infedu.2016.07

Minson, V., & McLean, K. (2023). Playgroup families' experiences of play-based remote learning. *Australasian Journal of Early Childhood*, 48(2), 117–33. https://doi.org/10.1177/18369391221193

Morgan, G. (1986). *Images of organization*. Sage.

Morley, D. (1986). *Family television: Cultural power and domestic leisure*. Comedia.

Mumsnet Ltd (n.d.). *Mumsnet: by parents for parents*. Retrieved 21 March 2022 from https://www.mumsnet.com/

NAEYC (2020). *Developmentally appropriate practice: Position statement*. National Association for the Education of Young Children. https://www.naeyc.org/sites/default/files/globally-shared/downloads/PDFs/resources/position-statements/dap-statement_0.pdf

NAEYC (2022). *Developmentally appropriate practice in early childhood programs serving children from birth through age 8* (4th ed). National Association for the Education of Young Children (NAEYC). Washington, DC: NAEYC. https://www.naeyc.org/resources/pubs/books/dap-fourth-edition

Nelson, C. A., & Gabard-Durnam, L. J. (2020). Early adversity and critical periods: Neurodevelopmental consequences of violating the expectable environment. *Trends in Neuroscience*, 43(Mar), 133–43. https://doi.org/10.1016/j.tins.2020.01.002

Neumann, M. M. (2014). An examination of touch screen tablets and emergent literacy in Australian pre-school children. *Australian Journal of Education*, 58(2), 109–22. https://doi.org/10.1177/0004944114523368

Neumann, M. M. (2018). Using tablets and apps to enhance emergent literacy skills in young children. *Early Childhood Research Quarterly*, 42, 239–46. https://doi.org/10.1016/j.ecresq.2017.10.006

Neumann, M. M., & Neumann, D. L. (2017). The use of touch screen tablets at home and pre-school to foster emergent literacy. *Journal of Early Childhood Literacy*, 17(2), 203–20. https://doi.org/10.1177/1468798415619773

Nevski, E., & Siibak, A. (2016). The role of parents and parental mediation on 0–3-year olds' digital play with smart devices: Estonian parents' attitudes and practices. *Early Years: An International Journal*, 36, 227–41. https://doi.org/10.1080/09575146.2016.1161601

Nikken, P., & Opree, S. J. (2018). Guiding young children's digital media use: SES-differences in mediation concerns and competence. *Journal of Child and Family Studies*, 27(6), 1844–57. https://doi.org/10.1007/s10826-018-1018-3

Nimrod, G., Lemish, D., & Elias, N. (2019). Grandparenting with media: Patterns of mediating grandchildren's media use. *Journal of Family Studies*, 1–19. https://doi.org/10.1080/13229400.2019.1679660

O'Connor, H., & Madge, C. (2004). My mum's thirty years out of date. *Community, Work & Family*, 7(3), 351–69. https://doi.org/10.1080/1366880042000295754

Odgers, C. L., & Jensen, M. R. (2020). Annual research review: Adolescent mental health in the digital age: Facts, fears and future directions. *Journal of Child Psychology and Psychiatry*, 61, 336–48. https://doi.org/10.1111/jcpp.13190

Ólafsson, K., Green, L., & Staksrud, E. (2017). Is big brother more at risk than little sister? The sibling factor in online risk and opportunity. *New Media and Society*, 20(4), 1–18. https://doi.org/10.1177/1461444817691531

O'Neill, B., Staksrud, E., & Mclaughlin, S. (Eds.) (2013). *Towards a better internet for children: policy pillars, players and paradoxes*. Nordicom.

Palaiologou, I. (2016). Teachers' dispositions towards the role of digital devices in play-based pedagogy in early childhood education. *Early Years*, 36(3), 305–21. https://doi.org/10.1080/09575146.2016.1174816

Palfrey, J., & Gasser, U. (2008). *Born digital: Understanding the first generation of digital natives*. Read How You Want.

Parenting for a Digital Future (n.d.). *Data tables for reports 1–5*. [Data set]. https://www.lse.ac.uk/media-and-communications/assets/documents/research/projects/parenting-for-a-digital-future/All-data-tables-FINAL060121.pdf

Pasquale, L., Zippo, P., Curley, C., O'Neill, B., & Mongiello, M. (2020). Digital age of consent and age verification: Can they protect children? *IEEE Software*, 39(3), 50–7. https://ieeexplore.ieee.org/abstract/document/9295422?casa_token=NBu1g_8Bl5wAAAAA:iiNsGQM0eeWlW_0s8OVMns2899PoKTSqYS_lroVLzrMUMiAuvEwa0XXVh8AonKptRmQpGMu2ew https://doi.org/10.1109/MS.2020.3044872

Pearce, K. E., Yip, J. C., Lee, J. H., Martinez, J. J., Windleharth, T. W., Bhattacharya, A., & Li, Q. (2022). Families playing animal crossing together: Coping with video games during the COVID-19 pandemic. *Games and Culture*, 17(5), 773–94. https://doi.org/10.1177/155541202110561

Pelo, A. (2008). Embracing a vision of social justice in early childhood education. *Rethinking Schools*, 23, 14–18. https://rethinkingschools.org/articles/embracing-a-vision-of-social-justice-in-early-childhood-education/

Petrovčič, A., Vehovar, V., & Dolnicar, V. (2015). Landline and mobile phone communication in social companionship networks of older adults: An empirical investigation in Sloveni. *Technology in Society*, 45, 91–102. https://doi.org/10.1016/j.techsoc.2016.02.007

Pew Research Center. (2020). *Parenting Children in the Age of Screens*. https://www.pewresearch.org/internet/2020/07/28/parenting-children-in-the-age-of-screens/

Piaget, J. (1952). *Play, dreams and imitation in childhood*. W.W. Norton Co.

Piaget, J. (1954). *The construction of reality in the child*. Basic Books.

Piaget, J., & Cook, M. T. (Tr.) (1952). *The origins of intelligence in children*. International Universities Press.

Pic, A., Han, M., Whitaker, A., & Barnes, T. N. (2023). Early childhood educators' perspectives on the impact of COVID-19 on child care. *Social Education Research*, 4(2), 194–208. https://doi.org/10.37256/ser.422

Pink, S., & Leder Mackley, K. (2013). Saturated and situated: Expanding the meaning of media in the routines of everyday life. *Media, Culture & Society*, 35(6), 677–91. https://doi.org/10.1177/0163443713491298

Plantin, L., & Danebacc, K. (2009). Parenthood, information and support on the internet. *A literature review of research on parents and professionals online. BMC Family Practice*, 10(34). https://doi.org/10.1186/1471-2296-10-34

Plowman, L. (2015). Researching young children's everyday uses of technology in the family home. *Interacting with Computers*, 27(1), 36–46. https://doi.org/10.1093/iwc/iwu031

Plowman, L., & Stephen, C. (2003). A 'benign addition'? A review of research on ICT and pre-school children. *Journal of Computer-Assisted Learning*, 19(2), 149–64. https://doi.org/10.1046/j.0266-4909.2003.00016.x

Plowman, L., & Stephen, C. (2005). Children, play and computers in pre-school education. *British Journal of Educational Technology*, 36(2), 145–57. https://doi.org/10.1111/j.1467-8535.2005.00449.x

Plowman, L., & Stevenson, O. (2013). Exploring the quotidian in young children's lives at home. *Home Cultures*, 10(3), 329–47. https://doi.org/10.2752/175174213X13739735973381

Plowman, L., McPake, J., & Stephen, C. (2008). Just picking it up? Young children learning with technology at home. *Cambridge Journal of Education*, 38(3), 303–19. https://doi.org/10.1080/03057640802287564

Plowman, L., McPake, J., & Stephen, C. (2010). The technologisation of childhood? Young children and technology in the home. *Children & Society*, 24(1), 63–74. https://doi.org/10.1111/j.1099-0860.2008.00180.x

Plowman, L., Stephen, C., & McPake, J. (2010a). *Growing up with technology. Young children learning in a digital world*. Routledge.

Plowman, L., Stephen, C., & McPake, J. (2010b). Supporting young children's learning with technology at home and in preschool. *Research Papers in Education*, 25(1), 93–113. https://doi.org/10.1080/02671520802584061

Plowman, L., Stevenson, O., Stephen C., & McPake, J. (2012). Preschool children's learning with technology at home. *Computers and Education*, 59, 30–7. https://doi.org/10.1016/j.compedu.2011.11.014

Prensky, M. (2001). Digital natives, digital immigrants, Part 1. *On the Horizon*, 9(5), 1–6. https://doi.org/10.1108/10748120110424816

Quadrello, T., Hurme, H., Menzinger, J., Smith, P., Veisson, M., Vidal, S., & Westerback, S. (2005). Grandparents use of new communication technologies in a European perspective. *European Journal of Ageing*, 2, 200–7. https://doi.org/10.1007/s10433-005-0004-y

Rhodes, A. (2017). *Screen time and kids: What's happening in our homes. Detailed report*. Melbourne (VIC): The Royal Children's Hospital Melbourne. Retrieved on 28 August 2022 from https://rchpoll.org.au/wp-content/uploads/2017/06/ACHP-Poll7_Detailed-Report-June21.pdf

Rideout, V., Vandewater, E., & Wartella, E. (2003). *Zero to six: Electronic media in the lives of infants, toddlers and preschoolers*. Kaiser Family Foundation. https://www.kff.org/wp-content/uploads/2013/01/zero-to-six-electronic-media-in-the-lives-of-infants-toddlers-and-preschoolers-pdf.pdf

Roberts-Holmes, G. (2014). Playful and creative ICT pedagogical framing: A nursery school case study. *Early Child Development and Care*, 184(1), 1–14. https://doi.org/10.1080/03004430.2013.772991

Rouse, E., & Hadley, F. (2018). Where did love and care get lost? Educators and parents' perceptions of early childhood practice. *International Journal of Early Years Education*, 26(2), 159–72. https://doi.org/10.1080/09669760.2018.1461613

Savic, M., McCosker, A., & Geldens, P. (2016). Cooperative mentorship: Negotiating social media use within the family. *M/C Journal*, 19(2). https://journal.media-culture.org.au/index.php/mcjournal/article/view/1078

Schank, R. C., Berman, T. R., & Macpherson, K. A. (1999). Learning by doing. In C. M. Reigeluth (Ed.), *Instructional-design theories and models: A new paradigm of instructional theory*, Vol. II (pp. 161–81). Laurence Erlbaum Associates.

Schriever, V. (2021). Early childhood teachers' management of their changing roles regarding digital technologies in kindergarten: A grounded theory study. *Australasian Journal of Early Childhood*, 46(1), 32–49. https://doi.org/10.1177/1836939120979065

Schriever, V., Simon, S., & Donninson, S. (2020). Guardians of play: Early childhood teachers' perceptions and actions to protect children's play from digital technology. *International Journal of Early Years Education*, 28(4), 351–65. https://doi.org/10.1080/09669760.2020.1850431

Scott, F. (2018). Troublesome binaries. In P. K. Smith & J. L. Roopnarine (Eds.), *The Cambridge handbook of play: Developmental/and disciplinary perspectives* (pp. 240–57). Cambridge University Press. https://doi.org/10.1017/9781108131384

Selwyn, N. (2009). The digital native – myth and reality. *Aslib Proceedings*, 61(4), 364–79. https://doi.org/10.1108/00012530910973776

Share, M., Williams, C., & Kerrins, L. (2018). Displaying and performing: Polish transnational families in Ireland Skyping grandparents in Poland. *New Media & Society*, 20(8), 3011–28. https://doi.org/10.1177/1461444817739272

Shinomiya, Y., Yoshizaki, A., Murata, E., Fujisawa, T. X., Taniike, M., & Mohri, I. (2021). Sleep and the general behavior of infants and parents during the closure of schools as a result of the COVID-19 pandemic: Comparison with 2019 data. *Children*, 8(2), 168. https://doi.org/10.3390/children8020168

Shinskey, J. L. (2021). Can infants use video to update mental representations of absent objects? *Infant Behavior and Development*, 64. https://doi.org/10.1016/j.infbeh.2021.101623

Siibak, A., & Traks, K. (2019). The dark sides of sharenting. *Catalan Journal of Communication & Cultural Studies*, 11(1), 115–21. https://doi.org/10.1386/cjcs.11.1.115_1

Silverstone, R., & Hirsch, E. (Eds.) (1992). *Consuming technologies: Media and information in domestic spaces*. Routledge.

Silverstone, R., Hirsch, E., & Morley, D. (1992). Information and communication technologies and the moral economy of the household. In R. Silverstone & E. Hirsch (Eds.), *Consuming technologies: Media and information in domestic spaces* (pp. 15–31). Routledge.

Spera, C. (2005). A review of the relationship among parenting practices, parenting styles and adolescent school achievement educational. *Psychology Review*, 17, 125–46. https://doi.org/10.13007/s10648-005-3950-1

Spink, A., Danby, S., Mallan, K., & Butler, C. (2010). Exploring young children's web searching and technoliteracy. *Journal of Documentation*, 66(2), 191–206. http://dx.doi.org/10.1108/00220411011023616

Stephen, C. (2010). Pedagogy: The silent partner in early years learning. *International Journal of Research and Development*, 30(1), 15–28. https://doi.org/10.1080/09575140903402881

Stephen, C. (2021). Young learners in a digital age. In L. Green, D. Holloway, K. Stevenson, T. Leaver, & L. Haddon (Eds.), *The Routledge companion to digital media and children* (pp. 577–66). Routledge.

Stephen, C., & Edwards, S. (2018). *Young children playing and learning in a digital age: A cultural and critical perspective*. Routledge.

Stephen, C., & Plowman, L. (2003). Information and communication technologies in pre-school settings: A review of the literature. *International Journal of Early Years Education*, 11(3), 223–34. https://doi.org/10.1080/09669760320000147343

Stephen, C., & Plowman, L. (2008). Enhancing learning with information and communication technologies in pre-school. *Early Child Development and Care*, 178(6), 637–54. https://doi.org/10.1080/03004430600869571

Stephen, C., Stevenson, O., & Adey, C. (2013). Young children engaging with technologies at home: The influence of family context. *Journal of Early Childhood Research*, 11(2), 149–64. https://doi.org/10.1177/1476718X12466215

Stephen, S., McPake, J., Plowman, L., & Berch-Heyman, S. (2008). Learning from the children. Exploring preschool children's encounters with ICT at home. *Journal of Early Childhood Research*, 6(2), 99–117. https://doi.org/10.1177/1476718X08088673

Stevenson, K. J., Green, L., Holloway, D. J., & Jaunzems, K. (2019). Like mother, like daughter? Unboxing an Etsy childhood: At home with digital media. In L. Green, D. J. Holloway, K. J. Stevenson, & K. Jaunzems (Eds.), *Digitising early childhood* (pp. 212–25). Cambridge Scholars Publishing.

Stevenson, K. J., Green, L., Holloway, D. J., & Jaunzems, K. (2021). Screening language acquisition skills in a mediated childhood. In D. Holloway, M. Wilson, K. Murcia, C. Archer, & F. Stocco (Eds.), *Young children's rights in a digital world: Play, design and practice* (pp. 93–106). Springer. https://doi.org/10.1007/978-3-030-65916-5_8

Stevenson, K. J., Jaunzems, K., Green, L., & Holloway, D. J. (2019). Accounting for siblings in family-based research. In L. Green, D. J. Holloway, K. J. Stevenson, & K. Jaunzems (Eds.), *Digitising early childhood*. Cambridge Scholars Publishing.

Stiglic, N., & Viner, R. M. (2019). Effects of screentime on the health and wellbeing of children and adolescents: A systematic review of reviews. *BMJ Open*, 9(1), 1–15. https://doi.org/10.1136/bmjopen-2018-023191

Su, J., Ng, D. T. K., Yang, W., & Li, H. (2022). Global trends in the research on early childhood education during the COVID-19 pandemic: A bibliometric analysis. *Education Sciences*, 12(5), 331, 1–20, https://doi.org/10.3390/educsci12050331

Technavio (2021, June 6). *Global Education Apps Market | $ 46.88 Billion growth expected during 2020–2024*. https://www.prnewswire.com/news-releases/global-education-apps-market—46-88-billion-growth-expected-during-2020-2024–technavio-301306209.html

Temban, M. M., Hua, T. K., & Said, N. E. M. (2021). Exploring informal learning opportunities via YouTube Kids among children during COVID-19. *Academic Journal of Interdisciplinary Studies*, 10(3), 272–87. https://doi.org/10.36941/ajis-2021-0083

Thiele, D., & Whelan, T. (2006). The nature and dimensions of the grandparent role. *Marriage & Family Review*, 40(1), 93–108. https://doi.org/10.1300/J002v40n01_06

Third, A., Collin, P., Walsh, L., & Black, R. (2019). *Young people in digital society: Control shift*. Palgrave Macmillan. https://doi.org/10.1057/978-1-137-57369-8

Tizard, B., & Hughs, M. (1984). *Young children learning: Talking and thinking at home and at school*. Fontana Press.

Toh, W., & Lim, F. V. (2021). Let's play together: Ways of parent–child digital co-play for learning. *Interactive Learning Environments*, 1–11. https://doi.org/10.1080/10494820.2021.1951768

Tőkés, G. (2016). Digital practices in everyday lives of 4 to 6 years old Romanian children. *Journal of Comparative Research in Anthropology and Sociology*, 7(2), 93–111. https://www.ceeol.com/search/article-detail?id=552545

Tsaliki, L., & Chronaki, D. (Eds.) (2020). *Discourses of anxiety over childhood and youth across cultures*. Palgrave Macmillan.

UNCRC. (2021). General Comment (no. 25) on *Children's Rights in the Digital Environment*, United Nations Committee on the Rights of the Child. Retrieved on 18 April 2022 from https://tbinternet.ohchr.org/_layouts/15/treatybodyexternal/Download.aspx?symbolno=CRC/C/GC/25&Lang=en [in six languages with a child-friendly version linked through from https://www.ohchr.org/EN/HRBodies/CRC/Pages/GCChildrensRightsRelationDigitalEnvironment.aspx]

United Nations. (2011). *Guiding principles on business and human rights: Implementing the United Nations 'Protect, Respect and Remedy' Framework* (HR/PUB/11/04). https://www.ohchr.org/Documents/Publications/GuidingPrinciplesBusinessHR_EN.pdf

Valcke, M., Bontea, S., De Wevera, B., & Rotsa, I. (2010). Internet parenting styles and the impact on internet use of primary school children. *Computers & Education*, 55(2), 454–64. https://doi.org/10.1016/j.compedu.2010.02.009

Valkenburg, P., Krcmar, M., Peeters, A., & Marseille, N. (1999). Developing a scale to assess three styles of television mediation: Instructive mediation, restrictive mediation and social coviewing. *Journal of Broadcasting & Electronic Media*, 43(1), 52–66. https://doi.org/10.1080/08838159909364474

Verenikina, I., & Kervin, L. (2011). iPads, digital play and pre-schoolers. *He Kupu*, 2(5), 4–19. https://www.hekupu.nztertiarycollege.ac.nz/sites/default/files/2017-11/iPads-Digital-Play-and-Preschoolers.pdf

Vidal-Hall, C., Flewitt, R., & Wyse, D. (2020). Early childhood practitioner beliefs about digital media: Integrating technology into a child-centred classroom environment. *European Early Childhood Education Research Journal*, 28(2), 167–81. https://doi.org/10.1080/1350293x.2020.1735727

Vittrup, B., Snider, S., Rose, K., & Rippy, J. (2016). Parental perceptions of the role of media and technology in their young children's lives. *Journal of Early Childhood Research*, 14(1), 43–54. https://doi.org/10.1177/1476718X14523749

Vygotsky, L. S. (1962). *Thought and language* (Ed. & Trans. Eugenia Hanfmann & Gertrude Vakar). MIT Press & Wiley.

Vygotsky, L. S. (1978). *Mind in society: The development of higher psychological processes*. Harvard University Press.

Vygotsky, L. S. (2016 [1966]). Play and its role in the mental development of the child. *International Research in Early Childhood Education*, 7(2), 3–25. https://bridges.monash.edu/collections/International_Research_in_Early_Childhood_Education_2016_7_2_-_Special_issue/3594548

Wade, M., Prime, H., & Browne, D. (2023). Why we still need longitudinal mental health research with children and youth during (and after) the COVID-19 pandemic. *Psychiatry research*, 323(May), 115126. https://doi.org/10.1016/j.psychres.2023.115126

Wartella, E., Beaudoin-Ryan, L., Blackwell, C., Cingel, D., Hurwitz, L., & Lauricella, A. (2016). What kind of adults will our children become? The impact of growing up in a media-saturated world. *Journal of Children and Media*, 10(1), 13–20. https://doi.org/10.1080/17482798.2015.1124796

Williams, S., & Williams, L. (2005). Space invaders: The negotiation of teenage boundaries through the mobile phone. *The Sociological Review*, 53, 314–31. https://doi.org/10.1111/j.1467-954X.2005.00516.x

Wohlwend, K. E. (2015). One screen, many fingers: Young children's collaborative literacy play with digital puppetry apps and touchscreen technologies. *Theory into Practice*, 54(2), 154–62. https://doi.org/10.1080/00405841.2015.1010837

Wolfe, S., & Flewitt, R. (2010). New technologies, new multimodal literacy practices and young children's metacognitive development. *Cambridge Journal of Education*, 40, 387–99. https://doi.org/10.1080/0305764X.2010.526589

Wood, D., Bruner, J. S., & Ross, G. (1976). The role of tutoring in problem solving. *Journal of Child Psychology and Psychiatry*, 17(2), 89–100, https://doi.org/10.1111/j.1469-7610.1976.tb00381.x

World Health Organization. (2019). *Guidelines on physical activity, sedentary behaviour and sleep for children under 5 years of age.* https://apps.who.int/iris/handle/10665/311664

Yamada-Rice, D. (2021). Children's interactive storytelling in virtual reality. *Multimodality & Society*, 1(1), 48–67. https://doi.org/10.1177/2634979521992965

Yarosh, S., Chew, Y., & Abowda, G. (2009). Supporting parent–child communication in divorced families. *International Journal of Human-Computer Studies*, 67, 192–203. https://doi.org/10.1016/j.ijhcs.2008.09.005

YouTube (2011). *A magazine is an iPad that does not work.m4v* [video], UseExperiencesWorks: https://www.youtube.com/watch?v=aXV-yaFmQNk

Zaman, B., Nouwen, M., Vanattenhoven, J., de Ferrerre, E., & Van Looy, J. (2016). A qualitative inquiry into the contextualized parental mediation practices of young children's digital media use at home. *Journal of Broadcasting & Electronic Media*, 60(1), 1–22. https://doi.org/10.1080/08838151.2015.1127240

Zevenbergen, R. (2007). Digital natives come to preschool: Implications for early childhood practice. *Contemporary Issues in Early Childhood*, 8(1), 19–29. https://doi.org/10.2304/ciec.2007.8.1.19

Index

ABC Kids' iView app 126, 132
ABC Me TV programme 150
active learning 31
active mediation 53. *See also* restrictive mediation
Adam. *See* Campbell, Adam
aggressive behaviour of children 38, 62
Alice. *See* Spinner, Alice
Amanda 58
Amelia. *See* Lawe-Tammell, Amelia
American Academy of Pediatrics (AAP) 8, 26–8, 133, 136–7, 157, 159
  2x2 rule 37
  on 'Media and young minds' 28
Andrew. *See* Brent, Andrew
Andrew. *See* Greenfield, Andrew
Andrew. *See* Lim-Park, Andrew
Andrews-White, Ben 126, 136, 149–50, 208–9
Andrews-White, Kate 1, 58, 60–1, 65, 126–7, 132–3, 136, 149–50, 158, 160, 198, 201, 208–9
Andrews-White, Liam 10, 13, 126, 136, 139–40, 149–50, 158, 160, 198, 202, 204, 208–9
Andrews-White, Richard 126, 149, 208–9
Andrews-White, Scott 10, 13, 47, 65, 119–20, 126–7, 133, 136, 149, 194–5, 204, 208–9
Angie. *See* Govender, Angie
Anglosphere 114, 134
animations 62, 90, 109, 178, 225
apps 18, 35–6, 44–6, 59, 61–5, 74, 89, 99, 101–2, 103, 105–7, 116, 118, 120, 122–4, 126–7, 132–3, 144–7, 154, 158, 160–1, 164–6, 174, 176–87, 194, 208, 210, 216, 218–21, 226. *See also specific apps*
attachment style parenting 111–12, 214
Australian Research Council (ARC) 8
  Toddlers and Tablets project (*see* Toddlers and Tablets: Exploring the Risks and Benefits 0-5s Face Online*)

authoritarian parents 54, 165, 228 n.4
authoritative parents 54, 138, 165, 204

baby karaoke app 105, 116
babysitting 48, 56, 72, 75, 77, 79
Bakardjieva, M., *Internet society: The Internet in everyday life* 3
balance, child's technology use 9, 11, 14, 16–17, 41–2, 55, 59–60, 67, 85, 106, 113, 115, 191, 205
Barbara. *See* Petersen, Barbara
Baumrind, D., parenting styles 53–4
Bazalgette, C. 28, 31, 113, 115
  How Toddlers Learn the Secret Language of Movies 2–3
Beck-Gernsheim, E., on individualization 40
Beck, U., on individualization 40
Belle. *See* Spinner, Belle
Ben. *See* Andrews-White, Ben
Ben. *See* Lawe-Tammell, Ben
Berger, P. 21–2
Berlin, I., analysis of liberty 35
Bernard, Chloe 96–7, 210
Bernard, Connor 130–1, 135, 139–40, 142–3, 151–2, 158, 164, 195, 199, 203, 209–10
Bernard, Sarah 56, 75, 78, 130–1, 133, 142–3, 151–2, 164, 190, 195, 199, 209–10
Bernard, Scott 135, 151–2, 164, 199, 209–10
Bernard, Sean 131, 164, 199, 210
Bernard, William 119–20, 130–2, 135, 142–3, 151, 164, 196, 199, 209–10
Bernard, Xavier 130–1, 142, 152, 164, 210
bi-lingual 166
Blum-Ross, A. 200
  genres of digital parenting 41
  Parenting for a digital future: How hopes and fears about technology shape children's lives 3–4, 11, 36, 40, 42–3

Brent, Andrew 147, 159, 175, 191, 210
Brent, Elisabeth 65, 147, 159, 161, 175, 191, 209–11
Brent, Ellen 10, 13, 64–5, 140, 147–8, 159, 161, 175, 191, 206, 209–11
Brent, James 147, 159, 175, 191, 210
Brent, Ted 147, 175, 209–10
Bronfenbrenner, U. 22–5, 30
Brown, Jerry 124, 132, 135–6, 165, 209, 211–12
Brown, Klara 59, 61, 124, 132–3, 135–6, 165, 177, 209, 211–12
Brown, Simon 10, 12, 59, 64, 120, 124, 132–3, 135, 165, 191, 200, 209, 211–12
Bruner, J. S. 22–3, 175

Campbell, Adam 65, 103, 112–14, 116, 209, 212
Campbell, Jenna 57, 60, 63, 65, 81, 103, 112, 114, 116, 134, 203, 209, 212–13
Campbell, Julia 10, 12, 63, 65, 100, 103, 114, 116, 134, 194, 203, 209, 212–13
CBeebies 87, 144, 147, 159, 218
Cecilia. *See* Langridge, Cecilia
Chaudron, S. 53, 158
Cheun-Yeo, Jo 61, 64, 107–8, 112, 114, 116, 192, 213
Cheun-Yeo, Marie 59, 64, 107–8, 112, 114, 116, 209, 213
Cheun-Yeo, Samuel 10, 13, 64, 100, 107–8, 112, 114, 116, 134, 209, 213
childcare centres 17, 24, 33, 108, 114–16, 159, 220
child participants, data of 9–11. *See also specific participants*
child-rearing 54, 57, 110, 204, 213
children's rights in digital environment 29, 46, 48–9
Chloe. *See* Bernard, Chloe
Claire. *See* Petersen, Claire
Clark, L. S., *The parent app: Understanding families in the digital age* 3
cognitive development of children 16, 22, 24, 27, 111, 156, 174, 177, 182, 198
compulsory schooling in Australia 3, 17, 27, 139, 161, 197
computer games 36, 43, 46, 226
Connor. *See* Bernard, Connor
consumerism 18, 154, 160, 201

control paradigm 45
converged play 85
CookieSwirlC vlogger 154, 160, 199
co-play 18, 154, 156, 193. *See also* free play
Corkin, M., study on screen time 39
Covid-19 pandemic 15. *See also* post-pandemic (Covid-19) era
  online learning during 30–2
  play-based learning 32–3
Craig. *See* Jameson, Craig
creative play 160
Cullen, Adam 104, 214
Cullen, Alexa 104, 214
Cullen, Elle 104, 112, 179, 214
Cullen, Finn 10, 13, 100, 104, 112, 115, 179, 209, 214
Cullen, Sherryl 65, 104, 112–13, 115, 179, 209, 214
culture 17–18, 22, 25, 28, 33, 114, 125, 165–6, 180, 197, 206
  cultural capital 18, 31, 158, 197, 200
  cultural values 18, 41, 174

Daniel. *See* Spinner, Daniel
Danny. *See* Greenfield, Danny
Davis, Emma 10, 12, 119–20, 122–3, 134, 136, 140, 152, 195–6, 209, 214–15
Davis, Isabelle 61, 65, 81, 122–3, 132–3, 136, 140, 152–3, 157, 160, 194, 196, 202, 209, 214–15
Davis, Jacob 81, 123, 134, 136, 140, 152–3, 160, 193–4, 201–3, 214–15
Davis, Malcom 81, 136, 209, 214–15
Davis, Phoebe 11–12, 123, 136, 139–42, 152–3, 157–8, 160, 194, 201–3, 209, 214–15
Dean. *See* Langridge, Dean
Dee 73–7
Delia 74–5, 78
Denise 57, 66
diet metaphor 55
DigiLitEY project 47
digital engagement of children
  for babysitting 48, 75, 79, 96
  children's rights in digital environment 29, 46, 48–9
  guide for digital parenting 45–9
  learnings (*see* learnings through digital media)
  medical perspectives of 27–8

parents' approaches/perceptions of 11–14, 17
parent's role in supporting 175–6, 180–6, 204–6
digital future 1, 11, 15, 36
   parenting for 40–2
   parents' planning for children's (challenges) 201–4, 206–7
Digital Futures Commission, UK 21, 46–7
digital immigrants 43, 74, 84, 228 n.3 (Ch 5)
digital inequality 4
digital literacy 36, 47, 52, 162
digital natives (digital natives myth) 35–6, 83–4, 228 n.3 (Ch 5)
digital parenting 1, 7, 11, 15–17, 104, 116, 127, 134, 205
   challenges 15, 32, 41–2, 48
   genres of (by Livingstone and Blum-Ross) 41
   guide for 45–9
   motivations for using digital apps (parents of under-fives) 45–6
digital play 7, 90, 103, 141, 144, 150, 158, 173, 198
digital skill development 16, 18–19, 63, 113, 130–1, 133, 135, 138, 151, 156, 161, 197, 199, 204, 206, 215
digital technology 7, 23, 36, 40–1, 46–7, 49, 51–6, 60, 63, 67, 84–5, 90–1, 98, 117, 127, 137, 156, 158, 161–2, 193, 198–9, 204–5, 208, 212–15
disability/disabled children 36, 49
diversity in children's digital lives 199–200
divorced/separated parents 11, 18, 163, 200
   children in divorced families 169–71
Dora the Explorer 103
dose-response relationship 38

early childhood educators/education (ECE) 19, 26–7, 33
   bibliometric analysis during Covid-19 30
ecological systems theory 24
educational apps 18, 36, 44, 89, 166, 177–8, 186–7. *See also* apps
educational games 88, 176
Elaine 75, 77–9
elective kindergarten 139
Elisabeth. *See* Brent, Elisabeth

Eliza. *See* Govender, Eliza
Elle. *See* Cullen, Elle
Ellen. *See* Brent, Ellen
Elsa. *See* Petersen, Elsa
embrace, child's technology use 11, 16–17, 41, 135, 164, 191, 199, 204, 206
Emily. *See* Lim-Park, Emily
Emma. *See* Davis, Emma
emotional skills 17–18, 27, 42, 139, 143, 155–61
Erin 74, 76, 78
ethnicity 18, 163, 199
ethnography/ethnographic study 2–3, 15, 18, 25, 30, 33, 37, 40, 99, 119, 131, 137, 155, 187, 189, 198
ethnotheories 16, 54, 56–60, 63, 66, 112, 190–1, 201, 203
EU Kids Online project 8
   Zero to Eight: Young Children and Their Internet Use 8
Evan. *See* Jameson, Evan
evidence-based approach 8, 18–19, 29, 38–9, 70, 110, 112, 143, 155–61, 194, 198, 206
evolving capacity of children 27, 29, 48
exosystem 24, 32–3
extending knowledge 84

Facebook 33, 58, 81, 101, 130, 134, 216
Facetime 63, 80, 103, 114, 134, 144, 170, 194, 208, 216, 222
'Families need Fathers' (FNF) organization 169–70
family-based research 3–4, 14, 18, 30, 33, 112, 121, 194, 198
'Family Media Plan' 137, 157
field collaborators, parents as 7, 101
Finn. *See* Cullen, Finn
Flewitt, R. 22, 25–6, 85
Floyd. *See* Jameson, Floyd
formal education 3, 36, 139, 198, 207
Francoise. *See* Jameson, Francoise
Frankie. *See* Ross, Frankie
freedom, children's 35–6, 47, 99, 110, 165, 225
free play 47, 61, 175. *See also* co-play
Freya. *See* Petersen, Freya
friendship-formation 197
fun 28, 45, 70, 103, 158, 165, 167, 182
future lives 1, 186, 210

games 4, 36, 43–4, 46, 61–2, 64, 120–1, 129–30, 153, 155–6, 167–8, 176–9, 182, 194–5, 198–9, 202, 209, 215, 217–18, 220, 223–4, 226
gender 5, 9–10, 18, 30, 44, 71, 150, 163, 198–9
General Comment (No. 25) on *Children's Rights in the Digital Environment*, UNCRC 14, 26, 29, 48
Google 57–8, 155
Govender, Angie 56–8, 81, 101–2, 114, 203, 209, 216
Govender, Eliza 100–2, 112, 114, 203, 209, 216
Govender, Yussef 101, 114, 209, 216
grandparents/grandparenting 9, 15–16, 19, 36, 40, 43, 57, 63, 69–72, 121, 125, 163, 192–3, 195, 202, 228 nn.1–2 (Ch 5), 228 n.7
  actions and digital media rules 76–9
  difficulties when using technology 71
  diversity of grandparents' experiences (*Toddlers and Tablets* findings) 72–3
  experience of technology 72–3
  grandparents-grandchild interaction 71–2
  haven strategy of 16, 78–9, 82
  parents' observations and perspectives 80–2
  parents' *vs.* grandparents' views on digital media 73–6
  study on grandparenting norms 71
  styles and variations 70
Greenfield, Andrew 10, 12, 57, 59, 65, 100, 108–9, 114–16, 209, 215–16
Greenfield, Danny 9, 57, 59, 65, 108, 114–16, 209, 215–16
Greenfield, Trish 81, 108–9, 114–16, 209, 215–16
Green, L. 14
Growing Up in New Zealand longitudinal cohort study 39
guided interaction 16, 84, 175

Haddon, L. 6–7, 9, 11, 14, 101, 106–7, 109, 111, 113, 132, 144–5, 147–9, 154, 156–9, 168, 180, 182, 198, 203
hand-me-down culture 8, 160, 202, 210, 223
haven strategy of grandparents 16, 78–9, 82
Helen 58, 79, 95

Holloway, D. 14
hula hoops game 6, 120–1
Human Research Ethics Committees of Edith Cowan University 5–6
hyperactivity 39, 103, 113

ICTs (Information and Communication Technologies) 52, 84, 90–1, 135, 164
imaginary companions 196–7
imagination, children's 28, 46, 61, 66, 87, 89, 129, 155, 177, 190
imaginative play 46, 199
Imelda. *See* Spinner, Imelda
imitative play 123, 134, 195
incidental learning 175
independent activities 5, 59, 63, 65, 67, 70
individualization 40
infants (birth to twenty-three months), digital media use 2–3, 5, 9, 17, 19, 28, 31, 44, 99–100, 133, 197
  during Covid pandemic in Japan 31
  factors for enabling 112–16
  participants 100–11 (*see also specific participants*)
  policy considerations 117–18
iPad 52, 61–2, 64–5, 75, 80–1, 87–90, 96, 103, 108–11, 120–1, 126, 129, 133, 136, 144–50, 152–4, 156, 158, 160–1, 177, 180, 193, 195–6, 203, 208–9, 211–12, 215, 217, 219, 221, 224–6. *See also* smartphones; tablets
Isabelle. *See* Davis, Isabelle

Jackie 74
Jacob. *See* Davis, Jacob
James. *See* Brent, James
Jameson, Craig 11, 61, 81, 129–30, 135, 154–5, 157–8, 202, 209, 217
Jameson, Evan 10, 12, 119–20, 129–30, 135, 154–5, 209, 217
Jameson, Floyd 129, 135, 139–40, 154–5, 157–8, 197, 201, 209, 217
Jameson, Francoise 11, 61, 81, 129–30, 135, 154–5, 203, 209, 217
Jasper. *See* Langridge, Jasper
Jeff. *See* Petersen, Jeff
Jenna. *See* Campbell, Jenna
Jerry. *See* Brown, Jerry
Jo. *See* Cheun-Yeo, Jo

joint media engagement 43
Julia. *See* Campbell, Julia

Karen 75–6, 81
Karla. *See* Spinner, Karla
Kate. *See* Andrews-White, Kate
Kath 58, 96
kindergarten/preschool 139, 146, 153, 166, 179, 193, 210, 220. *See also* preschoolers
Kindle 155, 212, 217–18, 224
Klara. *See* Brown, Klara
Kramer, Libby 10, 12, 56, 106–7, 113, 139–40, 143–4, 157–8, 167, 184–6, 198, 209, 217–18
Kramer, Michael 209, 217–18
Kramer, Owen 10, 12, 100, 106–7, 113, 115, 143, 157, 167, 198, 209, 217–18
Kramer, Stella 56, 60, 64–6, 106, 113, 115, 143–4, 158–9, 177, 179, 184–6, 209, 217–18

laissez-faire parenting 126, 219
Langridge, Cecilia 10, 13, 100, 105–6, 113, 115–16, 119, 128, 209, 218–19
Langridge, Dean 105, 115, 128, 132, 209, 218–19
Langridge, Jasper 105, 115–16, 119–20, 128–9, 135, 196, 209, 218–19
Langridge, Louisa 60, 105, 115–16, 128–9, 132, 135, 209, 218–19
language 22–3, 28, 57, 84, 109, 119, 120–1, 140, 146, 154, 166–7, 176, 178–9, 226
  bi-lingual 166
  mother-tongue 165, 220
Lavinia. *See* Zhang/Chen, Lavinia
Lawe, Rosalie 65, 150–1, 156–7, 159, 165, 209, 219–20
Lawe-Tammell, Amelia 150, 156, 201
Lawe-Tammell, Ben 10, 13, 65, 140, 150–1, 156, 160, 195, 198–9, 201, 203, 209, 219–20
Lawe-Tammell, Richard 150–1, 157, 209, 219–20
Lawe-Tammell, Samantha 150, 156, 201
learnings through digital media 18–19, 31–2, 35, 42–4, 164, 186
  active learning 31
  incidental learning 175

language learning 64, 179
  parents' evaluation (perceptions) of 200–1
  importance of digital media for learning 173–5
  parent's role in (supporting) learning process 175–6, 180–6, 204–6
  potty training, references for 120, 175, 178
  scaffolding of children's learning 23, 32, 48, 175–6, 181, 186
Leela. *See* Palmer, Leela
Lenka 74, 76, 79
Leopoldo. *See* Tosetti, Leopoldo
Liam. *See* Andrews-White, Liam
Libby. *See* Kramer, Libby
Lily. *See* Zhang/Chen, Lily
Lim-Park, Andrew 145–6, 220
Lim-Park, Emily 10, 12, 100, 109–10, 113, 116, 146, 195, 209, 220
Lim-Park, Michael 10, 12, 109–10, 113, 139–40, 145–6, 156, 159, 193, 196, 209, 220
Lim-Park, Mi Na 57, 62, 65, 109–10, 113, 116, 145–6, 156, 159, 196, 220
Lim-Park, Yu Na 145, 220
Livingstone, S. 4, 14, 37, 200
  genres of digital parenting 41
  Parenting for a digital future: How hopes and fears about technology shape children's lives 3–4, 11, 36, 40, 42–3
  on screen time 39
Liza 58, 94–5
London School of Economics and Political Science (LSE) 5, 8
Lorenzo. *See* Tosetti, Lorenzo
Louisa. *See* Langridge, Louisa
Luckmann, T. 21–2
Lucy 75–8
Lull, J., *Media, communication, culture: A global approach* 3

macrosystem 24, 32
Malcom. *See* Davis, Malcom
Mansi, Nadia 63, 65, 110–15, 136, 166, 179–80, 192, 209, 221
Mansi, Rohan 60, 63, 65, 110–12, 114–15, 136–7, 166, 179–80, 209, 221

Mansi, Sergei 10, 12, 63, 65, 100, 110–11, 114–15, 136–7, 166, 179–80, 191, 201, 209, 221
Marcy 73, 78
Marie. *See* Cheun-Yeo, Marie
Marissa. *See* Palmer, Marissa
medical perspectives of digital engagement of children 27–8
mesosystem 24, 32–3
Michael. *See* Kramer, Michael
microsystem 24, 33
Mi Na. *See* Lim-Park, Mi Na
Minecraft 131, 150, 177, 199, 209, 215, 220
Mirabella. *See* Tosetti, Mirabella
moral panics about technology 37, 51–2, 85
Morley, D., *Family television: Cultural power and domestic leisure* 3
mother-tongue 165, 220. *See also* language
motor skill development 17, 19, 99, 105, 112, 161, 176, 194, 197
Mr Tumble programme 147, 161
mum and baby yoga 111
Mumsnet Ltd 57, 127, 215

Nadia. *See* Mansi, Nadia
National Association for the Education of Young Children (NAEYC), US
  child development and learning 26–7
  Developmentally Appropriate Practice in Early Childhood Programs 26
neglectful parents 43, 54
Netflix 103, 210, 218
nursery(ies) 16–17, 56, 60, 84, 86–97, 108, 115, 164, 193. *See also* preschool settings/education; *specific nurseries*

Office for Standards in Education, Children's Services and Skills (Ofsted) 87, 91
O'Neill, B. 14
online advice/sources 16, 44, 54–5, 58–9, 66
ontology 22
operational knowledge/skills 18, 84, 90, 174, 179, 186, 205
Our Family TV programme 147
overuse of digital devices/technology 60, 71, 89, 93
Owen. *See* Kramer, Owen

Palmer, Leela 140, 148–9, 156, 159, 167, 179, 182–4, 186, 195–9, 209, 221–2
Palmer, Linda 57, 60–2, 148–9, 156, 177, 179, 182–3, 186, 197, 209, 221–2
Palmer, Marissa 148–9, 167–8, 182, 198, 221–2
parallel parenting 170
parental controls 44–5, 208–10
parental evaluations 60, 67, 179–80
parental mediation 16–18, 43–5, 49, 52–5, 59, 66–7, 77, 171
  active mediation 53
  restrictive mediation 53
parental/parenting styles 16, 54, 59–60, 112. *See also specific styles*
parent-child interactions 43, 51, 55. *See also* co-play
parenting and digital media 190–2
  findings by Toddlers and Tablets project (*see* Toddlers and Tablets: Exploring the Risks and Benefits 0-5s Face Online)
  review 52–6
parenting organizations 138, 187
parents' online forums 57–9, 190
password privacy 150
Pemberton Nursery, UK 87–92, 97
  Carmen (staff) 87–92, 94
  Leo (staff) 88, 90–3, 97
  Sita (staff) 92–3
Penny. *See* Ross, Penny
Peppa Pig 89, 125–6, 134, 136, 166, 180, 197
permissive parents 54
Peter Pan Nursery, UK 86–91, 97, 195
  Bridget (staff) 87, 89, 92–4
  Ivanka (staff) 87, 89–94
  Maria (staff) 87, 94
Petersen, Barbara 153, 176, 178, 186, 222
Petersen, Claire 56, 62–3, 65, 72, 74–6, 78–81, 95–7, 141–2, 153–4, 156–7, 159–60, 176, 178, 205, 209, 222–3
Petersen, Elsa 64, 141, 153–4, 156, 176, 178, 186, 199, 201–2, 222
Petersen, Freya 11, 12, 140–2, 153–4, 156, 159–60, 176, 178, 186, 199, 201–2, 209, 222
Petersen, Jeff 142, 153–4, 160, 176, 178, 186, 199, 209, 222–3
Phoebe. *See* Davis, Phoebe

Piaget, J. 18, 23, 175
Play and Learn Nursery, Australia 88–9, 92, 96–7
  Abbey (staff) 91
  Carey (staff) 96
  Trisha (staff) 96
play-based research activity 6, 189
playgroup model (play-based learning) 32–3
Plowman, L. 54, 84, 191. *See also* ethnotheories
policymakers 15, 28, 35, 44–6, 138, 204
positive feedback for children 46, 84, 180
positive learning dispositions 84
post-pandemic (Covid-19) era 30–4. *See also* Covid-19 pandemic
potty/toilet training 120, 125–6, 128, 140, 175, 178, 202, 219
preschoolers (four and five years old) 2–3, 8–9, 16–17, 19, 31, 48, 139–43, 194–8
  participants 140–1 (*see also specific participants*)
  policy considerations 161–2
  social and emotional skills in digital engagement 155–61
preschool settings/education 16, 25, 52, 57, 193
  and digital media 83–6
    parents' view of children's learning in preschool 94–7
    relationship between home and school 86, 92–4, 98
    Toddlers and Tablets findings 86–92
  preschool practitioners 192–3
pretend-play 141, 195, 198
psychology 8, 21, 23, 38
public health model 26, 38, 133, 135
public place, use of digital media in 1, 192

Reading Eggs app 123, 127, 136, 143, 158
restrictive mediation 53. *See also* active mediation
restrict/resist, child's technology use 11, 14, 28, 41, 44–5, 46, 53, 61, 73, 104, 109, 122, 128, 135–6, 159–60, 165, 191, 213
Richard. *See* Andrews-White, Richard
Richard. *See* Lawe-Tammell, Richard
rights-based approach 14, 29

Rita. *See* Zhang/Chen, Rita
Rohan. *See* Mansi, Rohan
Ron. *See* Ross, Ron
Rosalie. *See* Lawe, Rosalie
Ross, Frankie 127, 133, 168, 223–4
Ross, Penny 120, 127–8, 132–3, 168, 179–82, 186, 195, 206, 209, 223
Ross, Ron 59, 62, 127–8, 160, 209, 223
Ross, Sandra 59, 62, 127–8, 132–3, 179–83, 186, 192, 209, 223
Royal Children's Hospital, Melbourne 160
Royal College of Paediatrics and Child Health, UK 38

Safer Internet plus Programme, EU 8
safety 37, 43, 46, 57, 117, 138, 162, 204, 210, 219
Samantha. *See* Lawe-Tammell, Samantha
Samuel. *See* Cheun-Yeo, Samuel
Sandra. *See* Ross, Sandra
Sarah. *See* Bernard, Sarah
scaffolding of children's learning 23, 32, 48, 175–6, 181, 186
Scott. *See* Andrews-White, Scott
Scott. *See* Bernard, Scott
Scott, F. 47
screen time 14–15, 28, 31, 57, 85, 96, 98, 107, 114, 117, 158, 165, 201, 209, 213
  guide for digital parenting 45–9
  injunctions to parents 35–6
  parenting for digital future 40–2
  rise and fall of 37–40
  sedentary activities 38
  study on excessive screen time 39
  survey findings 42–5
Sean. *See* Bernard, Sean
sedentary screen time 38
Sergei. *See* Mansi, Sergei
sexuality 190
sexualization 62
shared activities (child-parent) 4, 43–4. *See also* co-play
sharenting 117
Sherryl. *See* Cullen, Sherryl
siblings, engagement in technology use 18, 57, 65, 104–7, 113, 131, 133, 140, 143, 166–8, 171, 191, 206, 229 n.3 (Ch 10)

sign language 87
Simon. *See* Brown, Simon
Siri 148, 156, 196, 208, 222
Skylanders 149, 151, 158, 198
Skype 63, 71–2, 80–1, 107, 114, 121, 130, 134, 194, 208, 212, 215–16, 222
smartphones 1, 4, 8, 36, 40, 52–3, 61, 64–5, 71–3, 80–1, 83, 111, 124, 144, 179, 211–15, 217–19, 221–2, 224. *See also* iPad; tablets
Snapchat 149, 159, 182–3, 198–9, 216
social constructionism 21–2, 25, 82, 190, 193
social context 21, 40, 56
social interaction 21, 32, 55, 175, 200
socialization 37, 41, 224
social media 40, 58, 153, 212. *See also specific companies*
socio-cultural tradition 22, 24, 198, 205
socioeconomic 5, 18, 38, 43–4, 49, 163, 215
socio-materiality 25
software 47, 84, 87–8, 91, 94–5, 174, 186, 205, 212, 223
sole-parent households 9, 200
Spera, C., parental practices 53
Spinner, Alice 144, 160, 168, 176, 202, 224
Spinner, Belle 144–5, 160, 168, 176, 202–3, 224
Spinner, Daniel 61, 66, 144–5, 159, 176–7, 209, 224
Spinner, Imelda 10, 12, 66, 140, 144–5, 168, 176, 203, 209, 224
Spinner, Karla 56, 59, 66, 144–5, 156, 158, 160, 176–7, 204, 209, 224
Stampylonghead vlogger 153, 199
Stanley. *See* Zhang/Chen, Stanley
Statutory Framework for the Early Years' Foundation Stage: Setting the Standards for Learning, Development and Care for Children from Birth to Five (Department for Education, UK) 27
stay-at-home parenting 58, 214, 224
Stella. *See* Kramer, Stella
Steve language teaching programme 147, 159, 211
Stevenson, K. J. 14, 101, 105, 120–1, 123, 129, 131, 133, 141–3, 150–3, 158, 196, 198, 203

storytelling 38, 46
Subway Surfer game 145

tablets 1, 4, 59–66, 74, 83, 88–90, 97, 132, 166, 174, 179, 202, 208, 210–11, 213, 215, 217–18, 221–4. *See also* iPad; smartphones
Tang 81
Tapestry 92, 229 n.8
technological orientations of parents 18, 126, 163–6
Ted. *See* Brent, Ted
Toddlers and Tablets: Exploring the Risks and Benefits 0-5s Face Online,
  findings of 2, 8, 14–16, 18, 51, 61, 69–71, 101, 143, 160, 191, 193, 202
  characteristics of parents 163–6
  developing ethnotheories 56–60
  diversity of grandparents' experiences 72–3
  parental concerns on digital media use 60–4
  parents' evaluations of children's learning through digital media 176–80
  parents letting children access touchscreens 64–6
  use of digital media in preschool 86–92
toddlers (two and three years old), digital media use 2–3, 9, 17, 19, 28, 31, 36, 44, 119, 195–7
  awareness of parents 132–7
  participants 119–21 (*see also specific participants*)
  policy considerations 137–8
Tosetti, Leopoldo 10, 13, 61, 63, 120–2, 133, 164–5, 175–8, 180, 186, 195, 199, 209, 224–5
Tosetti, Lorenzo 61–2, 122, 132–3, 164–5, 175–6, 180, 186, 190–1, 195, 199, 204, 209, 224–5
Tosetti, Mirabella 59, 62–3, 80, 121–2, 164–5, 175–8, 180, 186, 190, 195, 199, 209, 224–5
touchscreens 8, 51–3, 59–60, 62–6, 74, 79, 83, 99, 111–13, 115–16, 132, 149, 160, 164, 169–71, 174, 177, 179, 186, 194, 213
traditional play 85
Trish. *See* Greenfield, Trish

United Nations Committee on the Rights of the Child (UNCRC) 26, 29, 48
United Nations Convention on the Rights of the Child 26, 48
United Nations Office of the High Commissioner on Human Rights 29
US Centers for Disease Control and Prevention 2

violence (violent cartoons/games) 38, 62, 127, 190, 209, 220
virtual teaching educators, survey 32
Vygotsky, L. S. 18, 22–3, 175

whatever works approach 126, 206
WhatsApp 57–8, 169, 216
The Wiggles 103
William. *See* Bernard, William
World Health Organization (WHO), *Guidelines on Physical Activity, Sedentary Behaviour and Sleep for Children under 5 Years of Age* 38, 115

Xavier. *See* Bernard, Xavier

yoga 111, 213
YouTube 60, 62, 65, 80, 90, 94, 96, 109, 114–15, 122–4, 131, 152–3, 168, 177–8, 186, 209–10, 212, 215–16, 222–3, 225
YouTube Kids 31, 62, 146, 148, 156, 162, 220
Yu Na. *See* Lim-Park, Yu Na
Yussef. *See* Govender, Yussef

Zhang/Chen, Lavinia 120, 125–6, 134, 136, 166, 179, 197, 199, 201, 209, 225–6, 229 n.1 (Ch 8)
Zhang/Chen, Lily 125, 166, 225–6
Zhang/Chen, Rita 57, 72, 80, 125–6, 132, 134, 136, 146, 158, 166, 179–80, 197, 199, 209, 225–6
Zhang/Chen, Stanley 72, 80, 125, 132, 146, 166, 209, 225–6
zone of proximal development 22, 33

www.ingramcontent.com/pod-product-compliance
Lightning Source LLC
Chambersburg PA
CBHW071817300426
44116CB00009B/1346